LEGALLYWED

▼

Same-Sex Marriage and the Constitution

Mark Strasser

CORNELL UNIVERSITY PRESS   *Ithaca and London*

First published 1997 by Cornell University Press
First printing, Cornell Paperbacks, 1998

Printed in the United States of America

Library of Congress Cataloging-in-Publication Data

Strasser, Mark Phillip, 1955–
    Legally wed : same-sex marriage and the constitution / Mark Strasser.
        p.   cm.
    Includes bibliographical references and index.
    ISBN 0-8014-3406-8 (cloth : alk. paper). —ISBN 0-8014-8429-4 (pbk. : alk. paper)
    1. Marriage law—United States.   2. Husband and wife—United
States.   3. Gay couples—Legal status, laws, etc.—United States.   I. Title.
KF511.S77   1997
346.7301'6—dc21   96-50344

Cornell University Press strives to use environmentally responsible suppliers and materials to the fullest extent possible in the publishing of its books. Such materials include vegetable-based, low-VOC inks and acid-free papers that are recycled, totally chlorine-free, or partly composed of nonwood fibers.

Cloth printing   10 9 8 7 6 5 4 3 2 1
Paper   10 9 8 7 6 5 4 3 2 1

TO GEORGE

CONTENTS

▼

PREFACE TO THE

CORNELL PAPERBACKS EDITION

▼

A court in Hawaii has held that the state's same-sex marriage ban is unconstitutional. However, that ruling has been appealed and will not be given legal effect until the state supreme court has had a chance to consider the issues raised. The Hawaii Supreme Court is expected to affirm the lower court's ruling in 1998 and may well have done so by the time this edition of *Legally Wed* appears.

The Hawaii case involves an interpretation of the existing *state* constitution. In November, 1998, the Hawaii citizenry will decide whether to amend their state constitution to allow the legislature to reserve marriage for opposite-sex couples. Should that occur, the Hawaii decision will have been legislatively overruled—basically, the decision will no longer be legally binding because the constitution upon which it had been based will itself have changed.

Even if the Hawaii citizenry passes the proposed amendment and even if the legislature passes the relevant statute, however, that will not settle whether the same-sex marriage bans in Hawaii and other states violate federal constitutional guarantees. The reasoning that has already been offered by a plurality of the Hawaii Supreme Court provides a strong basis upon which to challenge such marital bans. The United States Constitution prohibits discrimination on the basis of sex. Same-sex marriage bans involve such discrimination.

To make classifications based on sex, states must show that they have important interests at stake. It is not at all clear that the state has legitimate, much less important, interests that are served by prohibiting same-sex couples from marrying. Further, the right to marry involves interests that are of fundamental importance to all individuals. The state cannot deprive individuals of such a right without compelling reasons. Finally, the state interest in *promoting* marriage and family has long been recognized. Preventing a whole group of people from marrying *undermines* the state's own interests.

Should the Hawaii Supreme Court rule as expected and should the Hawaii citizenry not pass the proposed amendment, the same-sex couples will be permitted to marry in Hawaii. Other states will then have to confront at least two issues: whether their own same-sex marrige bans are constitutional and, even if so, whether to recognize same-sex marriages performed in Hawaii. As a general matter, merely because a state does not allow certain marriages to be celebrated within its own borders does not establish that it will refuse to recognize a marriage from elsewhere. For example, some states refuse to allow first cousins to marry within their own borders but recognize a marrriage of first cousins if performed in a state that permits such unions.

While it might be argued that the Defense of Marriage Act (DOMA) permits states to refuse to recognize any same-sex marriages celebrated in Hawaii, that Act arguably was only intended to allow states to refuse to recognize the same-sex marriages of their own citizens who had gone elsewhere to marry. There is some question whether a state would be permitted to refuse to recognize a marriage celebrated in Hawaii by Hawaiians who, for example, had decided to move to that state a few years after their marriage had taken place. Moreover, the constitutionality of DOMA itself is open to challenge on a number of different grounds. Regardless of the outcome of events in Hawaii, same-sex marriage bans will be challenged in the courts for the foreseeable future. Eventually, the United States Supreme Court will have to make clear how the numerous issues raised by current marital laws should be resolved.

MARK STRASSER

ACKNOWLEDGMENTS

▼

I have discussed some of these subjects in various law reviews:

Loving the Romer Out for Baehr: On Acts in Defense of Marriage and the Constitution, 58 U. Pitt. L. Rev. 279–323 (1997).

Judicial Good Faith and the Baehr Essentials: On Giving Credit Where It's Due, 28 Rutgers L.J. 313–366 (1997).

Fit to Be Tied: On Custody, Discretion, and Sexual Orientation, 46 Am. U. L. Rev. 841–895 (1997).

Legislative Presumptions and Judicial Assumptions: On Parenting, Adoption, and the Best Interests of the Child, 45 U. Kansas L. Rev. 49–111 (1996).

Domestic Relations Jurisprudence and the Great, Slumbering Baehr: On Definitional Preclusion, Equal Protection, and Fundamental Interests, 64 Fordham L. Rev. 921–986 (1995). Reprinted with permission of the Fordham Law Review.

Unconstitutional? Don't Ask; If It Is, Don't Tell: On Deference, Rationality, and the Constitution, 66 U. Colo. L. Rev. 375–460 (1995). Reprinted with permission of the University of Colorado Law Review.

Suspect Classes and Suspect Classifications: On Discriminating, Unwittingly or Otherwise, 64 Temple L. Rev. 937–975 (1991). Copyright 1991, Temple Law Review. Reprinted with permission.

Family, Definitions, and the Constitution: On the Antimiscegenation

Analogy, 25 *Suffolk U. L. Rev.* 981–1034 (1991). Reprinted with permission of the Suffolk University Law Review.

I thank each of the law reviews, without whose cooperation this book would not have been possible. I would also like to thank David Ralston for his secretarial assistance, and Alison Shonkwiler and the readers for Cornell University Press, whose help greatly enhanced this book.

M. S.

INTRODUCTION

▼

Although same-sex couples have sought marriage licenses at various times over the past three decades, the issue of same-sex marriage has never been as prominent in the public mind as it is today. This prominence has several causes, not the least of which is a 1993 plurality decision by the Supreme Court of Hawaii which may eventually result in that state's recognizing same-sex marriages.

The Hawaii decision may affect other states in a variety of ways. For example, if Hawaii comes to recognize such marriages, each state will have to decide whether to recognize the same-sex unions of individuals domiciled there who go to Hawaii to marry. Contrary to popular belief, the Constitution's Full Faith and Credit Clause allows each state to make its own decision; the clause does not force states to recognize marriages which the state legislatures either have declared void or have explicitly declared will not be recognized.

Many members of Congress do not seem to understand how the Full Faith and Credit Clause works. The ostensible reason for Congress's passing the Defense of Marriage Act (DOMA)—to prevent states from having to recognize the same-sex marriages of their domiciliaries—is not a reason at all, since domiciles already have that power. Not only is DOMA unnecessary, but it is unconstitutional because it is the antithesis of a full faith and credit measure, because it lacks sufficient generality and because, without adequate justification, it encroaches upon an area traditionally reserved for state regulation. Further, the act unreasonably restricts interstate travel and is motivated by a desire to impose an undeserved burden on a disfavored group.

That Hawaii *may* come to recognize same-sex marriages should lay to rest one of the arguments offered to establish why states need not recognize such unions, namely, that such marriages are a contradiction in terms and thus *cannot* be recognized. That there was a remand to a lower court to enable the state to try to offer compelling reasons to prevent the recognition of such marriages implied that such marriages were conceptually possible. Were they precluded by definition, there would have been no remand.

Same-sex marriage bans can be challenged on Equal Protection or Substantive Due Process grounds. Equal Protection issues are implicated in a few different ways by the refusal to give legal recognition to same-sex unions. For example, the class of lesbian, bisexual, and gay people meets the standards for being declared a suspect or quasi-suspect class. Ironically, this designation has not been accorded, *despite the class's having the relevant characteristics to merit that protection*, because courts have not applied the relevant criteria in good faith.

When denying that sexual orientation deserves the kind of protection that has already been extended to race, religion, ethnic and national origin, alienage (noncitizenship), illegitimacy, and gender, courts explain their holdings by discussing the standards that allegedly have not been met. The difficulty with these analyses is that the *wrong* standards are offered: *none* of the classes already recognized as deserving protection meets the standards offered to establish that sexual orientation does not deserve heightened judicial protection from invidious discrimination. Courts cannot sincerely claim that they are applying the relevant criteria when their analyses yield results that would simply do away with the protections that have been built into the system.

Notwithstanding this judicial unwillingness to apply the relevant criteria in good faith, the Equal Protection Clause may still require that same-sex marriage bans be invalidated. The Equal Protection Clause already prevents discrimination on the basis of sex. In Hawaii, the case was remanded precisely because the same-sex marriage ban was held to discriminate on the basis of sex: a man can marry a woman but not a man, and a woman can marry a man but not a woman. Such bans also involve sex discrimination because they involve the state's impermissibly promoting stereotypical gender roles. Each sex is implied to have specific roles that should not be performed by a member of the other sex.

Thus far, most courts have refused to grant the class of lesbians, bisexuals, and gays the kind of heightened protection against discrimination that is deserved and, further, have rejected that same-sex marriage bans involve sex discrimination. Nonetheless, state prohibitions of same-sex marriages are unconstitutional because they are not rationally related to legitimate state purposes. The Equal Protection Clause prohibits states from imposing disabilities solely for the purpose of disadvantaging despised minorities.

Even if courts reject that the Equal Protection Clause is violated by state refusals to recognize same-sex marriages, the Due Process Clause is also violated by such bans. The right to marry is fundamental and it is a violation of Substantive Due Process for states to abridge fundamental rights without compelling reasons to do so. The Supreme Court has articulated several interests that are served by marriage, all of which apply to same-sex as well as opposite-sex unions. Thus far, states have failed to articulate the compelling interests that are served by same-sex marriage bans.

Some courts and commentators argue that there is no fundamental right to marry a same-sex partner. The test cited to establish that thesis, however, is not the appropriate test, since it might also be used to establish that there are no fundamental rights to contraception, abortion, or interracial marriage. Indeed, most commentators and judges seem to underappreciate the striking parallels between the current refusal to recognize same-sex marriages and the former refusal to recognize interracial marriages. Many denied that the latter were marriages at all, claiming that such unions were unnatural, immoral, and demeaning to the institution of marriage.

The reason most often articulated to justify the refusal to recognize same-sex marriages is that the alleged purpose of marriage is to provide a setting for the production and raising of children. Yet, lesbians, bisexuals, and gays both have and raise children, whether those children are the product of a previous marriage, adoption, surrogacy, or artificial insemination. Were courts serious about promoting the alleged purpose of marriage, they would require states to recognize same-sex marriages rather than support state refusals to do so. The state refusal to recognize same-sex marriages undermines rather than promotes the state's legitimate purpose of providing a setting for the production and raising of children.

The states' refusal to recognize same-sex marriages and the courts' complicity in upholding those refusals have implications that affect everyone. The law of domestic relations has to be turned on its head to justify such bans. Such fundamental changes in the law bode poorly for the protection of fundamental rights generally and numerous kinds of families specifically. Everyone's rights are put at risk when the current justifications and rationales are accepted as good law. This is a price which a society like ours should never be willing to pay.

I MARRIAGE BARRED BY DEFINITION

▼

The United States Constitution guarantees that each individual's fundamental rights will be respected unless compelling state interests require that those rights be overridden. If the right to marry, which is fundamental,[1] includes the right to marry one's same-sex partner, then states prohibiting same-sex marriage will have to establish that they have compelling state interests which justify the maintainence of such a prohibition. Because, as Gerald Gunther has suggested, states must bear "especially high burdens of justification" for the infringement of an individual's fundamental right,[2] it would be much easier for a state to justify its same-sex marriage ban if no fundamental rights were implicated.

THE CONTRADICTION-IN-TERMS ARGUMENT

A variety of arguments have been offered to establish that there is no fundamental right to same-sex marriage, the most ambitious of which suggests that there *cannot* be a right to same-sex marriage because such a right would involve a contradiction in terms. When one suggests that something is logically impossible because it involves a contradiction in terms, one might simply be asserting that a particular concept is logically incoherent *if one accepts certain definitions.* For example, given the definition that marriage involves one man and one woman, same-sex marriage is logically incoherent as is a marriage between one woman and more than one man or between one man and more than one woman. By the same token, if marriage is defined as involving two individuals of the same race, then an interracial marriage is simply a contradiction in terms. If marriage is defined as a union of two individuals of the same religion, then an interreligious marriage is a contradiction in terms.

Insofar as the refusal to recognize same-sex marriages is based on a particular definition of marriage, it is important to establish that the chosen definition is reasonable rather than simply question-begging. It is more difficult than it first appears to distinguish between reasonable and question-begging definitions of marriage. Consider whether marriage is reasonably defined as the union of one man and one woman. Arguably, that definition is reasonable because there is a long tradition of defining marriage that way. Yet, before 1967, the same argument would have established the reasonableness of many states' defining marriage as the union of two people of the same race. One of the lessons to be learned from the history of antimiscegenation statutes is that even a long historical pedigree does not establish the legitimacy of a state definition or policy. As Justice Harry Blackmun suggested in his dissent in *Bowers v. Hardwick,* it is "revolting to have no better reason for a rule of law than that it was laid down in the time of Henry IV."[3]

Suppose that reasons in addition to historical pedigree could be offered to establish that marriage is reasonably defined as the union of one man and one woman. Even so, the issue would not thereby be resolved. It would further have to be established that defining marriage to include same-sex unions would *not* be reasonable. Else, two "reasonable" definitions of marriage would conflict with respect to the point at issue, namely, whether same-sex unions are included within the concept of marriage. Same-sex marriage would be a contradiction in terms using one reasonable definition and would not be using another. If the contradiction-in-terms argument is to have any force, it cannot simply depend upon which "reasonable" definition one happens to employ.

There are a variety of ways that one might seek to establish the reasonableness of a definition. One might consult a dictionary,[4] although this approach is problematic insofar as courts or commentators want to use a dictionary definition to establish why the state cannot recognize same-sex unions. Terms may mean one thing in common usage and another in the law. For example, *The Random House Dictionary of the English Language* defines "information" as "knowledge communicated or received concerning a particular fact or circumstance."[5] However, it has a separate listing for law in which "information" is defined as "an official criminal charge presented, usually by the prosecuting officer of the state, without the interposition of a grand jury."[6] When one consults a dictionary to establish the meaning of a particular term in law, one must remember that the terms do not always mean the same thing in law as they do in ordinary usage.

Merely because some terms have a special meaning in law does not mean that all terms are ambiguous in that way. Perhaps, then, marriage does mean the same thing in law as it does in common parlance. In everyday speech, however, people use the term marriage to refer to longterm, same-sex relationships.[7] Further, journalists, theorists, and everyday speakers discuss same-sex marriages.[8] Thus, if common parlance is to determine whether same-sex marriage involves a contradiction in terms, those maintaining such a claim will be unable to establish their position.

Theorists might not look at standard dictionaries but instead at a legal dictionary to establish their claim that same-sex marriage is a *legal* contradiction in terms. They might cite *Black's Law Dictionary*, in which marriage is defined as the "[l]egal union of one man and one woman as husband and wife."[9] However, *Black's Law Dictionary* cites *Singer v. Hara* as authority for that definition.[10] The *Singer* court looked at ordinary usage to determine the legal meaning, suggesting that "words of a statute must be understood in their usual and ordinary sense in the absence of a statutory definition to the contrary."[11] Indeed, the court believed it unnecessary to consult a dictionary to establish that marriage "in the usual and ordinary sense refers to the legal union of one man and one woman."[12] Thus, the legal definition was based on ordinary usage. Were *current* ordinary usage the relevant standard, it is not at all clear that the *Singer* court would have reached the same result.

THE DIFFICULTY WITH DEFINITIONS

A fundamental difficulty with using the contradiction-in-terms approach is that it involves a misunderstanding of the purposes behind consulting a dictionary. When a legislature has passed a law that one must interpret, it may be appropriate and is certainly acceptable to consult a dictionary to help discern legislative intent. If a particular term has never before referred to "X" and has never before included "X" within its scope, then it is sensible to assume that the legislature, when using the term, was not intending to include "X" in the prohibition or permission which had been enacted.[13] In this kind of case, the dictionary is not being used to establish what the legislature could or could not do but merely as a tool to facilitate interpretation of a statute.

A legislature can decide to define marriage as the union of one man and one woman,[14] assuming that no state or federal constitutional guarantees are thereby being violated. As a general matter, states are given some discretion with respect to deciding which marriages they will consider valid. For example, states may but need not allow first cousins to marry,[15] adoptive siblings to marry,[16] or a stepparent to marry his or her (former) spouse's child.[17] However, states are limited in the amount of discretion they have with respect to the statutory classifications they can make. Thus, even if a court has accurately characterized legislative intent, that will not settle the issue if the legislature has exceeded constitutional limits.

Consider interracial marriage. In 1804, a Virginia court explained why *interracial* marriages should be considered a nullity. "The law concerning marriages is to be construed and understood in relation to those persons only to whom that law relates; and not to a class of persons clearly not within the idea of the legislature when contemplating the subjects of marriage and legitimacy."[18] Yet, as the Supreme Court has made eminently clear, legislatures do not have the power to prohibit certain marriages.[19]

Presumably, the Virginia court had accurately characterized legislative intent when it held that interracial marriages were a nullity. Yet, legislatures take a chance that their intentions will be misconstrued if those intentions are not clearly stated. States fearing that courts will misconstrue legislative intent can help assure that such mistakes will not occur. For example, states that have decided not to recognize particular unions can define marriage to exclude the union in question or they can specifically prohibit that union.[20] Although either method will clearly demonstrate the legislative will, it should not be thought that constitutional protections can somehow be avoided if definitional preclusions rather than statutory prohibitions are employed. Regardless of the method by which the legislature makes its intent clear, the legislature must limit it enactments to those that will pass constitutional muster. Were definitions somehow immune from constitutional scrutiny, legislatures would be able to thwart constitutional protections by offering definitions rather than prohibitions. For example, notwithstanding the Supreme Court's having made clear that states cannot prohibit interracial couples from marrying, a state would be able to avoid this constitutional guarantee by simply defining interracial marriage as a contradiction in terms.[21]

Certainly, there are differences between interracial and intrasexual marriage bans. However, the relevant substantive analysis cannot simply be avoided by positing a definition. As the Supreme Court made clear in a different context, "It is too late in the day . . . for decisions on the merits to be avoided on the basis of such [methods],"[22] especially since the definition of marriage might as easily be employed to require recognition of same-sex marriages as to prohibit their recognition.

When a legislature creates a definition that passes constitutional muster, that definition will have legal weight. It is important, however, to understand how much and what kind of legal weight that definition will have. A legislature's having adopted a definition will not preclude that legislature from later modifying or changing that definition. Thus, a legislature which currently defines marriage as involving a man and a woman could change that definition to allow same-sex unions. By the same token, a legislature which had adopted a definition of marriage which allowed same-sex couples to marry could amend that definition to preclude such unions, assuming that such a modification would be permitted by the Constitution.[23]

A much stronger form of definitional preclusion argument must be offered if legislatures are to be *precluded* from defining marriage to include same-sex marriages. For example, one might argue that the definition of marriage is fixed and unchanging and that the state cannot permit same-sex marriages even if it so desires.[24]

THE NATURE OF THINGS

Some argue that same-sex marriage is definitionally precluded not merely in the weak sense that, for example, a particular legislature has decided not to include those unions within its own definition of who may marry whom, but in the strong sense that a legislature *could* not include such unions within its definition of marriage, legislative desire to do so notwithstanding. In *Jones v. Hallahan*, the Kentucky Supreme Court suggested that the state of Kentucky was not invidiously discriminating against two women by refusing to allow them to marry: the two women were "prevented from marrying, not by the statutes of Kentucky or the refusal of the County Court Clerk of Jefferson County to issue them a license, but rather by their own incapability of entering into a marriage as that term is defined."[25]

When a court suggests that the definition of the term *rather than* the marital statute prevents two individuals from marrying, the court implies that the legislature is not responsible for that definition. Otherwise, the legislature could simply change the definition and permit the individuals to wed. By suggesting that the statutes of Kentucky were not preventing the women from marrying, the *Hallahan* court implied that the state was precluded from defining marriage to include same-sex partners.

States may be precluded from passing particular laws for a variety of reasons. For example, a state cannot pass laws that deprive citizens of their fundamental rights unless compelling state interests are implicated. However, this rationale is inapplicable here, since individuals do not have a fundamental right to have *others* precluded from marrying. It would be as if allowing same-sex couples to marry would so devalue the institution of marriage that the right of opposite-sex couples to marry would somehow have been abridged.

It is not difficult to imagine someone's *claiming* that allowing same-sex marital unions would cheapen the institution of marriage,[26] just as it is not difficult to imagine someone's claiming that interracial or interreligious unions cheapen the institution of marriage. Yet, it is not at all clear that such a claim should be taken any more seriously when it is made about intrasexual marriages than when it is made about interracial or interreligious marriages, and it is *not* taken seriously when the latter unions are discussed.

Indeed, one might imagine someone's claiming not only that interreligious or interracial marriages should be precluded but that people of a particular race or religion should not be allowed to marry at all because unions involving such people cheapen the institution of marriage. Although such a view might be sincerely held, that is hardly the test for whether individuals should be allowed to marry. Bigoted views should not be allowed to circumscribe the rights of others, regardless of the sincerity with which such views are held. So, too, prejudice should not be allowed to prevent same-sex partners from marrying, regardless of the depth or sincerity of such views.

The point is not that individuals who believe that members of despised groups should not be allowed to marry would admit that they are wrong were they to sit down and have a rational discussion. Indeed, reasoning with them may be impossible.[27] Rather, the point is that their bigotry should not be allowed to abridge the rights of others.

John Stuart Mill discusses a religious bigot who, "when charged with disregarding the religious feelings of others, has been known to retort that they disregard his feelings, by persisting in their abominable worship or creed."[28] Mill suggests that "there is no parity between the feeling of a person for his own opinion and the feeling of another who is offended at his holding it."[29] So, too, there is no parity between the feelings of the person whose fundamental right to marry is at issue and the feelings of someone else who does not want that person to be able to marry.

GOD'S WILL

Perhaps it will be argued that the state should not recognize same-sex marriages because God refuses to countenance such unions. Such a claim would require at least two subclaims:

1. One would have to establish that it is clear that God does not recognize such unions. This claim might be supported through examination and interpretation of various religious texts. However, it is important to distinguish between what a particular sect or denomination believes and what *all* religions believe. If one wishes to argue that the state should not recognize same-sex marriages because God does not recognize them, then one is presumably offering a fairly comprehensive claim about what (nearly) all traditions believe. However, *some religious traditions accept and recognize same-sex unions*.[30] Indeed, the state of Hawaii has expressly stated its unwillingness to inhibit religious organizations from sanctifying such unions,[31] implicitly accepting that some religious traditions recognize same-sex marriages.

Those invoking God's alleged refusal to recognize same-sex marriages to support the state's not recognizing such unions are implicitly claiming that traditions recognizing such unions either (1) are *wrong* about their own faith or (2) are somehow *not* faiths. Presumably, those arguing against same-sex unions do not want to adopt either of those tacks, at least in part, because whatever criteria are used to disqualify Quakers, Unitarians, Buddhists, Reconstructionist Jews, etc., from belonging to a religion or from understanding their own religion will be ad hoc and at least potentially used to disqualify a variety of religions from being veridical faiths or a variety of individuals from understanding their own religious views.

Those contending that marriage should be defined as the union of one man and one woman because it is in accord with God's Will face yet another difficulty. The same justification was offered to establish the reasonableness of limiting marriage to intraracial unions. The trial court in *Loving v. Virginia* stated that "Almighty God created the races white, black, yellow, malay and red, and he placed them on separate continents. . . . The fact that he separated the races shows that he did not intend for the races to mix."[32] The Supreme Court reversed, notwithstanding God's alleged stamp of approval on prohibiting interracial unions.

Theorists might suggest that individuals were mistaken when arguing that God refuses to countenance interracial unions. Yet, the same argument might be made about God's alleged refusal to countenance intrasexual unions, especially given that various religions recognize such unions. If jurists and commentators are concerned about their own integrity and credibility, they must refrain from using the kinds of arguments that were used to justify the refusal to recognize interracial marriages.

2. One would have to establish that God's (alleged) refusal to recognize same-sex marriage entailed that the state should not recognize them. Yet, even were there unanimity among religious faiths about which marital unions God recognizes, it is a separate question whether that would have any import for which marital unions states may recognize. It is clear that merely because a religion recognizes a particular marital union will not establish that the state must recognize that union. Otherwise, polygamous unions would be recognized.[33] Thus, a religion's recognizing a marriage is not a *sufficient* condition for a state's recognizing that union.

Yet, there is no reason to believe that God's recognizing a marital union is a *necessary* condition for the state's recognizing that union. For example, suppose that no religion recognized interreligious unions. Or suppose that God did not recognize interreligious unions. Neither of these suppositions, even if true, would establish that the state should not recognize such unions if the state interests promoted by recognizing marriages generally would also be promoted by recognizing interreligious unions. Thus, at least two points should be noted with respect to the contention that the state should not recognize same-sex marriages because God does not recognize them. First, there is no requirement that God recognize a marital union in order for the state to do so. Second, even were there such a requirement, that would still not be a reason to refuse to recognize such marriages, since some religions celebrate same-sex unions and, presumably, believe that God recognizes such unions.

THE CONTRADICTION-IN-TERMS ARGUMENT REFUTED

In *Baehr v. Lewin*,[34] a plurality of the Hawaii Supreme Court held that the state's prohibition of same-sex marriage involved sex discrimination and could be justified only if the state could establish that it had compelling state interests in supporting such a ban. The lower court to whom the case was remanded had to decide whether the state interests were sufficiently compelling and the statute sufficiently narrowly tailored to justify the ban. When the lower court decided that they were not, it was *not* deciding whether same-sex marriage involves a contradiction in terms; that question, which is logically prior to the question of whether the state can justify the prohibition,[35] had already been answered in the negative.

Given that Hawaii may actually come to recognize same-sex marriages, it might be expected that judges would no longer offer the canard that such unions are definitionally precluded in the strong sense that states cannot recognize such unions even if they wish to do so, and thus that governmental bodies cannot be held responsible for refusing to recognize same-sex marital unions. However, in *Dean v. District of Columbia*, Judge John Terry concluded that it makes no "difference that the District of Columbia, or any agency of its government, discriminates against these two appellants by refusing to allow them to enter into a legal status which the sameness of their gender prevents them from entering in the first place."[36] Yet, it is difficult to understand how a judge could conclude that "appellants cannot enter into a marriage because the very nature of marriage makes it impossible for them to do so"[37] when it was already clear that the state of Hawaii might come to recognize such marriages and that two individuals with those "natures" might be able to marry in Hawaii.

The point here does not depend upon whether Hawaii in fact comes to recognize such unions. The fact that there was a remand

and that the state *may* recognize such unions already establishes the falsity of the claim that states *cannot* recognize such unions. Were the very nature of marriage to make it impossible for same-sex couples to marry, there would have been no remand.

Judge Terry's position would have been more understandable had *Dean* preceded the first *Baehr* decision. Although the position would still have been in error (because Judge Terry would have had to have shown not merely that there *had not yet* been a decision like *Baehr* but that there *could not have* been such a decision), the position at least would not have already been refuted in the case law. Judge Terry's position also would have been more understandable had he been unaware of the Hawaii decision. However, *Baehr* was cited by a different judge in the *Dean* opinion.[38] It is regrettable that jurists continue to offer specious arguments so that they can avoid addressing the substantive issues implicated in same-sex marriage bans.

Ironically, those states that have explicitly refused to permit same-sex couples to marry have at least implicitly recognized that same-sex marriage is not definitionally precluded in the strong sense. For example, the relevant Texas statute reads, "A license may not be issued for the marriage of persons of the same sex."[39] This hardly implies that such couples are conceptually barred from marrying. On the contrary, the existence of this prohibition suggests that such unions are not so barred.

The Utah statute which states that marriages "between persons of the same sex" are "prohibited and void"[40] might seem to pose more difficulties. Perhaps it will be argued that a statute which classifies a union as prohibited and void implicitly categorizes the union as conceptually barred. The Utah statute, however, also specifies that marriages involving a "male or female . . . under 18 years of age"[41] will also be considered prohibited and void unless the appropriate consents are obtained.[42] Yet, clearly, it is not a contradiction in terms for individuals under 18 years of age to marry, even if they do not have parental consent. Indeed, such marriages may be valid. For example, the Georgia marital statute allows individuals under the age of majority to consent to marriage, even without parental consent, "upon proof of pregnancy on the part of the female or in instances in which both applicants are the parents of a living child born out of wedlock."[43] Thus, even the Utah statute which makes same-sex marriage prohibited and void implicitly suggests not that the forbidden union is a contradiction in terms but, rather, merely that the union will not be recognized in Utah.

Perhaps a marital statute like Maryland's which specifies, "Only a marriage between a man and a woman is valid in this State"[44] would seem to support the definitional preclusion argument. Yet, such a statute does not suggest that such unions cannot be recognized anywhere but merely that the state has chosen not to recognize such marriages within its borders. Certainly, this kind of statute suggests that the particular state has consciously decided not to recognize same-sex marital unions. Yet, it also suggests that such unions are not definitionally precluded in the strong sense.

Whether states are acting constitutionally permissibly by restricting marriage to opposite-sex couples is a different question that requires separate analysis, but the point remains that states explicitly prohibiting same-sex marriages implicitly recognize the speciousness of the claims that same-sex marriage is a contradiction in terms and, further, that same-sex partners are not being prevented from marrying by the state statutes. Were there no need for such statutes the legislatures would not have passed them. Statutes prohibiting same-sex unions and statutes declaring such unions void suggest that the legislatures do not want to recognize such unions but also suggest that the contradiction-in-terms argument is merely a specious attempt to evade the real issues.

FAMILY

Just as same-sex marriages have been said to be precluded because marriage by definition requires one man and one woman, same-sex families have been said to be precluded because family by definition requires legal or blood ties. The latter position is objectionable both because it is parasitic on the state's refusal to recognize legal ties between same-sex couples[45] and because the legal-or-blood-ties requirement has *not* been imposed in a variety of cases where the outcome turned on the definition of family.

The issue of who constitutes a family has often arisen in the context of challenges to zoning ordinances. Courts deciding these cases have had to choose between using a definition of family which (a) was limited to legal ties (marriage or adoption) or blood ties (including extended family)[46] or (b) used a functional approach in which groups of individuals with the characteristics of a family,[47] albeit no legal or blood ties, were nonetheless treated as a family. Courts have often been willing to use the latter approach. A functional definition of family has been used to allow the following groups of individuals to constitute family for zoning purposes: ten nonbiologically related students,[48] a group of nurses,[49] a group of priests,[50] and a group of nuns.[51]

The issue of who constitutes a family has arisen in other contexts as well. In *Braschi v. Stahl Associates Co.*,[52] the New York Court of Appeals held that because Miguel Braschi and Leslie Blanchard had a family relationship, Braschi could not be evicted after his same-sex partner's death. The court suggested that a "more realistic, and certainly equally valid, view of a family includes two adult lifetime partners whose relationship is long term and characterized by an emotional and financial commitment and interdependence."[53] Had Braschi and Blanchard not constituted a family, Braschi would have been evicted because his partner had been the sole tenant of record.

Regrettably, courts have been unwilling to adopt this functional definition of family in other contexts. For example, in a different New York case, Sandra Rovira and her two children sought to be declared beneficiaries of a life insurance policy when her life partner, Marjorie Forlini, died.[54] This relationship, like the one in *Braschi*, was "characterized by an emotional and financial commitment and interdependence"[55]: the two women had been together for twelve years, had pooled their resources, had joint ownership of a home, and had shared responsibility for important decisions.[56] They had formalized their relationship in a ceremony in which they had exchanged rings and vows.[57] Nonetheless, the benefits were denied because the court refused to recognize them as a family.[58] Other courts have denied life partners dental benefits,[59] insurance benefits,[60] sick leave,[61] or the right to elect against a will.[62] Thus, although the definition of family has been held to include same-sex partners in some limited contexts, it has not been so held in a variety of other contexts.

ADULT ADOPTIONS

Given court unwillingness to classify gay and lesbian couples as family in many situations, couples have explored other avenues to secure legal recognition of their relationships. For example, some have tried to avail themselves of the mechanism of adult adoption. If the partner has been legally adopted, it will be more difficult for family members to later contest a will which names the partner as a beneficiary.[63]

The notion of adult adoption might itself seem to be an abuse of the system,[64] if adoptions are to be reserved for parent-child relationships.[65] However, as a New York appellate court made clear in *In re Adult Anonymous II*, adult adoptions have long "served as a legal mechanism for achieving economic, political, and social objectives rather than the stereotype parent-child relationship."[66] If adult adoption is a mechanism designed to allow individuals to achieve those objectives, then adoption of one's partner would not be an abuse of the system, since one might thereby achieve economic goals (unifying property rights and assuring that the partner would receive economic benefits which might otherwise be at risk), political goals (promoting equal rights for lesbian, bisexual, and gay individuals), and social goals (on both a societal and personal level).

In New York, the law "is well settled that adoption of an adult by an adult is permissible so long as the parties' purpose is neither insincere nor fraudulent."[67] Notwithstanding the permissibility of adults' adopting adults for economic, political, and social objectives, some courts have been reluctant to approve gay adult adoptions because of an unwillingness to appear to be condoning gay families. In *In re Adoption of Adult Anonymous*, the court approved an adult adoption involving gay partners, although the court made quite clear that it did not "wish to allow the adoption statute to be used as a shield for the protection of homosexuality, or even to give the appearance of approving or encouraging such practice, must less express approval."[68] The court was careful to point out that the parties were not "attempting to use the adult adoption statute to create, in effect, a pseudo-marriage."[69] Rather, the parties both wished to "enter into a consensual adoption for credible and uncontroverted legal and economic reasons valid on their face."[70] The court apparently believed that it was more legitimate for two individuals to become family members for economic reasons than for reasons involving love and commitment.

In *Anonymous II*, a New York appellate court took a more enlightened approach, recognizing that the individuals wished "to formalize themselves as a family unit, for the purposes of publicly acknowledging their emotional bond and more pragmatically to unify their propery rights."[71] The court recognized that the "'nuclear family' arrangement is no longer the only model of family life in America," understanding that nontraditional families also seek the rights and responsibilities that more traditional families have and noting that "the best description of a family is a continuing relationship of love and care, and an assumption of responsibility for some other person."[72]

Although it is clear that the *Anonymous II* court recognized that the individuals seeking to avail themselves of the adult adoption mechanism met the criteria for constituting a family, the court's decision was not predicated on that recognition. After examining the relevant statutes and finding that the legislature had not precluded same-sex adult adoptions, the court held that the "statutes involved do not permit this Court to deny a petition for adoption on the basis of this court's view of what is the nature of a family."[73] Thus, the court suggested that even if it had had a different view of family, the court would have been precluded from imposing that view, given the legislature's failure to limit adult adoptions beyond those which were insincere or fraudulent.

In *In re Adoption of Robert Paul P.*, the New York Court of Appeals held that adult adoption is "not a quasi-matrimonial vehicle to provide nonmarried partners with a legal imprimatur for their sexual relationship, be it heterosexual or homosexual."[74] The court reasoned that if the "adoption laws are to be *changed* so as to permit sexual lovers, homosexual or heterosexual, to adopt one another for the purpose of giving a nonmatrimonial legal status to their relationship, . . . it is for the Legislature, as a matter of State public policy, to do so."[75] There is good reason to believe that the court was misrepresenting then-current law. As Judge Bernard Meyer pointed out in his dissent, "nothing in the statute require[d] an inquiry into or evaluation of the sexual habits of the parties to an adult adoption or the nature of the current relationship between them."[76] Indeed, it seems that the court was not imposing the legislature's will but its own, since the legislature had not set the requirements suggested by the court and *adult adoptions involving gay couples had already been permitted in the state.*[77]

The New York Court of Appeals claimed that while the "adoption of an adult has long been permitted under the Domestic Relations Law, there is no exception made in such adoptions to the expressed purpose of legally formalizing a parent-child relationship."[78] The court further argued that "deference to the narrow legislative purpose is especially warranted with adoption, a legal relationship unknown at common law."[79] The court believed that "where the relationship between the adult parties is utterly incompatible with the creation of a parent child relationship between them, the adoption process is certainly not the proper vehicle by which to formalize their partnership in the eyes of the law."[80]

Certainly, one might imagine a statute which operated as the court implied.[81] However, that simply was not descriptive of the New York statute. A legislature that is willing to grant adult adoptions to promote economic, social, or political objectives clearly does not intend to limit adoptions to those that involve parent-child relationships.

The *Robert Paul P.* opinion is especially surprising given the *Anonymous II* opinion two years earlier. The appellate court felt constrained by the relevant statute to *permit* an adult adoption involving a gay couple. That opinion was published and the legislature did not react. Two years later, New York's highest court allegedly felt constrained to *refuse to permit* a similar adoption, despite (1) the statute's not prohibiting such adoptions, (2) a lower court's having earlier construed the statute as requiring recognition of such adoptions, and (3) the legislature's having failed to act despite its having been put on notice that the statute was being construed to allow same-sex adult adoptions. Although it of course is true that a lower court cannot bind a higher court, the above chronology casts doubt on the accuracy or even sincerity of the *Robert Paul P.* interpretation. Indeed, Judge Meyer in dissent in *Robert Paul P.* pointed out that had the legislature "intended to impose limitations of age, consent of others, sexual orientation, or other such condition upon adult adoption, it could easily have done so."[82]

In *333 East 53rd Street Associates v. Mann*,[83] a New York appellate court considered whether an 83-year-old woman's adoption of a 67-year-old woman was valid. The plaintiff suggested that the adoption had not been to establish a legally recognized mother-daughter relationship but, rather, that the "adoption [was] motivated by a desire to bring the adopted person within the protection of the rent control laws."[84] The court held that even if the "motivation alleged with regard to the adoption" was accurate,[85] i.e., even if the adoption was *not* designed to legally formalize a parent-child relation but, instead, was to bring the younger woman within the protection of the rent control laws, the adoption would nonetheless be valid. In *Mann*, there was no discussion of the filial nature of the relationship between the two women, except implicitly in the dissent where Judge Theodore Kupferman suggested that the majority had decided the case incorrectly. After all, he pointed out, in *Robert Paul P.* "adoption was denied among mature adults where there was no true filial relationship."[86] The *Mann* majority explained that it "perceive[d] no reason why an adoption motivated by a desire to enlarge the adopted person's right to inherit should be considered as presenting a problem."[87] The majority was correct, as long as there was no implicit requirement that the purpose of an adult adoption is to legally formalize an existing parent-child relationship.

The point is not that the adoption should have been declared invalid. Further, the two women might have met the criteria for family later enunciated in *Braschi*; perhaps they had a relationship which was "long term and characterized by an emotional and financial commitment and interdependence."[88] Rather, the point is that there should be some uniformity with respect to the standards used. If indeed there is a requirement that adoptions not be permitted unless there is a parent-child relationship, then that requirement should be enforced even when nongay or nonlesbian couples seek to make use of the adult adoption option. If there is no such requirement, then it should not suddenly be invented so that an adoption can be prevented which in fact seems to fulfill the statutory requirements.

It seems clear that the New York courts were not so worried about requiring the filial bond as they were about not wanting to appear to be condoning a same-sex relationship, notwithstanding the permissibility of adult consensual sodomy in New York.[89] This kind of judicial approach does not inspire confidence in the integrity and impartiality of the courts.

In *Robert Paul P.*, the court was not implying that it was beyond the legislature's power to create a quasi-matrimonial, legal status for same-sex couples. Presumably, the court also believed that it was within the legislature's power to allow same-sex couples to marry. The court was merely suggesting that a statute explictly creating that matrimonial or quasi-matrimonial status would have to be enacted before the relation would be legally recognized. It is not at all clear, however, that legislatures have it within their power to *refuse* to recognize same-sex marriages. Arguably, legislatures prohibiting same-sex unions are creating an invidious classification which abridges fundamental individual rights. The implications of a legislature's creating an invidiously discriminatory classification are discussed in the next chapter.

II EQUAL PROTECTION

▼

Whether legislatures are free not to recognize same-sex unions depends upon how much discretion legislatures are accorded with respect to the content of their marital statutues, which in turn depends upon how closely such statutes will be scrutinized by the courts. Some kinds of legislation will receive very close scrutiny while other kinds of legislation will be presumed to be within legislative discretion. Regrettably, the necessary and sufficient conditions for the imposition of this closer scrutiny are surprisingly unclear.

The Supreme Court has indicated that legislation which discriminates against classes with certain indicia or indicators will be examined with heightened scrutiny. The class of lesbians, bisexuals, and gays has the relevant characteristics to the required degree, although the Court has not yet recognized that and does not seem likely to do so. Even if the Court refuses to recognize that sexual orientation is a legislative classification which should trigger closer scrutiny, however, this does not mean that statutes prohibiting same-sex partners from marrying will be presumed to be within legislative discretion. Arguably, such statutes discriminate on the basis of gender, a classification which the Court has already recognized as meriting heightened solicitude.

Thus far, most courts have rejected that orientation is a classification meriting heightened scrutiny and have rejected that orientation discrimination involves discrimination on the basis of gender. Yet, a court refusing to impose heightened scrutiny when examining a statute prohibiting same-sex marriage might nonetheless strike down such a statute on Equal Protection grounds, since such state bans involve attempts to invidiously discriminate against lesbians, bisexuals, and gays and thus do not even meet the least exacting standard used by the courts. It would clearly be easier to establish the invalidity of such bans, however, were a more rigorous standard employed and, in any event, the issues facing the courts and legislatures will not be comprehensible without an understanding of the differing levels of judicial scrutiny.

THE THREE-TIERED APPROACH

When the Supreme Court has to decide whether a particular statute passes constitutional muster, it will employ one of three standards to determine whether the statute is constitutionally infirm: (1) strict scrutiny, (2) heightened scrutiny, or (3) the rational basis test. Strict scrutiny requires that the examined statute be narrowly tailored to promote a compelling state interest; heightened scrutiny requires that the statute be substantially related to an important state interest; and the rational basis test requires that the statute be rationally related to a legitimate state goal.

Strict scrutiny involves the most demanding standard. If the state interests are not compelling or the chosen means is not sufficiently narrowly tailored, the statute will be held unconstitutional.[1] Almost invariably, statutes examined with strict scrutiny do not pass constitutional muster.[2]

Heightened scrutiny involves an intermediate test which is less exacting than strict scrutiny; the government interest must be important rather than compelling and the means chosen to promote that interest must be substantially related rather than narrowly tailored. Although this level of scrutiny will not always result in the statute's being held unconstitutional,[3] it does impose a tougher standard than the rational basis test.

The rational basis test is the least rigorous standard.[4] In *Williamson v. Lee Optical*, the Court suggested that as long as there was "an evil at hand for correction" and "the particular legislative measure was a rational way to correct it,"[5] the statute would pass the rational basis test. Yet, in *City of Cleburne v. Cleburne Living Center*,[6] the Court indicated that the rational basis test may be a more rigorous test than many suppose. The *Cleburne* Court used a *rational basis* test to overturn a denial of a zoning permit for a home for the mentally handicapped, despite that denial being a rational way to address legitimate state concerns.[7] The Court's using the rational basis test in this way has caused (1) some debate whether there is only *one* rational basis test (the test used in *Lee Optical* seems much weaker than the test used in *Cleburne*)[8] and (2) some confusion in the lower courts. For example, in *High Tech Gays v. Defense Industrial Security Clearance Office*, one three-judge panel in the Ninth Circuit suggested that the military policy concerning gays and lesbians could easily pass the rational basis test.[9] In *Pruitt v. Cheney*, a different three-judge panel in the *same* circuit suggested that the *Cleburne* rational basis test might be used to overturn the constitutionality of that very policy.[10]

In *Romer v. Evans*, the Supreme Court considered an amendment to the Colorado Constitution which withdrew "from homosexuals, but no others, specific legal protection from the injuries caused by discrimination, and . . . [forbade] reinstatement of these laws and policies."[11] The Court recognized that "if a law neither burdens a fundamental right nor targets a suspect class," it will be upheld "so long as it bears a rational relation to some legitimate end."[12] However, the Court found the amendment "inexplicable by anything but animus toward the class that it affect[ed]," and held it unconstitutional because it lacked "a rational relationship to legitimate state interests."[13]

The *Romer* dissent suggested that the standard employed by the Court was more robust than the usual rational basis test.[14] Basically, the disagreement between the majority and the dissent with respect to the rational basis test is best understood as a disagreement about whether the *Cleburne* rather than the *Lee Optical* test was appropriately used, although the Court has never explicitly admitted that the rational basis test in reality involves two different tests.

The Supreme Court will employ a more exacting standard than

the rational basis test when the legislation adversely affects *either* (a) certain specified classes, implicating the Court's suspect class analysis, *or* (b) certain specified interests, implicating the Court's fundamental interest analysis. To understand these analyses, it will be helpful to understand why these safeguards were developed and the purposes they were designed to serve.

WHAT IS A SUSPECT CLASS?

A suspect class is a group of individuals whom the Court recognizes as deserving special protection from our majoritarian political process because the group has a history of having been subjected to purposeful, unjustified discrimination, and also has a history of political powerlessness.[15] A quasi-suspect class is a group that has the same indicia as does a suspect class, although to a lesser degree. Because such groups tend to be shut out of the political process, they will be unable to avail themselves of one of the safeguards built into our political system to bring about changes in legislation adversely affecting them.[16] Realizing that such groups will not be adequately protected by the political process, the Court will compensate by more carefully examining relevant legislation to make sure that it is serving a legitimate purpose and is not simply discriminating against an unprotected minority.[17]

The Supreme Court has refused to provide an explicit rule or definition to establish which classes are suspect or quasi-suspect. Instead, it has offered the following list of qualities to help determine which groups merit this protected status. The group must be "discrete and insular,"[18] individuals of the class must have a "disability" over which they do not have control,[19] and the defining characteristic of the class must bear no rational relation to a legitimate state purpose.[20] Further, the group must have "experienced a 'history of purposeful unequal treatment' or have been subjected to unique disabilities on the basis of stereotyped characteristics not truly indicative of their abilities."[21] Finally, class membership must be stigmatized by society.[22]

The Court is wise to insist that laws that discriminate against groups exemplifying the above characteristics be examined with close scrutiny. Although a law that adversely affects such a class *might* be serving a legitimate interest, it might instead involve an attempt by the State to continue discriminating against the disfavored class. As the Supreme Court made clear in *Skinner v. Oklahoma ex rel. Williamson*, strict scrutiny of certain classifications "is essential, lest unwittingly, or otherwise, invidious discriminations are made against groups or types of individuals in violation of the constitutional guarantee of just and equal laws."[23] Indeed, over a hundred years ago, the Supreme Court recognized in *Strauder v. West Virginia* that unless closer scrutiny is sometimes imposed, "[s]tate laws might be enacted or enforced to perpetuate the [invidious] distinctions that had before existed."[24] As the *Romer* Court explained, "By requiring that the classification bear a rational relationship to an independent and legitimate legislative end, we ensure that classifications are not drawn for the purpose of disadvantaging the group burdened by the law."[25]

The Court has offered various examples of suspect classes: race,[26] nationality,[27] religion,[28] and alienage.[29] This list is not exhaustive, however. In *Massachusetts Board of Retirement v. Murgia*, Justice Thurgood Marshall recognized in his dissent that there are "classes, not now classified as 'suspect', that are unfairly burdened by invidious discrimination unrelated to the individual worth of their members."[30]

DISCOVERING NEW SUSPECT CLASSES

In his *Murgia* dissent, Justice Marshall noted that the Court has "apparently lost interest in recognizing further . . . 'suspect' classes."[31] If indeed the Court is unwilling to recognize "new" suspect classes, it may be open to criticism, depending upon whether that refusal is justified or instead merely arbitrary.

Whether such a refusal is arbitrary will itself depend upon what is involved in "discovering" new suspect classes. For example, the Court might believe that it should simply use its "intuition" to discover which groups have suspect status. If this is the correct method, then the Court is not open to criticism merely because it in good faith fails to discover any additional suspect classes. If the Court fails to intuit a class's suspect status, then the class is not suspect; there is no independent ground upon which a class's suspect status could be based.

Perhaps the Court believes that it does not directly discover the suspect status of classes, but instead discovers or intuits the relevant indicia and then judges whether the group in question meets those criteria. The Court's unwillingness to recognize new suspect classes might simply mean that it is unwilling to recognize additional criteria or indicia by which to determine which classes are suspect. If this accurately reflects the Court's position, the Court should not be criticized because it in good faith fails to discover or recognize any additional criteria. If the Court does not recognize additional criteria, then there are none. There is no independent ground upon which the appropriateness of a nonrecognized criterion could be based.

Another possibility is that when refusing to recognize new suspect classes, the Court is suggesting that no unrecognized classes have the relevant characteristics to the extent that already recognized classes have them. If this accurately reflects the Court's position, the Court may not deserve criticism merely because it has failed to extend protected status to groups that suffer invidious discrimination to a lesser extent than do suspect and quasi-suspect classes. Although one might argue that the degree to which groups must have the relevant qualities should be relaxed so that new groups may be included, one would not thereby be criticizing the Court for failing to apply the existing criteria but, instead, suggesting that the current standards are too strict. Certainly the Court might be open to criticism for requiring that groups have the relevant indicia to too great a degree. This kind of criticism, however, has much less force than the criticism that the Court is failing to apply the criteria already recognized as appropriate.

Finally, the Court might not believe that it directly discovers or recognizes the relevant criteria. Rather, it recognizes certain principles regarding the appropriate treatment and protection of persons in the United States. This approach suggests that the criteria are derivable from the relevant principles. If other criteria more closely capture the spirit of those principles, those criteria should either supplant or be added to the current ones and the Court deserves criticism for failing to *revise* the relevant indicia to more accurately reflect the purposes which underlie suspect class jurisprudence.

Insofar as the indicia of suspectness are based on some underlying principle like respect for persons, the class of lesbians, gays, and bisexuals will have whatever characteristics are (objectively) chosen to reflect that principle, at least insofar as the currently recognized classes provide any guidance. However, the Court has not stated that the criteria are derived from some neutral principle, and thus criticizing the Court for failing to recognize that gays, lesbians, and bisexuals have the *revised* indicia may not seem particularly damning. One might imagine a defender of the Court responding, "*Were* those the applicable criteria, the Court *would* recognize that gays, lesbians, and bisexuals compose a suspect or quasi-suspect class. However, because those *are not* the relevant characteristics, the Court *does not* recognize that the class is protected."

Yet, one need not assert that the indicia are derivable from some underlying principle in order to justly criticize the Court for its failure to recognize that lesbians, gays, and bisexuals compose a suspect or quasi-suspect class. Indeed, unless the Court maintains that it directly intuits suspectness, a claim that presumably has been rejected because the Court has already articulated the relevant indicia, the Court is open to criticism because the class of lesbians, bisexuals, and gays already has the recognized characteristics of suspectness.

For present purposes, it does not matter whether the Court pictures itself as somehow intuiting the relevant criteria or, instead, as deriving them from some neutral principle. Having recognized the indicia of suspectness, the Court cannot simply announce that it is unwilling to recognize new suspect classes if those classes have the relevant characteristics as least as much as classes already recognized as suspect or quasi-suspect have them. While the Court may not be open to criticism for failing to recognize additional principles or criteria, it clearly is appropriately criticized for failing to apply the criteria it has already recognized as relevant.

The class of lesbians, gays, and bisexuals, although not yet recognized as suspect or quasi-suspect, deserves to be so recognized because it already meets the relevant standards. Thus, as a matter of *fairness*, this "new" class should be recognized as suspect or quasi-suspect. Indeed, because the class of lesbians, bisexuals, and gay men already meets all of the Court's announced criteria for suspectness, the Court cannot deny that status without either (a) admitting that some classes already recognized as suspect or quasi-suspect do not in fact merit that status, or (b) admitting that classes are recognized as suspect or nonsuspect at the whim of the Court. The Court cannot choose either (a) or (b) without further supporting the view that it determines suspect status capriciously and arbitrarily.

APPLYING THE RELEVANT CRITERIA

Various theorists and jurists have noted the Court's unwillingness to recognize that lesbians, gays, and bisexuals constitute a suspect or quasi-suspect class in light of the currently accepted criteria, and have attempted to justify that unwillingness by showing which of the relevant standards have not been met.[32] Some have denied that lesbians, gays, and bisexuals constitute a discrete, insular, and powerless group;[33] others have denied that they are defined by a characteristic that is uncontrollable or immutable;[34] while still others deny that gays, lesbians, and bisexuals are discriminated against on the basis of a characteristic that is generally irrelevant as a basis for legislation.[35]

Powerlessness

The reason that courts have viewed legislation that is passed out of animus with disfavor is that such legislation is not likely to have a rational basis and is not likely to be corrected by the normal democratic processes. If such animus is absent, the courts will assume that the standard political processes will provide the necessary correction when unwise legislation has been passed. Thus, the courts provide an additional check on legislation when there is reason to believe that the normal political processes are not operating properly.[36]

The belief that the normal political processes are not operating correctly suggests that the targeted group lacks political power. Regrettably, the Supreme Court has not made clear how powerless a group must be to qualify as potentially meriting protection. Not surprisingly, this has led to confusion in the lower courts, sometimes resulting in exaggeration of the degree to which a group must be powerless to merit that status. For example, some courts have suggested that the relevant "test is whether the particular group has 'no ability to attract the attention of lawmakers.'"[37] That this is an exaggeration becomes evident when one considers that some of the *current* suspect and quasi-suspect classes could not meet this standard. For example, classifications on the basis of race or gender would not then deserve heightened scrutiny. The same might be said of religion.

Perhaps it will be thought that religion would still be suspect because some of the identifiable religious groups have not yet attained political power.[38] Yet, if this is the correct mode of analysis, then one should look at the individually identifiable groups within sexual orientation. For example, it does not seem that bisexuals are a particularly powerful group. In any event, it would at best be ironic to suggest that lesbians have too much political power for sexual orientation to be considered a quasi-suspect class but that women in general are not too powerful as a class to merit heightened scrutiny.

The above discussion assumes for the sake of argument a point that is by no means obvious, namely, that lesbians, gays, and bisexuals in fact have a great deal of power. The mere assertion that a group has "sufficient" political power does not make it so.[39] Further, it is clear that the relevant test for suspect status is not simply whether, in the *Cleburne* Court's words, the group "lacks [any] political power."[40] Rather, it is how much power that group has and whether that group is as discrete, insular, and shut out of the political process as *other groups meriting heightened or strict scrutiny.* Were the inability to attract the attention of lawmakers the real criterion, there would be a radical change in who qualified as a suspect class.

Certainly, gays, lesbians, and bisexuals are more powerful politically now than they were years ago. When deciding whether they meet the relevant standard, however, one must compare them to groups whom the Court has held to constitute suspect or quasi-suspect classes. African-Americans and other minorities are clearly more powerful politically than they were years ago; yet (one hopes) theorists would not claim that those groups should no longer be viewed as constituting suspect classes.[41]

Courts have misunderstood the degree of powerlessness required in order for a class to be suspect or quasi-suspect. That misunderstanding is due, at least in part, to a mistaken focus upon a particular passage in *City of Cleburne v. Cleburne Living Center*[42] without considering how that passage fits into the opinion as a whole. The *Cleburne* Court denied that mental retardation was a quasi-suspect classification because "those who are mentally retarded have a reduced ability to cope with and function in the everyday world . . . and the States' interest in dealing with and providing for them is plainly a legitimate one."[43] The Court also argued that the "legislative response, which could hardly have occurred and survived without public support, negates any claim that the mentally retarded are politically powerless in the sense that they have no ability to attract the attention of the lawmakers."[44]

Courts have zeroed in on *Cleburne*'s discussion of the inability "to attract the attention of the lawmakers" to conclude that gay and lesbian people cannot compose a suspect class because they can attract the attention of legislators,[45] without considering the Court's claim that the state's interest in dealing with and providing for the mentally handicapped was clearly legitimate. By solely focussing on the point concerning the ability to attract the attention of legislators, courts have come up with an absurd reading of the case. For example, if that passage is taken literally, it would imply that the paradigmatic suspect classification, race, would not be suspect. Given that the Civil Rights Act of 1964 was passed to protect racial minorities, there is "obviously" no need to make race a suspect classification. Indeed, if the passage about attracting attention is read literally, one might assume that legislation passed *against* minorities would establish that those minorities were not suspect; any group which is the subject of discriminatory legislation has obviously captured the attention of legislators.

Suppose that the courts admit the absurdity of a reading of the relevant criterion that implied that those who are most discriminated against would be without a remedy. Suppose instead that the courts were to say that as soon as a class secured some *protective* legislation, the class would obviously no longer need judicial protection. Yet, this reading would be only slightly less absurd than the previous one. Indeed, Justice Marshall recognized the self-defeating nature of the position that only completely powerless groups can be suspect classes. "Once society begins to recognize certain practices as discriminatory, in part because previously stigmatized groups have mobilized politically to lift this stigma, the Court would refrain from approaching such practices with the added skepticism of heightened scrutiny."[46]

When legislatures outlaw discrimination on the basis of sexual orientation, they do so by including sexual orientation among a list of characteristics which cannot legitimately be the basis of discrimination such as race, nationality, and gender. To conclude that sexual orientation cannot be suspect by virtue of its being on such a list but to refuse to draw the same conclusion about the other characteristics on that list suggests bias. When one considers that many more legislatures protect race than orientation, the fallacy of the position "if legislatures offer protection then the class cannot be suspect" becomes apparent.

Ironically, there have recently been attempts by the electorate in some localities and states to set up special obstacles to prevent lesbians, gays, and bisexuals from securing equal rights; it is claimed that the class does not merit special solicitude. Basically, these initiatives may be understood as statements to the various legislative bodies that voters do not want the class to receive protections against, for example, job and housing discrimination, because those voting in favor *want to be able to discriminate on the basis of sexual orientation.*[47]

Statutes preventing orientation discrimination do not create "special" rights but, instead, simply include sexual orientation among other characteristics that will not be an acceptable basis for the withholding of benefits.[48] Claims to the contrary notwithstanding, legislative attempts to preclude these kinds of protections do not involve attempts to maintain an equal playing field but, instead, to allow invidious discrimination. The *Romer* Court explained that it could not "accept the view that Amendment 2's prohibition on specific legal protections does no more than deprive homosexuals of special rights. To the contrary, the amendment imposes a special disability upon those persons alone."[49]

One of the more ironic facets of these initiatives is that they underscore the importance and appropriateness of gays, lesbians and bisexuals being declared a suspect or quasi-suspect class *by the courts.* Those that are relatively powerless and relatively unable to forge political alliances are less able to secure *continuing* protection through legislative bodies and, all else equal, *more suitable* for judicial protection. In what would be a wonderful tongue-in-cheek analysis were there only reason to believe that it was not written in utter earnestness, the *Romer* dissent characterized Amendment 2 as "a modest attempt by seemingly tolerant Coloradans to preserve traditional sexual mores against the efforts of a politically powerful minority to revise those mores through the use of the laws."[50] It is hard to imagine how an amendment which "withdraws from homosexuals, but no others, specific legal protection from the injuries caused by discrimination, and . . . forbids reinstatement of these laws and policies"[51] could be characterized as a modest attempt by tolerant individuals to rein in a powerful political group.

It is important to distinguish between two different ways in which groups might acquire protection from discrimination. One is through legislative bodies, whether city councils or state legislatures. Here, the groups may have enough political clout to acquire such status or, perhaps, may receive protection out of a recognition that such irrational discrimination is wrong. Another source of protection is through the courts.

It should not be thought that these judicial and legislative protections are mutually exclusive. Classes that have been recognized by the courts as suspect or quasi-suspect may also receive special protection from state legislatures or city councils. For example, the ordinance at issue in *Equality Foundation of Greater Cincinnati, Inc. v. City of Cincinnati* offered protection on the basis of race, gender, color, religion, and ethnic and national origin, in addition to a number of characteristics that did not involve suspect or quasi-suspect classifications.[52] It strains credibility to suggest that lesbians, gays, and bisexuals are too powerful to merit strict or heightened scrutiny but that classes with that designation who are receiving protection from legislatures are nonetheless not too powerful to deserve that classification.

Control

In order for a characteristic to be the basis of a suspect classification, it must be something which individuals cannot readily control. If the characteristic could be easily changed without cost to the possessor, there would be little point to subjecting all legislation adversely affecting all and only individuals with that characteristic to heightened scrutiny. If the characteristic cannot be changed, then it is sensible for that characteristic to be the basis of a suspect classification, assuming that the other standards have also been met. The important issue involves determining where along the continuum between "easily discardable without cost" and "immutable" the dividing line should be drawn.

Regrettably, there has been no consensus with respect to where that line lies. If a characteristic is immutable, it clearly is not within an individual's control; the individual would be unable to change it even were he or she so inclined. However, merely because a characteristic can be changed does not mean that it cannot be the basis of a suspect classification.

Currently, it is controversial whether sexual orientation is immutable. Insofar as it is biologically determined, the characteristic should be so classified. Two points should be emphasized, however. First, even if sexual orientation is not genetically based, it may nonetheless be immutable because orientation may be the result of environmental factors which occur early in life.[53] Second, even if orientation is a mutable characteristic, it may nonetheless be the basis of a suspect class.

Permanence

Some theorists suggest that the reason that lesbians, bisexuals, and gays do not compose a suspect class is that they are not shackled with a permanent disability. If homosexuality can be "cured," then it is not a permanent "affliction" and one criterion of suspect status will not have been met.

Yet, the Court does not require permanence in order for heightened or strict scrutiny to be imposed. Illegitimacy need not be permanent, since fathers may be able to legitimize their children. Nonetheless, statutes adversely affecting illegitimates merit heightened scrutiny. Further, religious affiliation is a mutable characteristic. One can renounce one's religion and have no religious affiliation or one can convert to another religion. Nonetheless, despite the mutability of this characteristic, religion is a suspect classification.

Obviousness

Others who question whether gays, lesbians, and bisexuals have a disability over which they have no control suggest that the characteristic in question, although perhaps permanent and uncontrollable, is easily hidden and thus others may be unable to discover that individuals have the "offending" characteristic.[54] For example, all else being equal, it is much easier to determine the race or sex of a particular person than it is to determine that person's sexual orientation.

Yet, this point is less telling than might first appear. Illegitimacy is a quasi-suspect classification, despite the possible difficulty in determining who was born out of wedlock. National origin is a suspect classification despite the nonobviousness of that characteristic. Further, religion is a suspect classification, despite the difficulty of determining the religious faiths of individuals "unless they elect to be so identifiable by conduct,"[55] for example, by wearing religious jewelry or by other sorts of self-identifying behavior. While it is true that one's orientation may not be as obvious as one's race or sex, it is not true that orientation is less obvious than other classifications which nonetheless have been deemed suspect or quasi-suspect.[56]

Status versus Activity
Many who claim that gays, lesbians, and bisexuals can rid themselves of their "affliction" assume that homosexuality involves an *activity* rather than an *orientation*.[57] Thus, because gays, lesbians and bisexuals can decide to refrain from engaging in sexual relations with members of the same sex (thereby supposedly not becoming or continuing to be gay, lesbian, or bisexual), they have control over their "disability".

There are at least two difficulties with the "activity" view. First, it is wrongheaded. This can be seen most clearly if one thinks about how heterosexuals would analogously be defined. It would approach absurdity to suggest that *only* those who engage in sexual relations with the opposite sex are heterosexual. On such an account, individuals who refrained from having sexual relations, citing health or religious reasons, would seem to be neither heterosexual nor homosexual. Presumably, courts do not want to imply that individuals who have not yet been sexually active (and indeed may have consciously chosen not to have sexual relations) do not and indeed *cannot* have a sexual orientation. Individuals who wait until they marry before having sexual relations have a sexual orientation even if they have not yet been sexually active.

Courts must not conflate choosing an orientation with choosing to act in light of an orientation. Presumably, no one would argue that individuals who choose to act in light of their heterosexual orientation *thereby choose their orientation*. The individuals had a particular orientation and then acted in light of it. Even had they not acted in light of it, they still would have had that orientation. Thus, a court that looks at whether individuals choose to have sexual relations in order to determine whether individuals choose their orientation is simply looking at the wrong criterion. Even if one's orientation is fixed, one can usually choose whether to have sexual relations.

The Supreme Court has made clear that it is important to distinguish between activity and status, regardless of the likelihood that people with a particular status will engage in that activity. In *Robinson v. California*,[58] the Court considered whether California's punishing an individual for his drug addiction violated the Fourteenth Amendment. The Court overturned the conviction because the California statute made "the 'status' of narcotic addiction a criminal offense."[59] In *Powell v. Texas*,[60] the Court affirmed its view expressed in *Robinson* that status and activity can be distinguished even when the defining characteristic of the status is to engage in a particular activity. The *Powell* Court explained, "Punishment for a status is particularly obnoxious . . . because it involves punishment for a mere propensity, a desire to commit an offense; the mental element is not simply one part of the crime but may constitute all of it."[61] In *Powell*, the individual was punished not for his status but for his action.[62] If the Court can distinguish between the activity of drinking from the status of alcoholism and the activity of drug-taking from the status of drug addiction, it strains credibility that the activity of having sexual relations cannot be distinguished from the status of sexual orientation.

Robinson may be used to establish another important point. While the *Robinson* Court made clear that the state could not punish an individual on the basis of his status as a drug addict, the Court did not preclude the state from punishing people for taking drugs. Thus, a state's being allowed to punish an act does not allow it to punish the class. Precisely because of the difference between status and conduct, it would be false to conclude that a state's being constitutionally permitted to criminalize sodomy would "entitle" the state to discriminate against the class of individuals who might desire to commit sodomy.[63] Indeed, the *Bowers* Court made clear that it was not addressing any Equal Protection issues when it held that states were permitted to criminalize homosexual sodomy.[64] Thus, in

Padula v. Webster, the court was wrong to conclude that the Supreme Court's refusal to strike down sodomy laws implied that discrimination against lesbian, bisexual, and gay people was permissible.[65] The court in *Woodward v. United States* made the same mistake.[66] Even if states may criminalize sodomy,[67] sexual orientation itself may not be punished and, further, may nonetheless be a suspect or quasi-suspect class.[68]

Sexual orientation, as opposed to sexual activity, is not behavioral. Even if it were, however, that would not establish that it could not be the basis of a suspect classification. Religion is a suspect classification and it arguably should be defined in terms of behaviors (when or how one prays, customs observed, etc.). Indeed, if "behavioral" may be defined in terms of desires and inclinations in addition to observable activities, it is even more plausible to define religion in terms of behaviors, because some of the internal desires and inclinations associated with religion and spirituality might then nonetheless count as religious "behaviors."

Religion is important to consider in any analysis of suspect class jurisprudence. We consider some of the reasons offered to explain why sexual orientation cannot be the basis of a suspect classification: the characteristic is not genetic in origin, the characteristic is mutable, the defining characteristic is behavioral, the characteristic is nonobvious, and the targeted group is politically powerful.

Although it is unclear whether these claims are true of homosexuality, it is clear that they are true of religion and religion is nonetheless suspect. Religion is not immutable, neither in the sense that it is genetically determined nor in the sense that it is unchangeable (because of the possibility of conversion). Religion might be defined in terms of behaviors: when and where one prays, how one lives, etc. Further, it may be nonobvious: unless one wears religious jewelry, discusses one's religious practices, etc., others may have no idea what faith one observes. Finally, religious groups are not politically powerless.

To some, the idea that sexual orientation might be compared to religion might seem absurd.[69] At least for some individuals, religion is an essential part of personal identity. It is not merely a simple, easily identifiable behavior or a tendency to perform such a behavior, for example, when and where one prays, but instead is a part of the core of the person's personality. Thus, insofar as one is going to claim that religion is behavioral, one will have to include a fairly complex set of behaviors. Religion is not merely something that one considers on Friday or Saturday or Sunday but something that affects one's entire life.

Similarly, sexual orientation does not merely involve a simple, easily identified behavior or tendency to perform such behavior, but instead is a vital part of one's personality. Thus, for some, sexual orientation does not merely involve what one does on a Friday or Saturday night but involves something that affects one's entire life. Religion and sexual orientation cannot be distinguished by claiming that the former is important in the structure of personal identity but that the latter is not.

It is not argued here that religion and orientation are analogous in all relevant respects. It may well be easier to change one's religion than one's sexual orientation.[70] Nonetheless, it is important to examine these two categories together because even if many of the controversial claims made about homosexuality are true, the Court's treatment of religion indicates that the (alleged) truth of those claims would not be a bar to orientation's being a suspect category.

The point here is not that religion, alienage, and illegitimacy do not merit heightened scrutiny, but merely that orientation should not be denied suspect status because the class allegedly fails to meet the applicable standards when the class has the relevant characteristics to an equal or greater extent than those classes already recognized as suspect or quasi-suspect. If courts wish to maintain even an appearance of fairness and disinterestedness, they must stop applying the relevant criteria in bad faith to achieve the results that they desire. Otherwise, they will continue to undermine society's increasingly shaky belief in the rule of law and the objectivity of the courts.

Irrelevance
Some theorists who believe that orientation is not a suspect classification argue that gays, lesbians, and bisexuals are not discriminated

against on the basis of a characteristic that is generally irrelevant as a basis for legislation. They contend that because homosexuality is immoral, the characteristic in question is relevant as a basis for legislation; morality is promoted by punishing or discouraging homosexuality.[71]

Yet, one must be very careful when justifying the imposition of burdens on one specific group of people because of their alleged moral, spiritual, or physical inferiority. Suspect class jurisprudence is based on the inappropriateness of stigmatizing groups.

Over one hundred years ago, the Court in *Strauder v. West Virginia* supported the right of African-Americans to be free "from legal discriminations, implying inferiority in civil society, lessening the security of their enjoyment of the rights which others enjoy, and discriminations which are steps towards reducing them to the condition of a subject race."[72] In *Brown v. Board of Education*, the Court worried that segregating children on the basis of race might generate "a feeling of inferiority."[73] Even the Court in *Plessy v. Ferguson*[74] worried about the state's imposing a stigma on a group. That Court, however, upheld segregation in railway cars, denying that "the enforced separation of the two races stamps the colored race with a badge of inferiority."[75] The *Plessy* Court apparently believed that if segregation does somehow impose a stamp of inferiority, "it is not by reason of anything found in the act, but solely because the colored race chooses to put that construction upon it."[76]

Those who justify discrimination against gay, bisexual, and lesbian people on moral inferiority grounds seem to forget that racial discrimination was once justified on the same basis.[77] There are at least two reasons to be wary of such arguments. First, they may justify policies which cause great and undeserved harm to the adversely affected group. Second, there is reason to believe that such "moral" arguments mask an antipathy towards the "inferior" group; these "moral" arguments allow policies to be adopted which cannot otherwise be supported.

In *Palmore v. Sidoti*, the Court recognized that "[c]lassifying persons according to their race is more likely to reflect racial prejudice than legitimate public concerns; the race, not the person, dictates the category."[78] It is no less irrational to discriminate on the basis of sexual orientation than it is on the basis of race. In striking a West Virginia law excluding African-Americans from jury service, the *Strauder* Court made clear that it was the *irrationality* of the classification that was offensive.[79] Further, that Court established that the Fourteenth Amendment was broad in scope. "The Fourteenth Amendment . . . speaks in general terms . . . [which] are as comprehensive as possible. The language is prohibitory; but every prohibition implies the existence of rights and immunities, prominent among which is an immunity from inequality of legal protection, either for life, liberty, or property."[80] The equal protection of the laws must be respected. As the Supreme Court explained in *Rose v. Mitchell,* "Equal protection of the laws is . . . a command which the State must respect, the benefits of which every person may demand."[81]

One must wonder what is being claimed when a whole group is characterized as immoral and thus appropriately subject to discriminatory treatment. Is it that individuals in that group lie, cheat, steal, murder, etc.? There is no reason to believe that gays, lesbians, and bisexuals are more guilty of those offenses than are other individuals. Is it that the whole class is immoral because they are all sodomites? Even were there reason to think sodomy immoral, one still would have to ask (1) What of those who do not commit sodomy?, and (2) What of those heterosexuals who commit sodomy with their opposite-sex partners?[82]

It is sometimes argued that there is no desire to punish the class of lesbians, gays, and bisexuals but, instead, to punish a particular activity in which they might engage, namely, sodomy. Yet, there is reason to reject that contention. If that were the goal, one would expect increased enforcement of sodomy statutes in the minority of states that have such statutes and would not expect the class to be penalized in areas of life where that activity was not implicated. Further, one would not expect discriminatory treatment in those states in which the commission of sodomitic acts by consenting adults is not illegal. That sodomy laws tend not to be enforced and that the majority of states do not have such laws anyway suggest that the prevention of sodomy is not the real goal but instead is being used as a pretext to invidiously discriminate against an unpopular group.

What is eminently clear is that the evils of sodomy have been greatly exaggerated, both with respect to what will happen if such conduct is not punished and with respect to what states are constitutionally permitted to do in their efforts to punish such conduct. One commentator, Harry Jaffa, has suggested that "if sodomy is not unnatural, then nothing is unnatural. And if nothing is unnatural, then nothing—including slavery and genocide—is unjust."[83] Fortunately, various states disagree, as is evidenced by their decriminalizing sodomy but their not decriminalizing murder, rape, etc.

Even were sodomy evil, states would not thereby be given carte blanche to enact statutes designed to punish individuals merely suspected of committing sodomy. The Constitution demands that there be some rational relation between the desired end and the means chosen to achieve that end. Thus, if one wishes to prevent sodomy, one should pass laws criminalizing sodomy rather than impose penalties in areas of life which are totally unrelated to individuals' sexual practices. Further, our entire constitutional system is predicated on preventing the State from imposing penalties without observing Due Process requirements. Thus, before punishing someone for having committed sodomy, one must first establish that the person did indeed perform the prohibited act. That penalties are imposed in states where the "evil" behavior is not criminally proscribed speaks to the pretextual nature of this rationale.

A paradigmatic example of the type of specious reasoning alluded to above was offered by Justice Antonin Scalia in his *Romer* dissent. Justice Scalia suggested that Amendment 2 was "constitutional as applied to those who engage in homosexual conduct,"[84] even though Colorado had repealed its antisodomy law in 1971[85] and even though, in any event, Amendment 2 had nothing to do with sodomy. If Coloradans had in fact wanted to punish the practice of sodomy rather than the class of lesbians, gays, and bisexuals, then they should have passed a law criminalizing sodomy. That they did not try to pass such a law but instead passed an amendment which "withdraws from homosexuals, but no others, specific legal protection from the injuries caused by discrimination, and . . . [which] forbids reinstatement of these laws and policies"[86] suggests animus rather than a "legitimate" desire to criminalize sodomy.

A separate question is whether laws that criminalize sodomy, especially one like Texas's which criminalizes only same-sex relations,[87] will continue to be upheld following *Romer*. In any event, *Romer* seems to preclude states from using the pretense of an interest in the prevention of sodomy to justify the imposition of penalties on lesbians, bisexuals, and gays for "offenses" that have nothing to do with that sexual practice.

SEX DISCRIMINATION

The above discussion involves whether lesbians, gays, and bisexuals compose a suspect or quasi-suspect class. Although that class has the relevant indicia to the required extent, courts have nonetheless been reluctant to subject legislation adversely affecting the class to heightened or strict scrutiny. However, it should not be thought that the refusal to recognize the suspectness of the class forecloses challenges to same-sex marriage bans on Equal Protection grounds, since those bans discriminate on the basis of sex.

In *Baehr v. Lewin*, a plurality of the Hawaii Supreme Court held that the Hawaii marriage statute "on its face and as applied, regulates access to the marital status and its concomitant rights and benefits on the basis of the applicants' sex."[88] Although sex is a quasi-suspect classification on federal constitutional grounds, it is a suspect classification according to Hawaii's constitution, and thus a statute discriminating on the basis of sex will be subjected to strict scrutiny. The classification must be "justified by compelling state interests" and must be "narrowly drawn to avoid unnecessary abridgements of the applicant couples' constitutional rights."[89]

Explicit Discrimination
The *Baehr* plurality reasoned that because a man may marry a woman but not a man, and because a woman may marry a man but

not a woman, the Hawaii statute discriminated on the basis of sex.[90] The Supreme Court has made clear its aversion to statutes which invidiously discriminate on that basis. In *Orr v. Orr*, the Court struck down an alimony system that disadvantaged males, noting that "Mr. Orr bears a burden he would not bear were he female."[91] Thus, the Court found that Orr was being disadvantaged because of his sex, and held that the statutory scheme was unconstitutional.[92]

In *Orr*, the Court made clear that not all males would be disadvantaged by the statute under examination. "As compared to a gender-neutral law placing alimony obligations on the spouse able to pay, the present Alabama statutes give an advantage only to the financially secure wife whose husband is in need."[93] Thus, the Court invalidated the statutory scheme, despite its not adversely affecting all males.

Arguably, the alimony system at issue in *Orr* was unconstitutional because it imposed a burden on *some* males but on *no* females. But the Hawaii marital statute imposed a burden on *both* sexes. Indeed, the dissent in *Baehr* argued that the statute did not involve an equal protection violation because all males and females were treated alike. "A male cannot obtain a license to marry another male, and a female cannot obtain a license to marry another female."[94]

The *Baehr* plurality rejected the dissent's argument, correctly pointing out that the Supreme Court had rejected an analogous line of reasoning in *Loving*.[95] The *Loving* Court had to evaluate the state of Virginia's argument that "because its miscegenation statutes punish equally both the white and the Negro participants in an interracial marriage, these statutes, despite their reliance on racial classifications, do not constitute an invidious discrimination based upon race."[96] The Supreme Court rejected the "notion that the mere 'equal application' of a statute containing racial classifications is enough to remove the classifications from the Fourteenth Amendment's proscription of all invidious racial discriminations."[97] Just as the statute at issue in *Loving* discriminated on the basis of race, notwithstanding that both whites and blacks would be disadvantaged, the statute at issue in *Baehr* discriminates on the basis of sex, notwithstanding that both sexes are disadvantaged by the law.

It might seem that the statute at issue in *Baehr* discriminates on the basis of sexual orientation rather than on the basis of sex. Yet, on its face, the statute applies to all individuals, regardless of their orientation.[98] While it may fairly be assumed that most individuals wanting to marry a same-sex partner will be lesbian, gay, or bisexual, it should not be assumed that *only* people with a same-sex orientation will want to choose this option. For example, some individuals might want to marry someone of the same sex for economic, political, or social reasons rather than for sexual or emotional ones. Indeed, bans on same-sex marriage have been criticized as *overbroad* because they are not narrowly tailored to discriminate *solely* against lesbians, bisexuals, and gays.[99]

Gender Discrimination

Same-sex marriage bans involve discrimination on the basis of gender because such bans reinforce traditional sex roles. In *Personnel Administrator of Massachusetts v. Feeney*, the Supreme Court recognized that "[c]lassifications based upon gender, not unlike those based upon race, have traditionally been the touchstone for pervasive and often subtle discrimination."[100] Four years earlier, the Supreme Court had established in *Stanton v. Stanton* that gender classifications may not permissibly promote the view that the "female [is] destined solely for the home and the rearing of the family and only the male for the marketplace and the world of ideas."[101] Although Justice Joseph Bradley in his *Bradwell* concurrence suggested that the "natural and proper timidity and delicacy which belongs to the female sex evidently unfits it for many of the occupations of civil life," and that the "paramount destiny and mission of woman are to fulfil the noble and benign offices of wife and mother,"[102] the Supreme Court made clear in *Frontiero v. Richardson* that statutes that promote such views will no longer be countenanced even if they are "rationalized by an attitude of 'romantic paternalism.'"[103]

The Supreme Court has not restricted its notion of what constitutes impermissible role promotion to those classifications promoting the view that women should stay home and rear the children. In

Mississippi University for Women v. Hogan, the Court struck down a classification that tended to "perpetuate the stereotyped view of nursing as an exclusively woman's job."[104] The Court insisted that state classifications be "free of fixed notions concerning the roles and abilities of males and females."[105] The *Orr* Court had already pointed out that classifications based on gender "carry the inherent risk of reinforcing stereotypes about the 'proper place' of women."[106] The *Hogan* Court suggested that it would be vigilant to prevent reinforcement of archaic and stereotypic notions.[107] As the Supreme Court made clear in *Roberts v. United States Jaycees* two years later, discrimination "based on archaic and overbroad assumptions about the relative needs and capacities of the sexes forces individuals to labor under stereotypical notions that often bear no relationship to their actual abilities."[108]

In *Craig v. Boren*, the Court held that because of the "weak congruence between gender and the characteristic or trait that gender purported to represent," the legislature that had created sex-specific drinking ages had to make some changes: either "realign their substantive laws in a gender-neutral fashion" or "adopt procedures for identifying those instances where the sex-centered generalization actually comported with fact."[109] One of the questions at issue is whether statutes prohibiting same-sex marriages need to be changed because they involve a weak congruence between gender and the traits it is supposed to represent.

Many of the functions of marriage can be fulfilled as well by a same-sex couple as by an opposite-sex couple. A state barring same-sex marriages must explain why it has made a sex-based distinction. The state might claim that gender is being used as a proxy for the ability to procreate through the union of the two parties. Because the ability to procreate is not a requirement in opposite-sex marriages, however, it seems more plausible that the state is using gender to promote its own view of the proper roles of the sexes. The *Boren* rationale suggests that a state must either adopt a gender-free classification in its marriage statues or tailor a classification that more precisely captures gender differences. For example, a state could require that the would-be marital partners be able and willing to have a child through their union, although it is doubtful that such a requirement would be constitutional.

The same-sex marriage ban promotes stereotypical gender roles in various ways. It suggests that marital fulfillment (whether sexual, psychological, or emotional) is only appropriately sought by males from females and by females from males. Although there is nothing wrong with seeking such fulfillment from a member of the opposite sex, there is also nothing wrong with seeking it from a member of the same sex.

The *Baehr* plurality made clear that it was not declaring orientation a suspect or quasi-suspect classification.[110] Although the class merits that status, it is unlikely that the class will be accorded that designation. Were sexual orientation recognized as a suspect or quasi-suspect classification, same-sex marriage bans would be held unconstitutional, because the parallels with *Loving* would then be even more striking.[111] Yet, even if orientation is not recognized as a suspect or quasi-suspect classification and even if same-sex marriage bans are not viewed as discriminating on the basis of gender, such bans do not pass constitutional muster.

The *Romer* Court made clear that a statute which "seems inexplicable by anything but animus toward the class that it affects . . . lacks a rational relationship to legitimate state interests."[112] Insofar as same-sex marriage bans involve an attempt to penalize the class of gays, lesbians, and bisexuals because that class is a despised minority, the Equal Protection Clause is violated even under the rational basis test.

Suppose that notwithstanding the clear Equal Protection difficulties, a court were to conclude that the Equal Protection Clause was not violated by same-sex marriage bans. Even so, such bans are unconstitutional because the Due Process Clause is also implicated by statutes prohibiting same-sex unions. The next chapter discusses why the state interests in banning such marriages do not suffice for constitutional purposes to justify such bans.

III THE FUNDAMENTAL INTEREST

IN MARRIAGE

▼

If lesbians, gays, and bisexuals compose a quasi-suspect class or if same-sex marriage bans are recognized as a form of gender-based discrimination, statutes forbidding such unions will be subjected to heightened scrutiny at the very least. Yet, a violation of the Equal Protection Clause is not the only way to trigger the requirement that the Court closely examine such statutes. If the right to marry one's same-sex partner involves a fundamental interest, then courts will examine statutes which abridge that interest with strict scrutiny. If, however, the right to marry one's same-sex partner is a mere liberty interest and if statutes banning such marriages do not violate the Equal Protection Clause, courts will use a rational basis test to determine whether such statutes pass constitutional muster.

SUBSTANTIVE DUE PROCESS

The Supreme Court may decide to examine a statute with strict scrutiny on a ground other than that it adversely affects a suspect class. Sometimes the Court will strictly scrutinize a law because it abridges a fundamental right rather than because it is aimed at a protected class. In these cases, the Court's focus is on the importance of the interest adversely affected.[1] The Court's close examination is not motivated by a belief that the State is being unfair to a particular class but simply by the realization that a very important individual interest hangs in the balance.

Basically, the Court examines legislation either because something very important is at risk, in which case it seems prudent to require more proof from the State that the legislation is necessary since vital interests may be at stake, or because there is reason to believe that the checks built into our system to prevent discrimination against particular classes might not be operative. Thus, although one may rightly infer that if a class is deemed suspect or quasi-suspect the relevant law will be examined with strict or heightened scrutiny, one should not infer that if no suspect or quasi-suspect classes are involved the statute will be examined in light of the rational basis test. The Court may examine a particular law with strict scrutiny solely because fundamental rights are at issue.

Certainly, one should not infer that laws may involve protected classes or fundamental rights but will never involve both. On the contrary, laws have too often been passed to abridge the fundamental rights of suspect classes. Nonetheless, it is important to remember that these are two separate considerations. A law that is prejudicial to the fundamental interests of a nonsuspect class may be declared unconstitutional and a law that is prejudicial to the nonfundamental interests of a suspect class may be upheld. Indeed, even a law that adversely affects the fundamental interests of a suspect class may be upheld if the State's goal is sufficiently compelling and the law is narrowly tailored to promote that goal.[2]

FUNDAMENTAL INTERESTS

The Supreme Court has recognized that the Constitution affords "protection to personal decisions relating to marriage, procreation, contraception, family relationships, child rearing, and education."[3] Courts hearing challenges to state bans on same-sex marriages have had to decide whether the fundamental right to marriage includes the right to marry a same-sex partner. Thus far, courts addressing this have suggested that the fundamental right to marry does not include same-sex marriage because the importance of that right lies in its allowing individuals to raise their own biological children. This is a misinterpretation of the relevant case law which could have significant implications for domestic relations law.

When discussing the right to marry, it is important to establish (a) how important that right is, and (b) why that right is important.

Once these are made clear, courts should not be tempted to accept the kinds of analyses thus far offered to establish that no fundamental rights are abridged by statutes banning same-sex marriages.

THE FUNDAMENTAL INTEREST IN MARRIAGE

In *Loving v. Virginia*, the Court recognized that the "freedom to marry has long been recognized as one of the vital personal rights essential to the orderly pursuit of happiness by free men."[4] That Court also described marriage as "one of the 'basic civil rights of man,' fundamental to our very existence and survival,"[5] and spoke glowingly about the institution of marriage. In *Griswold v. Connecticut*, the Court described marriage as an "association for as noble a purpose as any involved in our prior decisions" that is "intimate to the degree of being sacred."[6] In *Santosky v. Kramer*, the Court discussed "this Court's historical recognition that freedom of personal choice in matters of family life is a fundamental liberty interest protected by the Fourteenth Amendment."[7] The question then is not whether the right to marry is fundamental—it clearly is—but whether the fundamental right to marry includes the right to marry one's same-sex partner. That question cannot be answered without examining the purposes of marriage.

WHY THE RIGHT TO MARRY IS FUNDAMENTAL

Whereas courts agree that the right to marry is fundamental, they disagree about why that right is fundamental. That disagreement is due, at least in part, to the failure of many lower courts to understand or appreciate the numerous, constitutionally significant functions that the institution of marriage serves. For example, although the *Baehr* plurality recognized that the right to marry is as fundamental as rights related to procreation, childbirth, child rearing, and family relationships, it erred in its analysis of why that is so.[8] Its misunderstanding was due to its interpretation of *Zablocki v. Redhail.*[9]

The *Zablocki* Court recognized that the right to marry has been placed on the same level of importance as the right to have and raise one's children.[10] The Court suggested that it "would make little sense to recognize a right of privacy with respect to other matters of family life and not with respect to the decision to enter the relationship that is the foundation of the family in our society."[11] The *Baehr* plurality looked at this passage and concluded, "Implicit in the *Zablocki* Court's link between the right to marry, on the one hand, and the fundamental rights of procreation, childbirth, abortion, and child rearing, on the other, is the assumption that the one is *simply the logical predicate* of the others."[12] Yet, this analysis is faulty, both logically and legally, and cannot credibly be attributed to the Supreme Court.

PROCREATION OUTSIDE OF MARRIAGE

The *Baehr* analysis notwithstanding, marriage is neither a logical nor a legal predicate of procreation. While groups disagree about how to solve or even characterize the problems posed by out-of-wedlock births,[13] it is not credible to claim that marriage is a logical predicate of reproduction, because the illegitimacy rate is high[14] and is projected to go higher.[15]

Perhaps it will be thought that the *Baehr* plurality was simply being hyperbolic. Marriage is not the *logical* but the *legal* predicate of having and raising children. Yet, that analysis must also be rejected because marriage is a legal predicate neither of having a child[16] nor of raising one.[17] Thus, marriage is *neither* a logical *nor* a legal predicate *either* of having *or* of raising a child. *Zablocki* cannot plausibly be understood to be as limited as the *Baehr* plurality implied. Indeed, since in most states gay or lesbian individuals can adopt children, it is hard to understand how the court could have construed *Zablocki* that way.

What is at issue here is an interpretation of Supreme Court precedents regarding who may marry whom. The *Baehr* plurality offered an interpretation of the relevant precedents that both ignores the case law and defies common sense. That the court's interpretation was in error becomes even more obvious when one considers other implications of the opinion. Not only is marriage neither a logical nor a legal predicate of parenthood, but the contrapositive is also true; potential parenthood is neither a logical nor a legal predicate of marriage. Nonetheless, courts have upheld state refusals to issue marriage licenses to same-sex couples because of their alleged inability to have children.

MARRIAGE WITHOUT PROCREATION

It is sometimes argued that because the purpose of marriage is to provide a setting for the production and raising of children, individuals (such as gays and lesbians) who cannot have children need not be afforded the right to marry. This argument is faulty because (1) there is no requirement that married couples be able or willing to have children, and (2) even were there such a requirement, gay and lesbian couples nonetheless could not be precluded on that account.

It is obvious that there is no procreational requirement for marriage, because opposite-sex couples who will not or cannot procreate may nonetheless marry. Courts only claim that the ability to procreate is a precondition of marriage to prevent couples from marrying when same-sex partners wish to be joined together in matrimony. Yet, no unbiased court would hold that opposite-sex couples unable to procreate are permitted to marry but that same-sex couples are prohibited from marrying precisely because of their alleged inability to procreate. Although there may be justifications for distinguishing between opposite-sex and same-sex couples, those justifications should be stated. Courts lose credibility when they impose requirements on one group but not on another when the two groups are similarly situated.

In *Adams v. Howerton*,[18] the court tried to explain why there were no equal protection issues implicated by a policy that distinguished among couples unable to procreate, allowing the opposite-sex couples to marry but prohibiting the same-sex couples from doing so. The court reasoned that because "the state has a compelling interest in encouraging and fostering procreation of the race and providing status and stability to the environment in which children are raised,"[19] the state is permitted "to allow legal marriage as between *all* couples of opposite sex,"[20] even though some of those couples will be unable to have children.

The court understood that there were other ways the state might seek to promote its compelling interest in procreation. For example, the state could "inquire of each couple, before issuing a marriage license, as to their plans for children."[21] Further, the state might "give sterility tests to all applicants, refusing licenses to those found sterile or unwilling to raise a family."[22] The court rejected this approach, believing that "[s]uch tests and inquiries would themselves raise serious constitutional questions."[23]

Yet, one must wonder why these policies would be constitutionally offensive if indeed the state has a compelling interest in making sure that only people willing and able to procreate are joined in matrimony. The state would be narrowly tailoring its procedures to promote its compelling interest.

The *Adams* court failed to notice that even more constitutional issues are raised by the state's allegedly having a compelling interest in procreation but only seeking to promote that interest at the expense of one particular group. Theorists mirror this tendency of selectively applying theories to the disadvantage of one particular group when they claim that the purpose of sexual relations is to produce offspring but then make an exception for heterosexual couples unable or unwilling to procreate.[24] At the very least, these thinkers are open to the charge of intellectual inconsistency.[25]

Commentators defending the exception involving heterosexual couples unable to procreate do not admit that they are offering an intellectually inconsistent view and, indeed, offer an explanation of why their position is perfectly consistent. For example, John Finnis has argued that a "husband and wife who unite their reproductive organs in an act of sexual intercourse which, so far as they can make it, is of a *kind* suitable for generation" function as the appropriate kind of unit and thus "can be actualizing and experiencing the two-in-one flesh common good and reality of marriage, even when some biological condition happens to prevent that unity resulting in generation of a child."[26] Thus, it is claimed that those couples who, for example, are born sterile may nonetheless be married.

This argument is circular, however, because it depends on how one distinguishes between different "kinds." Although it is true that the sterile couple's sexual relations are of a kind suitable for generation *so far as they can make it*, their relations are no more likely to yield offspring than are the relations of a same-sex couple. More argument must be offered to establish why the sterile couple's love-making is of the appropriate kind, especially considering the kinds of couplings these theorists would presumably want to exclude. For example, this theory implies that lesbian sexual relations would be "acceptable" as long as artificial insemination was included as part of the lovemaking.[27] If the theory somehow does not imply this, perhaps because of some analysis that does not beg the question of what is "intrinsic" to the lovemaking, the commentators would be in the paradoxical position of asserting that (same-sex) couples who are capable of procreating are precluded from marrying because they do not engage in a kind of behavior suitable for generation, but that (heterosexual) couples who are incapable of procreating are allowed to marry because they engage in the "correct" kind of behavior.

The above position has other paradoxical implications as well. Even were the claim about the naturally sterile couple accepted as a persuasive response which disposed of the "problem" posed by those *unwillingly* unable to have children, the proposition that opposite-sex couples, but not same-sex couples, should be allowed to marry would still not have been established. Suppose, for example, that the reason that a couple could not reproduce was not because of some biological accident but because they had not wanted to have children and had both been sterilized to prevent conception. In this example, nature cannot be "blamed" for the "misfortune" of being unable to have a child, since this was something the couple had chosen. Should these individuals be prevented from marrying?

Commentators seem not to appreciate the difficulty that such an example poses. They can answer that such a couple should be allowed to marry (and no United States court wishing to avoid being overturned would deny such a couple a marriage license). However, such a position would seem to undermine the commitment to the importance of procreation. Or, these theorists might respond that such a marriage should not be permitted.[28] By denying the marriage license, however, these theorists would not only lose credibility but would also be undercutting the claim that in general opposite-sex couples, but not same-sex couples, should be allowed to marry. Further, these theorists would have to explain why these voluntarily sterile couples are not engaging in relations of a kind suitable for generation. To respond that such individuals are disqualified because they subjectively know that they cannot have children will not be helpful, since the same might be said of those involuntarily sterile. To talk about the past acts that resulted in their sterility would not explain why *these* acts are not of the right kind, unless one has a complicated theory which links past and present acts.[29] Further, these theorists will have to decide what to do with those individuals who became sterile because they knowingly worked in a job that increased their chances of becoming sterile, although the sterility was neither desired nor intended.[30] In short, no matter how these theorists address these examples, the argument offered simply will not credibly establish the proposed distinction between opposite-sex couples on the one hand and same-sex couples on the other.

Consider those commentators who suggest that marriage is intrinsically good and that gay and lesbian couples simply cannot partake of the intrinsic goodness of marriage.[31] Such critics may understand the difficulties involved in demonstrating what in fact has intrinsic value, but seem confident that same-sex unions simply cannot have such value.[32] These commentators seem utterly unaware of the possibility that lesbian and gay couples believe that their relationships are also intrinsically valuable, perhaps because such theorists cannot themselves appreciate the worth of such relationships. Indeed, these critics do not seem to appreciate the difficulties associated with determining which of two kinds of relationships is *more* intrinsically valuable.

John Stuart Mill offers a method by which to determine which of two pleasures is intrinsically superior. He asks that it be supposed that one of two pleasures "is, by those who are competently acquainted with both, placed so far above the other they they prefer it, even though knowing it to be attended with a greater amount of discontent, and would not resign it for any quantity of the other pleasure which their nature is capable of."[33] In that case, Mill claims that we would be "justified in ascribing to the preferred enjoyment a superiority in quality, so far outweighing quantity as to render it, in comparison, of small account."[34]

Here, of course, we would be comparing relationships and not pleasures. Nonetheless, perhaps one could ask those who had been in both kinds of relationships which was preferable. It is unclear which relationships would be chosen as intrinsically preferable or even that one would universally be chosen over the other. What does seem clear is that the theorists alluded to above have not taken seriously the implications of their own positions, which could be used to support the recognition of same-sex marriages as easily as their nonrecognition and which, in any event, ignore the relevant case law. It would be helpful if theorists stopped offering obviously specious arguments to support their positions.

Suppose that one ignores the "intrinsic goodness" argument if only because it is obvious that such an argument is unhelpful; those in favor of same-sex marriage might be expected to argue that same-sex unions are intrinsically good or, perhaps, intrinsically superior and those against it might be expected to deny such claims. Suppose instead that one discusses the common claim that the sole purpose of marriage is to provide a setting for the next generation. Even were marriage solely for the production and raising of children, constitutional questions would be raised by precluding couples from marrying based on their inability to produce a child together if the state does not in fact have a compelling interest in preventing individuals from marrying who are incapable of producing children *through their union*. After all, such a couple might adopt a child or one of the individuals might have a child. In either of these scenarios, the court would need a different justification for upholding the state prohibition of that marriage.

The *Adams* court might have believed that asking individuals about their procreational plans would itself invade their privacy: if the court could know those plans without asking, then no privacy

issues would be implicated. Because same-sex couples cannot produce a child through their union and opposite-sex couples may be
able to do so (absent information establishing that they cannot), the
court might have believed that it could justify making the distinction
that it did. Yet, there is no basis in law for such a position. A man
and a woman who voluntarily signed an affidavit stating that each
was incapable of reproduction could not be prevented from marrying on that ground and, presumably, not even the *Adams* court
would have upheld a statute that prevented two such people from
marrying.

The point here is not that couples unable or unwilling to procreate should not be allowed to marry if gay and lesbian couples cannot. The Supreme Court noted in *Carrington v. Rash* that "the fact
that a State is dealing with a distinct class and treats the members of
that class equally does not end the judicial inquiry."[35] There is no
reason that nonprocreating couples should be prevented from marrying and thus no reason that the whole class should have that
burden placed upon it. But additional difficulties are raised when a
group is selectively burdened. In *Eisenstadt v. Baird*, the Court
pointed out that "nothing opens the door to arbitrary action so
effectively as to allow . . . officials to pick and choose only a few to
whom they will apply legislation and thus to escape the political
retribution that might be visited upon them if larger numbers were
affected."[36] Were states to generally enforce laws precluding individuals from marrying who were unable or unwilling to have children,
there would be such an outcry that such laws would be repealed.
Further, courts would never say that such laws passed constitutional
muster if they were applied to heterosexual couples.

The *Singer* court reasoned that because "marriage exists as a protected legal institution primarily because of societal values associated
with the propagation of the human race" and because "it is apparent
that no same-sex couple offers the possibility of the birth of children
by their union," the state's refusal to authorize same-sex marriage
does not involve invidious discrimination.[37] The court recognized
that "married couples are not required to become parents and . . .
some couples are incapable of becoming parents and . . . not all

couples who produce children are married."[38] It claimed, however, that these involved exceptional situations.[39]

The *Singer* court's analysis was faulty on both empirical and conceptual grounds. First, there is reason to believe that the *Singer* court's demographic analysis was inaccurate at the time[40] and is even less accurate now.[41] It was not and is not true that only the exceptional married couple does not have children. Even were such a demographic analysis accurate, however, the court's opinion would still have been unpersuasive. Presumably, "societal values associated with the propagation of the human race" also involve the nurturing and raising of children. Thus, same-sex couples who have children fall *within* the protected category rather than outside of it. When the *Adams* court argued that "the state has a compelling interest in . . . providing status and stability to the environment in which children are raised,"[42] it conveniently overlooked that its argument *supported* rather than undermined allowing same-sex couples to marry, precisely because such couples may have children to raise. Both the *Adams* and *Singer* courts paradoxically asserted that the state's compelling interest in providing a stable environment for the raising of children justified denying marital status to individuals who did have children to raise and granting marital status to individuals who did not. Opinions like these undermine the belief that the courts are approaching the same-sex marriage issue fairly and in good faith.

ON PRODUCING AND RAISING CHILDREN

The state's compelling interest in providing a stable home for the raising of children is a reason to allow rather than prohibit same-sex marriage. To use it as a reason to prohibit such unions is to turn the rationale on its head. Indeed, even if one arbitrarily limited the state's interest to the production of children, the argument still could not be used in good faith to prohibit same-sex marriages. The state's refusal to allow same-sex couples to marry might deter gay and lesbian individuals from *procreating*, precisely because they are barred from marrying. Neither the state nor the courts can in good faith use the state's compelling interest in the production or raising of children as a reason to prohibit lesbian and gay couples from marrying when such couples both have and raise children.

The argument that the state's compelling interest in children justifies prohibiting certain marriages has a sad and embarrassing history. It has been used to establish the invalidity of interracial marriages, either because such unions allegedly would produce offspring who might not be able to reproduce with their chosen mates[43] or because, in any case, the offspring of interracial marriages would allegedly be inferior.[44] This history alone should give courts reason to pause before asserting such a rationale, especially because a related rationale was rejected in *Loving*.[45]

In *Skinner*, the Court held that "[m]arriage and procreation are fundamental to the very existence and survival of the race."[46] Yet there is no reason to think that the very existence and survival of the human race should or will rest on the shoulders only of those individuals who are raised by *both* of their biological parents. Otherwise, the human race would be in great danger indeed, given the number of individuals raised by single parents or by two parents, at least one of whom is not biologically related to the child.

When the Court has discussed the fundamental right to raise one's children, the Court has not limited that right only to those parents who were raising their own biological children.[47] Thus, even had the Supreme Court held that marriage was a fundamental right because of its relationship to procreation,[48] marriage would still be fundamental for gays and lesbians who are also having and raising children who need a stable and loving environment.[49] It is thus difficult to understand how judges who understand that gay and lesbian couples have children through adoption, surrogacy, and artificial insemination[50] can nonetheless believe that such families do not warrant constitutional protection.

In *Moore v. City of East Cleveland*,[51] the Supreme Court struck down housing restrictions that were based on an overly narrow definition of family. Were courts correct that the Supreme Court's domestic relations jurisprudence is based on the model of two parents who raise their own biological children, *Moore* would have been decided differently. When the *Moore* Court noted that it "is through the family that we inculcate and pass down many of our most cherished values, moral and cultural,"[52] the Court could not have been limiting its discussion of the family to two parents who were raising children biologically related to both of them. Rather, the Supreme Court has recognized what the lower courts discussed here apparently have not, namely, that many of our most cherished values are passed down in settings that do not involve two parents raising children biologically related to each of them.

The *Moore* Court made clear that courts must not close their "eyes to the basic reasons why certain rights associated with the family have been accorded shelter under the Fourteenth Amendment's Due Process Clause."[53] As the *Roberts* Court emphasized, families "have played a critical role in the culture and traditions of the Nation by cultivating and transmitting shared ideals and beliefs."[54] All kinds of families may play that role, not just those in which the children are biologically related to both adults.

Perhaps the difficulty is not that gay and lesbian parents will be unable to communicate values to their children, but that they will communicate the "wrong" values.[55] Yet, there is no reason to believe that the "wrong" values would be transmitted—commitment, loyalty, tolerance, and respect for self and others are values that should be transmitted. Further, there is no one set of values exhausting the "permissible" values that may be imparted. Finally, were the relevant standard for raising children whether the "wrong" values would be imparted, many parents teaching their children intolerance of other races, nationalities, or religions, etc., would seem vulnerable to losing their children.[56]

The *Zablocki* Court recognized the right to marry as fundamental because it is the "foundation of the family in our society."[57] Families, however, need not and often do not involve children. Marriage and family serve a variety of important functions in addition to the production and raising of children.

Were one to read the court opinions that suggest that same-sex relationships are not afforded constitutional protection, one would infer that the sole reason that marriage is important is that it facilitates the begetting and raising of the couple's own biological children. This analysis, which makes marriage only instrumentally important for the production and rearing of children, misrepresents the nature of the interest in marriage. The right to marry is itself of fundamental importance,[58] just as the right to procreate is itself fundamental, whether the procreator is married or single.[59] Further, the Supreme Court has never said that only heterosexuals have a fundamental interest in marriage; on the contrary, the right to marry is of fundamental importance for all individuals.[60]

INTIMATE ASSOCIATION

In *Board of Directors of Rotary International v. Rotary Club of Duarte*, the Court recognized that "the freedom to enter into and carry on certain intimate or private relationships is a fundamental element of liberty protected by the Bill of Rights."[61] The Court discussed a number of intimate associations that are protected: marriage, begetting and bearing children, child rearing and education, and cohabitation with relatives.[62] The Court explicitly rejected the argument that only those relationships that implicate all of these intimate associations would be protected.[63]

In *Turner v. Safley*,[64] the Supreme Court had to decide whether prisoners have a right to marry while they are in prison. The Court recognized that the "right to marry, like many other rights, is subject to substantial restrictions as a result of incarceration."[65] Thus, a restriction that might not pass constitutional muster outside of the prison context might be permissible within that context. Nonetheless, legitimate corrections goals notwithstanding, the Court recognized that the prisoner's right to marry was constitutionally protected.

Turner is important because of the interests that the Court recognized as having constitutional significance. The Court upheld the prisoner's right to marry because (1) marriages "are expressions of emotional support and public commitment";[66] (2) marriage may involve "an exercise of religious faith as well as an expression of personal dedication";[67] (3) most marriages will be "formed in the expectation that they ultimately will be fully consummated";[68] and

(4) marriage is often a "precondition to the receipt of government benefits."[69]

The Court did *not* say that the fundamental interest in marriage was dependent upon the couple's having or raising children. Indeed, the Court did not say that marriage was dependent upon consummation, because *most* rather than *all* marriages would be formed in the expectation of their being consummated. Instead, the Court mentioned interests possessed by all individuals, including gays, lesbians, and bisexuals. If the interests articulated by the Court justify allowing opposite-sex couples to marry, legitimate penological concerns notwithstanding, it is hard to understand why those same individual interests are suddenly insufficiently weighty to allow same-sex couples to marry, even when no penological concerns are implicated.

Ironically, it was brought to the attention of the *Dean* court that *Turner* involved factors that applied to both same-sex and opposite-sex couples.[70] Nonetheless, the *Dean* court rejected the approach offered by the Supreme Court and instead seemed to accept the *Baehr* analysis linking marriage to procreation,[71] and then failed to recognize that the state's procreation concerns *support* allowing same-sex couples to marry.

The *Roberts* Court recognized that individuals are enriched emotionally in large part from their close ties with others.[72] These relationships must be protected from unjustified state interference, at least in part, because they safeguard "the ability . . . to define one's identity" independently.[73] The ability to develop one's own identity is central to any concept of liberty.[74] The *Roberts* Court recognized that intimate associations foster diversity and serve as a critical buffer between the individual and the power of the State.[75] Such relationships safeguard the individual freedom that is central to our constitutional scheme.[76] Insofar as intimate associations serve as a buffer between individuals and the state so that individuals can independently define themselves, same-sex intimate associations are especially deserving of protection, because unconventional associations are the most likely to be subject to discrimination.[77]

Several commentators have suggested that the right to same-sex marriage should be recognized as falling within the right to intimate association.[78] Insofar as marriage is protected because it involves an intimate lifelong commitment that may be central to the life of any individual, both opposite-sex and same-sex unions must be protected. As Justice Blackmun pointed out in his dissent in *Bowers*,

> The fact that individuals define themselves in a significant way through their intimate sexual relationships with others suggests, in a Nation as diverse as ours, that there may be many "right" ways of conducting those relationships, and that much of the richness of a relationship will come from the freedom an individual has to choose the form and nature of these intensely personal bonds.[79]

Same-sex couples seeking the right to marry are not merely seeking the right to live together, but to live together as a unit recognized by society. It is simply false that the fundamental interest in intimate association is satisfied as long as the individuals may live in the same household. Just as a state refusal to recognize interracial or interreligious marriages would not be upheld on grounds that the state was willing to allow such couples to live together, the state cannot escape its responsibility to recognize same-sex marriages by allowing intrasexual couples to live together.

In *Planned Parenthood of Southeastern Pennsylvania v. Casey*, the plurality explained that "choices central to personal dignity and autonomy, are central to the liberty protected by the Fourteenth Amendment."[80] It is hard to imagine which choices qualify as central to personal dignity and autonomy if one's choice of an intimate life partner does not.

The freedom of intimate association is not absolute. The government can regulate such relationships to promote very important interests. Those interests must be real, however; they cannot suddenly be compelling so that discrimination against gays and lesbians can be justified, and just as suddenly be noncompelling when heterosexual individuals seek benefits seemingly precluded by these same, formerly compelling, state interests. The *Loving* Court described marriage as "one of the vital personal rights essential to the orderly pursuit of happiness."[81] Courts that permit legislatures to prohibit individuals from marrying their same-sex partners are allowing states to abridge these vital personal rights.

WHAT THE RIGHT TO MARRY INCLUDES

Even were courts to recognize all of the interests that the institution of marriage serves, it would not follow that no restrictions on marriage would be permissible. The *Zablocki* Court recognized that "reasonable regulations that do not significantly interfere with decisions to enter into the marital relationship may legitimately be imposed."[82] The Court also recognized, however, that "[w]hen a statutory classification significantly interferes with the exercise of a fundamental right, it cannot be upheld unless it is supported by sufficiently important state interests and is closely tailored to effectuate only those interests."[83] This implies that a statutory classification significantly interfering with the right to marry must serve compelling state interests.[84]

It might be thought that the Court's close scrutiny of any state marital restriction would result in that restriction's being invalidated.[85] Yet, if that is true, then the state restrictions on bigamy and incest, for example, must not be serving important state interests and arguably should be invalidated.[86]

Justice William O. Douglas suggested that the state prohibition of bigamy will eventually be ruled constitutionally infirm.[87] At least thus far, however, his prediction has not come true. Courts have subjected the classification to strict scrutiny and have nonetheless upheld it.[88]

Incest regulations might also seem vulnerable if subjected to strict scrutiny.[89] Yet, there may be sufficiently compelling reasons to justify such prohibitions, such as genetic concerns[90] or the protection of the young. Insofar as those interests are not implicated or are not deemed sufficiently important and insofar as there are no other important interests served by the prohibition, perhaps such regulations should not be upheld. Indeed, where genetic concerns are not at issue and where the individuals are of age, there has been a tendency to relax incest prohibitions. For example, a man was allowed to marry his adopted daughter,[91] and a brother was allowed to marry his sister by adoption.[92]

Although regulations preventing minors from marrying have been upheld as promoting important state interests,[93] they have not been subjected to strict scrutiny.[94] However, such regulations might survive strict scrutiny; they seem less vulnerable to attack both because they concern minors who are less capable of making a mature, informed decision and because the regulation would defer rather than prohibit marriage.

The Supreme Court has held that reasonable regulations that merely defer marriage may pass constitutional muster. For example, when upholding residency requirements for divorce, the Court made clear that such requirements were permissible because they did not involve a total deprivation of the right to marry but only a delay.[95] It should be noted that the prohibition of same-sex marriage involves a total denial of the right to marry rather than a mere delay.

The point here is not that the state has (or does not have) an important interest in prohibiting polygamous or incestuous marriages, but merely that statutory classifications that significantly infringe on the fundamental right to marry must promote important or compelling interests if they are to be upheld. If the state is going to prohibit same-sex marriage, it must articulate the important state interests that would thereby be served.

ANTIMISCEGENATION LAWS

There are numerous reasons why the best analogue to the current state refusal to recognize intrasexual marriages is the former state refusal to recognize interracial marriages. Many of the same reasons justifying the Court's striking down antimiscegenation statutes justify striking down laws prohibiting same-sex marriages.[96]

In the context of racial intermarriage, the Supreme Court of California in *Perez v. Lippold* pointed out that "a statute that prohibits an individual from marrying a member of a race other than his own restricts the scope of his choice and thereby restricts his right to marry."[97] Individuals denied the right to marry their would-be spouse may be barred from marrying someone whom they find irreplaceable.[98] Further, as one of the concurring judges in *Perez* pointed out, the question was not whether many would choose to marry someone of another race; rather, it was whether those "who do so desire have the right to make that choice."[99]

Of course, interracial and intrasexual marriages are different. Thus, the Court's holding Virginia's antimiscegenation statute unconstitutional in *Loving* did not thereby invalidate all intrasexual marriage prohibitions.[100] The rationale behind *Loving*, however, implies that same-sex marriage bans are unconstitutional.

The *Baker* court suggested that "there is a clear distinction between a marital restriction based *merely* upon race and one based upon the fundamental difference in sex."[101] Yet, such a view misrepresents just how fundamental the difference in race was thought to be. At the time the Virginia anti-miscegenation law was invalidated, many did not think it obvious that the right to marry included the right to marry someone of a different race.[102] Interracial marriages were not envisioned as traditional marriages deserving the kinds of protections intraracial marriages deserved. Indeed, interracial marriages were described as violating God's Law.[103]

A NEW FUNDAMENTAL RIGHT?

When the *Baehr* plurality addressed whether there was a due process right to same-sex marriage, the court sought to determine whether such a union should be recognized as a new fundamental right. Not surprisingly, it concluded that a right to same-sex marriage is not "so rooted in the traditions and collective conscience of our people that failure to recognize it would violate the fundamental principles of liberty and justice that lie at the base of all our civil and political institutions."[104] It also concluded that the right to same-sex marriage is not "implicit in the concept of ordered liberty, such that neither liberty nor justice would exist if it were sacrificed."[105] The court failed to appreciate that same-sex marriages are not rooted in the consciences of the people, at least in part, precisely because lesbians, bisexuals, and gays have historically been subjected to discrimination.[106] The court further failed to appreciate that when *Loving* was decided, the right to interracial marriage was neither deeply rooted in the traditions and collective conscience of our people nor was it viewed as implicit in the concept of ordered liberty. Indeed, had the *Turner* Court based its decision on whether prison marriages were implicit in the concept of ordered liberty or deeply rooted in the collective conscience of the people, the result would have been much different.

The *Baehr* plurality's analysis was faulty in that it used the wrong level of specificity when describing the right to marry.[107] That error led the plurality to believe that a new fundamental right was at issue rather than a right already recognized. Further, when deciding whether the "new" right should be recognized, the plurality used a standard that would not have been met by many of the interests already included within the right to privacy.

The *Bowers* Court warned, "The Court is most vulnerable and comes nearest to illegitimacy when it deals with judge-made constitutional law having little or no cognizable roots in the language or design of the Constitution."[108] Certainly, the Court needs some standard by which to decide what the Due Process Clause protects. Just as certainly, however, the Court must not arbitrarily change its standards when deciding what is protected.

One such standard has been proposed by Justice Scalia. A practice "is not constitutionally protected . . . [if] (1) the Constitution says absolutely nothing about it, and (2) the longstanding traditions of American society have permitted it to be legally proscribed."[109] Such a jurisprudence, however, would mean that contraception, abortion, and miscegenation would all be proscribable. Further, such a view entails overturning a variety of precedents.

In *Roe v. Wade*, Justice Potter Stewart pointed out in his concurrence that the "Constitution nowhere mentions a specific right of personal choice in matters of marriage and family life."[110] Further, the *Roe* Court was well aware that abortion had been criminalized by many states for about a century.[111] According to Justice Scalia's analysis, abortion does not fall within the right to privacy.[112]

The right to use contraception or, more generally, the right to procreate is not mentioned anywhere in the Constitution.[113] Further, contraception has a history of being criminalized by the states. For example, in 1965, when *Griswold v. Connecticut*[114] was decided, Connecticut had criminalized the use of contraception for over eighty years.[115] When *Eisenstadt v. Baird* was decided in 1972, Massachusetts had criminalized the distribution of contraceptives for over ninety years.[116] Applying Justice Scalia's test, the distribution or use of contraception should not have been included within the right to privacy.

The right to marry someone of a different race is mentioned nowhere in the Constitution and, even more generally, the right to marry is not explicitly protected in the Constitution. Before *Loving*, some states had criminalized racial intermarriage for long periods of time.[117] Were the Court to have accepted Justice Scalia's jurisprudence, *Loving* would have had a different result. Indeed, much that is protected within the right to privacy would not be protected.

The *Casey* plurality described Justice Scalia's jurisprudence as "inconsistent with our law."[118] The plurality explained that "[n]either the Bill of Rights nor the specific practices of States at the time of the adoption of the Fourteenth Amendment marks the outer limits of the substantive sphere of liberty which the Fourteenth Amendment protects."[119] The question then becomes what jurisprudence should be used.

In *Casey*, the plurality described the Constitution's written terms as embodying ideas and aspirations in need of interpretation and elucidation.[120] That interpretation can be successfully performed only if the Court is willing to "accept [its] responsibility not to retreat from interpreting the full meaning of the [Constitution]`in light of all of [the Court's] precedents."[121] As the *Casey* plurality recognized, the interpretation process cannot simply be mechanistic, but instead must involve reasoned judgment.[122]

This reasoned judgment will involve the Court's making decisions about the appropriate level of abstraction when judging the constitutionality of state classifications. For example, the right to procreation involves a more abstract level of generality than the right to use contraceptives. As a general matter, it should not be surprising that the greater the specificity with which one describes a right at issue, the less likely it is that the right will have historically received protection. Thus, while the rights to marital privacy and to marry and raise a family[123] have historically been protected, the right to use contraception has not.[124]

Justice Scalia's jurisprudence has been criticized both because it selectively relies on tradition[125] and because it examines issues with an inappropriate level of specificity.[126] Both of these weaknesses underlie the due process approaches contained in both *Baehr* and *Dean*. The level of specificity chosen by these courts, if applied in other contexts, would have meant that privacy would not include rights to contraception, abortion, or interracial marriage. The *Bowers* Court's warning that there should be "great resistance to . . . redefining the category of rights deemed to be fundamental"[127] should also be taken to heart to prevent the Court's recategorizing as mere liberties those rights previously considered fundamental.

SODOMY

It might be thought that the Court's upholding states' rights to criminalize sodomy has important implications for same-sex marriage. That may be correct, although not for the reasons usually thought.

In *Bowers*, Chief Justice Warren Burger pointed out in his concurrence that the proscriptions against sodomy have ancient roots.[128] Regrettably, he neglected to mention that the proscriptions having ancient roots did not correspond to what was proscribed by the state of Georgia. For example, at common law, oral sex was not included within the crime of sodomy.[129]

A general difficulty with the *Bowers* analysis is that while the Court only addressed whether the Constitution protects homosexual sodomy,[130] the Georgia statute proscribed sodomy whether committed intrasexually or intersexually.[131] Those who suggest that *Bowers* precludes same-sex marriage seem to forget the Court's limited focus. States can criminalize sodomy between unmarried heterosexuals without thereby implying that sodomy between married heterosexuals is also precluded.[132] Likewise, states can criminalize sodomy between unmarried same-sex partners without implying that sodomy between married same-sex partners is so precluded.[133] Indeed, the case for the U.S. Constitution's protecting same-sex marriage may be stronger than for its protecting extramarital sodomy. Certainly, the Court could not in good faith echo its *Bowers* decision by claiming that there is "[n]o connection between family, marriage, or procreation on the one hand"[134] and same-sex unions on the other. Insofar as sexual activity is protected because it instrumentally promotes the fundamental interest in marriage and family, same-sex marriage may have to be recognized as a fundamental right before sodomy can be included within the right to privacy.

Certainly, other justifications can and have been offered to establish that adult, consensual sodomy should be included within the right to privacy. As Justice Blackmun explained in his *Bowers* dissent, "An individual's ability to make constitutionally protected 'decisions concerning sexual relations' is rendered empty indeed if he or she is given no real choice but a life without any physical intimacy."[135] Nonetheless, it should be easier to establish the connection between family, marriage, and procreation on the one hand and same-sex unions on the other than to establish the relevant connection to sodomy between unmarrieds.

SOCIETAL INTERESTS

A number of state interests have been offered to justify a state's refusal to recognize same-sex marriages. For example, some suggest that homosexuality should not be encouraged or condoned by the state so that individuals will not be induced to develop same-sex romantic relationships.[136] Even if one brackets the issue that the state should not recommend certain romantic partners over others, as long as the parties are consenting adults, there is an empirical claim to examine. Because decriminalization of sodomy has not led to a decrease in the marriage rate,[137] there is no reason to believe that allowing same-sex couples to marry would induce many people to choose same-sex rather than opposite-sex marriage.[138] It is quite unlikely that individuals with a same-sex orientation would pose a significant threat to the stability or number of opposite-sex marriages; rather, individuals with an opposite-sex orientation would more likely pose such a threat.[139]

Certainly, legalization of same-sex marriages might induce gays and lesbians not to enter into opposite-sex marriages. This inducement, however, would presumably benefit all concerned, because it is unlikely that a marriage between an individual with a same-sex orientation and an individual with an opposite-sex orientation would be happy or stable.

Closely related to the fear that recognition of same-sex marriage might induce people to choose same-sex rather than opposite-sex relationships is the claim that the state should not condone or endorse the "homosexual lifestyle."[140] Most Americans do not approve of gay marriage.[141] Yet, the state should not endorse certain but not other marital unions between consenting, autonomous adults. For example, the state should not implement policies which endorse intraracial or intrareligious marriages but not interreligious or interracial marriages. In any event, the state's recognition of intrasexual or interracial marriages does not entail an endorsement of those marriages.[142]

When commentators claim that the state should not be endorsing same-sex relationships, they may implicitly be claiming that the state should not promote "immorality." Yet, same-sex relationships are not immoral, just as interracial relationships are not immoral, majority view notwithstanding.[143] Neither type of relationship harms anyone.

Although the state has often claimed that punishing same-sex behavior somehow promotes the public welfare, the basis for that position has not been articulated.[144] There is no reason to believe that the failure to punish same-sex relationships will somehow lead to a greater incidence of murder or theft.[145] Indeed, alleged moral rules designed to penalize unpopular groups who themselves do no harm must be recognized for what they are: biases masquerading as moral or legal rules.[146]

Even if same-sex behavior and relationships were immoral, this would not imply that the promotion of morality is of sufficient importance to deny something so fundamental as the right to marry. The Supreme Court rejected the argument that morality would justify prohibiting access to contraception or abortion. Just as the courts and the state cannot claim in good faith that procreation through the union of the parties is a compelling state interest when people of the same sex want to marry, but a noncompelling (or nonexistent) state interest when people of the opposite sex wish to marry, so, too, neither the courts nor the state can in good faith use morality to define or delimit the fundamental rights of one group but not of other groups.

Even courts and commentators using morality as a justification for penalizing gays and lesbians admit that the interest in promoting morality is not substantial.[147] Further, as the *Casey* plurality recognized, men and women of good conscience can disagree about profound moral questions.[148] The Court's "obligation is to define the liberty of all, not to mandate [its] own moral code."[149] Indeed, part of the public morality of our society is to allow individuals to develop their private morality according to their own lights, as long as they do not harm others in the process. As Judge John Ferren suggested in his concurring and dissenting opinion in *Dean*, "a mere feeling of distaste or even revulsion at what someone else is or does, simply because it offends majority values without causing concrete harm" would not justify that state's "withholding the marriage statute from same-sex couples."[150] The Supreme Court has recognized that "mere public intolerance or animosity cannot be the basis for abridgment of . . . constitutional freedoms"[151] and it seems clear that public animosity is one of the major reasons that gays and lesbians are penalized by society. Public animosity against bisexual, lesbian, and gay people does not implicate a legitimate interest of the state, much less the kind of compelling interest that is required for such a burden on a fundamental right to be justified.[152] Indeed, there is a strong state interest in eradicating this kind of animosity and prejudice against gay, bisexual, and lesbian people.[153]

There are other state interests in promoting marriage, such as stability for children and adults, that *support* recognition of same-sex marriages. Public health concerns, such as the prevention of AIDS, support the recognition of same-sex marriage as a way of promoting long-term, monogamous relationships.

Perhaps it will be thought that not enough individuals would be interested in marrying to justify recognizing same-sex unions. Yet there is reason to doubt that the number would be insignificant.[154] Even were the number likely to be small, however, that would not justify a state refusal to recognize same-sex marriages. The right at issue is a personal one.[155] It is as an individual that a person seeking to marry his or her same-sex partner would be entitled to the equal protection of the laws.[156] Indeed, as the Supreme Court suggested in a different context in *McCabe v. Atchison, Topeka, and Santa Fe Ry.*, the very "essence of the constitutional right is that it is a personal one." Because it "is the individual who is entitled to the equal protection of the laws," the right to marry a same-sex partner could not be denied, even were it true that not many individuals would avail themselves of that opportunity.[157] Because a personal, fundamental right is at issue, the number of those wishing to exercise that right is beside the point.

One of the most underappreciated facets of the same-sex marriage controversy is the extent to which domestic relations jurisprudence must change in order to justify the prohibition. The understanding of substantive due process that is required to justify excluding same-sex unions from the right to marry would seem to put many "fundamental" rights at risk. The state's interests in "morality" or procreation could be used to justify a variety of surprising policies if they can be so used here.

Indeed, it is especially surprising that courts have accepted that the purpose of marriage is to provide a setting for the production and raising of children and that *therefore* gays, lesbians, and bisexuals do not have a fundamental right to marry. Courts must reexamine their thinking because, as the next chapter demonstrates, gays, lesbians, and bisexuals both have and raise children.

IV THE CUSTODY AND ADOPTION

OF CHILDREN

▼

Lesbians, gays, and bisexuals do have children, sometimes through a former marriage to an opposite-sex partner and sometimes through artificial insemination, surrogacy, or adoption. It may be thought, however, that merely because lesbians and gays can be biological parents does not settle the issue, since one's being able to help create a child does not mean that one will be a good or even adequate parent. To see whether the allegedly primary function of marriage is simply inappropriate in the context of same-sex relationships, it will be important to see whether lesbians, bisexuals, and gays can not only help create children but also can raise them. It is thus important to examine how the various states treat gay or lesbian parents in custody disputes and examine whether states allow lesbians, bisexuals, or gays to adopt.

A discussion of how lesbian, bisexual, and gay parents are treated in the law might concentrate on how they are *supposed to be* treated or on how they are *actually* treated. This chapter concentrates on the former, because there are important implications of the states' recognizing that sexual orientation and good parenting are quite compatible. However, it should not be thought that what is supposed to occur and what actually occurs always coincide. Just as courts and agencies may continue to act in ways reflecting racial or gender bias, the inappropriateness of such actions and attitudes notwithstanding, some courts and agencies continue to act in ways reflecting orientation bias, the inappropriateness of such actions and attitudes notwithstanding.

Most states have recognized that gays and lesbians can be good parents who deserve to be permitted to raise children. Indeed, because in most states gay and lesbian parents are in fact awarded custody of their children and in fact are allowed to adopt, one might expect courts to *require* states to recognize same-sex unions, since the primary purpose of marriage allegedly is to provide a stable setting for the production and rearing of children. That courts have not done so has important implications for the good faith of their analyses of the constitutionality of same-sex marriage bans.

THE FUNDAMENTAL RIGHT TO PARENT

The Supreme Court has recognized that parents have a fundamental interest in the care, custody, and management of their children.[1] Indeed, as the Supreme Court recognized in *Meyer v. Nebraska*, the right of individuals to establish a home and bring up children is "essential to the orderly pursuit of happiness by free men."[2] The *Casey* plurality made clear that family matters, which involve "the most intimate and personal choices a person may make in a lifetime . . . are central to the liberty protected by the Fourteenth Amendment."[3]

State courts have also expressed their appreciation of the great importance of parent-child relationships. The Utah Supreme Court describes the right of the parent to maintain a relationship with his or her child as "transcend[ing] all property and economic rights [and as] rooted . . . in nature and human instinct."[4] The court argued that the "integrity of the family and the parents' inherent right and authority to rear their own children [are] . . . presupposed by all our social, political, and legal institutions."[5] Other state supreme courts have also recognized the importance of the right of parents to the custody and companionship of their children.

If indeed family relationships are fundamental to the purpose and enjoyment of life, then states must be very careful before terminating parental rights. As Justice Blackmun pointed out in his dissent in *Lassiter v. Dept. of Social Services*, "there can be few losses more grievous than the abrogation of parental rights."[6] The interest that a parent has in maintaining a relationship with her child "occupies a unique place in our legal culture given the centrality of family life as the focus for personal meaning and responsibility."[7] Thus, the parent's right to maintain a relationship with his or her child is treated very seriously in the law.

PARENTAL RIGHTS TERMINATIONS

The parent's right to custody and companionship is not absolute, however. Parental rights may be forfeited if the parent is unfit or unable to care for the child. Rarely, other compelling circumstances will justify severing the tie between parent and child, for example, if the child and parent have been separated for a very long period of time.

The New York Court of Appeals has summed up the conditions under which parental rights might be terminated. A state may terminate parental rights "if there is first a judicial finding of surrender, abandonment, unfitness, persistent neglect, unfortunate or involuntary extended disruption of custody, or other equivalent but rare extraordinary circumstance which would drastically affect the welfare of the child."[8] As the Illinois Supreme Court explains, precisely because very important rights are at risk when parent-child ties are severed and because of "the devastating effect produced by a termination of parental rights, the evidence of a parent's unfitness has to be clear and convincing."[9]

If inappropriate parental rights terminations are to be avoided, great care must be taken before parental rights are terminated due to the parent's fault or incapacitation.[10] Courts may require a showing of very harmful activity before they will conclude that the parent is unfit. For example, in *In re Welfare of P.L.C.*,[11] grandparents sought to have their former son-in-law declared an unfit parent. The trial court had found that he had physically abused his ex-wife.[12] Further, there were indications that the children had suffered some physical abuse at the home of their father.[13] Finally, the father was living in an adulterous relationship.[14] Nonetheless, the court refused to find him unfit. In *Alsager v. District Court*,[15] the court considered the fitness of parents who "sometimes permitted their children to leave the house in cold weather without winter clothing on, 'allowed them' to play in traffic, to annoy neighbors, to eat mush for supper, to live in a house containing dirty dishes and laundry, and to sometimes arrive late at school."[16] The court concluded that they were not unfit.[17]

PARENTAL AUTONOMY

There are several reasons that parental rights are given such great protection. First, parents are presumed to want to promote the welfare of their children.[18] Because of the presumption that parents have the best interests of their children at heart, the state is willing to give parents a substantial measure of authority over their children.[19] Indeed, courts have recognized that parents have an interest in being allowed to raise their children in an environment free from government interference.[20] Unless parents are given a wide zone of latitude, there will be a chilling effect on what parents will do with and for their children.[21] The *Alsager* court suggested that because courts should not "inhibit parents in the exercise of their fundamental right to family integrity,"[22] courts should give much deference to parents to decide how their children should be raised.

The state assigns to parents numerous roles in the raising of their children. The "process of teaching, guiding, and inspiring by precept and example is essential to the growth of young people into mature, socially responsible citizens"[23] and this process is entrusted to the parents. Not only are parents better able to respond to the particularized needs of their children,[24] but parents will be able to provide a bulwark against the standardization and homogenization of children. The Utah Supreme Court has observed that family autonomy helps to assure the diversity which is characteristic of a free society such as ours.[25] Parents should be given great latitude in rearing their own children, since, as the court points out, much "of the rich variety in American culture has been transmitted from generation to generation by determined parents who were acting against the best interest of their children, as defined by official dogma."[26] The court further argued that "there is no surer way to threaten pluralism than to terminate the rights of parents who contradict officially approved values imposed by reformers empowered to determine what is in the 'best interest' of someone else's child."[27] Thus, the Utah Supreme Court suggests that even parents who "contradict officially approved values" may in fact be benefiting society by promoting diversity. The court made clear that the protection of parental rights "promotes values essential to the preservation of human freedom and dignity and to the perpetuation of our democratic society."[28]

UNFITNESS

While there is a strong presumption that parents have a right to care for their children and to instill within them those values which the parents believe appropriate, that presumption may be rebutted because of unfitness, a finding of which will result in the parents' loss of custody. Children will not be forced to endure great and unnecessary risks and hardships at the hands of anyone, including their parents.

Unfitness is not to be measured in degrees; the parent is either fit or unfit.[29] Further, unfitness cannot be established by a parent's having been guilty at one time or another of neglecting to give their children "proper" care.[30] One or two instances of less than adequate care will not suffice to establish that parental rights should be terminated. Rather, to "provide a jurisdictional basis for termination, neglect must be serious and persistent and be sufficiently harmful to the child so as to mandate a forfeiture of parental rights."[31] The standard is not merely whether someone else would be a better parent but whether continued custody by the parent would actually be harmful to the child. Were courts to terminate parental rights merely because other parents would be more loving or supportive or understanding or merely because other parents could provide better educational or financial opportunities for the children, there would be a staggering number of parental rights terminations.

As the Illinois Supreme Court pointed out in *In re Adoption of Syck*, when courts are determining parental unfitness, they must do so *without* considering whether awarding custody to someone else would better promote the child's best interests.[32] The best interests of the child will be considered only *after* a finding of parental unfitness has been made.[33] Indeed, courts or statutes which declare a parent unfit solely because the child's best interests would be better promoted by being placed elsewhere may violate the parent's constitutional rights.[34]

Unfitness analysis is complicated because there are a variety of ways in which a parent can be unfit. Courts must consider whether the parent can provide for the physical needs of the child. The physical needs may involve whether the child is well-fed and well-clothed, in a clean home, and free from physical abuse.

Courts must also consider the child's emotional needs. The court may examine the rapport between parent and child, and, depending upon the age of the child, the child's preferences with respect to who will have custody, although those preferences will not be followed if they would be contrary to the best interests of the child.[35] At the very least, the court will examine whether the child is happy and well-adjusted. If the child is thriving, courts will tend not to modify custody, since the relevant criterion is "whether the child is best located with the [parent] and there well behaved and cared for."[36]

MORAL NEEDS

When courts consider the moral needs of the child, they may have any of a number of concerns in mind. Some courts fear that a parent who acts immorally may set an example which the child will later attempt to emulate. Other courts are concerned that the child will not understand the moral views of society or, perhaps, that there will be some other kind of unspecified harm.

When courts presume that exposure to an illicit relationship will cause harm without specifying what that harm will be, it will be difficult if not impossible to overcome that presumption. Further, the very vagueness of the standard invites different judges to apply it differently, even in relevantly similar factual situations. At least partially because of the potential unfairness and inconsistency which will likely occur if a vague standard of harm is used, courts tend to require that the harm be described with some specificity and, further, that there be a showing of actual or likely harm before they will find a parent morally unfit to raise children.

The Virginia Supreme Court has pointed out that in custody decisions the moral environment in which the child is to be raised is an important consideration.[37] However, states have good reason to pause before enforcing their own version of the "proper" moral climate. As the Utah Supreme Court suggests, parents may enrich their children's lives even when contradicting "officially approved values." Further, as the Supreme Court made clear in *Bellotti v. Baird*, "affirmative sponsorship of particular ethical, religious, or political beliefs is something we expect the State not to attempt in a society constitutionally committed to the ideal of individual liberty and freedom of choice."[38]

The *Bellotti* Court did not suggest that it was inappropriate for states to affirmatively sponsor particular ethical, religious, or political views only when there was no consensus about those views. On the contrary, even if, for example, a large majority of the population shared a particular religious view, the state would nonetheless not be permitted to endorse that view.[39]

Suppose, however, that the Court had held that there was no impropriety in the state's affirmatively sponsoring particular ethical beliefs about which there was a consensus. Even so, that would not entail that states would be permitted to affirmatively sponsor ethical beliefs about which no consensus exists. A variety of issues are hotly debated precisely because there is no consensus about their moral permissibility. For example, the morality of abortion is something about which reasonable people disagree.[40] So is the moral permissibility of same-sex relations.[41] Thus, states which affirmatively sponsor the view that adult, consensual, same-sex relations are immoral are erring in two ways: (1) they are violating *Bellotti* by endorsing a particular ethical view that condemns a practice which harms no one, and (2) they imply that there is a moral consensus which does not in fact exist.[42]

FORNICATION

Historically, unmarried individuals who had a sexual relationship were viewed as morally unfit to raise children. Currently, however, at least in most states, such individuals are not barred from having custody as long as the children are not adversely affected by the relationship.

Consider two unmarried couples. Couple A involves two cohabiting individuals, at least one of whom is married to a third party. Couple B involves two cohabiting individuals, neither of whom is currently married to anyone. Although some would accuse either couple of "living in sin," the couples are nonetheless dissimilar in an important respect—couple B's relationship does not involve adultery or a breaking of marital vows. While some believe that individuals living together without benefit of marriage are immoral whether or not marriage vows have been broken, others believe that it is morally permissible to live with someone without benefit of marriage as long as, for example, no promises are thereby being broken to an unknowing spouse.

Same-sex relationships are more analogous to opposite-sex relationships without benefit of marriage than to adulterous relationships.[43] Of course, unmarried, same-sex couples and unmarried, opposite-sex couples are not analogous in an important respect. In most cases, unmarried, opposite-sex individuals who cohabit may marry, whereas unmarried, same-sex cohabitants do not have that option. Insofar as unmarried inhabitants are subject to criticism for failing to avail themselves of the option to marry, same-sex couples are not appropriately criticized. Individuals should not have their failure to marry held against them when that failure is not their own fault.

One of the reasons that courts may be reluctant to award custody to a parent living with a partner to whom she or he is not married is the belief that children need a stable home and that people living together without a long-term commitment would be less likely to provide such a home.[44] For present purposes, it is unimportant to establish whether people who can marry but choose not to do so provide sufficiently stable homes. What is important to note is that the failure to marry cannot be assumed to indicate a lack of a long-term commitment when the couple does not have the option to marry; an extremely stable, same-sex couple does not have a legally recognized counterpart to marriage to manifest this commitment.

Certainly, in some localities, individuals may register as domestic partners.[45] Domestic partnerships, however, do not involve either all of the rights or all of the responsibilities of marriage and thus cannot be thought a comparable mechanism.[46]

It may be that courts simply do not believe that same-sex couples can have long, stable, monogamous, committed relationships. The refusal to take seriously that same-sex couples can have such relationships may partially explain the Court's decision in *Bowers v. Hardwick*. In *Bowers*, the Court refused to declare that homosexual sodomy was included within the right to privacy,[47] implying that there would be no nonarbitrary way to exclude adultery from the right to privacy if sodomy were included within that right.[48] Yet, such a claim is obviously specious. In the paradigmatic case of adultery, one of the parties is breaking his or her agreement to be faithful, unbeknown to the other party. In the paradigmatic case involving consenting same-sex adults, no agreements are broken and no one is harmed. Further, same-sex relations between committed partners may help promote a stable, durable bond just as opposite-sex relations do for opposite-sex couples. The same cannot be said of most adulterous relations.

The *Bowers* Court's failure to appreciate that same-sex individuals can have committed, long-term relationships may have undermined its ability to understand why sodomitic relations are protected by the right to privacy even if adulterous relations are not. Certainly, a Court that appreciated that lesbians and gays have committed, long-term relationships would not have so cavalierly denied the "connection between family, marriage, or procreation on the one hand and homosexual activity on the other."[49] If the Court is unable to distinguish between sodomitic and adulterous relations for purposes of deciding what is protected by the right to privacy, despite the clear differences between the two, for example, that the paradigmatic case of adult, consensual sodomy, unlike the paradigmatic case of adultery, does not involve a broken agreement or harm to anyone and in fact may help to promote a stable, durable bond, then the foundations of domestic relations jurisprudence are very shaky indeed.

There is no consensus about the morality of same-sex relations, although some judges seem to believe otherwise. Although it is clear that a portion of the population believes same-sex relations immoral, that does not establish that such relations are immoral. Otherwise, interracial relationships would be immoral, since a significant minority believes that such unions are morally impermissible.[50]

The point here of course is not that interracial relationships are immoral. On the contrary, they are morally permissible, views to the contrary notwithstanding. Indeed, just as interracial couples have been burdened unfairly because of societal prejudice masked as moral indignation, so have same-sex couples.

Whether or not same-sex relations are morally permissible in some absolute sense, it might seem permissible to enforce the moral code of the majority and, at least in some states, it seems safe to assume that the majority of the populace does not approve of same-sex relationships.[51] Yet, the same reasoning would imply that interracial relationships are at risk,[52] and the Supreme Court has made quite clear that states cannot prohibit interracial unions, alleged moral views of the populace notwithstanding.[53]

THE NEXUS TEST

In most states, the moral views of the populace regarding the moral permissibility of a parent's relationship with his or her partner will not determine who will get custody of a child of a previous marriage. Rather, most states employ the nexus test.

The nexus test requires that a connection between parental conduct and harm to the child be established if the parent is to be deprived of custody because of that conduct. Without that nexus, there will be insufficient grounds to deny custody. The nexus requirement is designed to prevent courts from depriving parents of custody based on the mere possibility of harm,[54] but *not* to force courts to wait until harm to the child has actually occurred before depriving a parent of custody.[55] The nexus test strikes a balance between these two poles and is "limited to [the] present or reasonably predictable effect upon the children's welfare."[56] Thus, harm need not have already occurred in order for a parent to be deprived of custody, but the harm must be likely (reasonably predictable) and not merely possible.

HARM TO THE CHILD

When deciding whether a parent's having custody would be harmful to a child, courts consider several different types of harm: physical harm, emotional harm, moral harm, and other kinds of harm. Any of these might provide sufficient grounds for a parent to be deprived of custody.

Physical Harm
Given the growing number of reported child abuse cases, courts must be sensitive to concerns that children will be severely hurt of killed by their parents. However, when courts are considering gay or lesbian parents and physical abuse, they are more likely to concern themselves with sexual molestation than with other kinds of physical abuse, perhaps because many judges still labor under the misapprehension that gay men and lesbians are more likely to molest children than are heterosexual men and women.[57]

Yet, current empirical data demonstrate that gay or lesbian parents are no more likely than heterosexual parents to molest children.[58] Indeed, much evidence suggests that gays and lesbians are *less* likely to molest children than are heterosexual parents.[59]

Emotional Harm
When courts consider who should have custody, they consider whether one parent's having custody would cause emotional harm to the child. Emotional harm might be indicated by the child's being depressed or having few friends or, perhaps, by the child's not fulfilling her potential in school.

Yet, courts must be careful when confronted by a child who is emotionally upset, since the *cause* of the upset should not be presumed.[60] Consider a depressed child whose custodial parent is in a committed, same-sex relationship. The child might be upset by the relationship or by her parents' having divorced. This is the kind of case which is heavily fact-dependent and would require an objective, unbiased judge to decide where the best interests of the child would lie. While there would be cases in which a modification of custody would improve matters, there would be other cases in which a custody modification would only cause further harm.

Exposure to Sexual Practices
Courts make clear that sexual behavior should not take place in front of children, although they are less clear about which behaviors are prohibited. They sometimes presume that *illicit* sexual conduct will harm children,[61] although it seems safe to assume that they believe that any sex play, even between marrieds, is inappropriate in front of a child.

There is too little discussion of which behaviors constitute sex play and which behaviors are simply permissible displays of affection. Consider kissing and hugging versus other types of behavior. In *Pleasant v. Pleasant*, an Illinois appellate court rejected the contention that adults who hug and kiss in a friendly manner are engaging in sexual conduct which should not take place in a child's presence.[62] The court differentiated between sexual activity which may be inappropriate in front of a child and that which merely involves a demonstration of affection.[63]

A further distinction should be made. Some kinds of affection are *not* inappropriate to express in front of a child, even though nonromantically linked friends might not choose to express their affection for each other that way. For example, in *Bottoms v. Bottoms*, the mother and her partner displayed affection in front of the child by hugging, kissing, or patting one another on the buttocks.[64] This kind of display will not harm the child and, presumably, a court would have no qualms about the display of such behavior were the individuals married. Sometimes, a court's disapproval of a display of affection in front of a child is not that the display itself would harm the child, but that it is a display between unmarried individuals and thus represents "immoral" behavior.

When a court chastises a couple for exposing a child to a display of affection which would have been perfectly acceptable had the couple been married, it is misleading to talk about this as inappropriately exposing a child to sexual activity, since it is not the activity but the relation of the performers that is at issue. Perhaps the best illustration of this mischaracterization is the way that some judges describe what occurs when nonmarried partners *say* that they love each other in front of a child. To classify such *statements* as inappropriate sexual *activity* is simply to conflate two different categories.[65]

To complicate matters even further, when courts examine whether sexual behavior occurs "in front" of a child, they may be considering whether the child sees the behavior or, instead, is simply asleep in the same house where the behavior occurs. Certainly, the two are quite different and should not be treated in the same way. Regrettably, courts are inconsistent in this regard, sometimes considering sexual activity as a negative factor only when it is seen by the child and sometimes considering it a negative factor if the child is in the same house when it occurs. This inconsistency may mean that relevantly similar situations might be treated quite differently.

Teasing

Courts will sometimes consider whether the child's living with a parent and that parent's same-sex partner would subject the child to teasing or social condemnation. There are several points which should be considered, however. Courts have rejected using teasing as a factor in custody decisions in other contexts, for example, where at least one of the parents and the child are of different races, and it is not clear why it is any more appropriate in this one. Courts should not be taking into account the popularity of a group of which the parent is a member when deciding something as important as custody or visitation.[66] Otherwise, individuals belonging to unpopular racial, religious, or ethnic groups might be in danger of losing custody of their children.

In *Palmore*, a divorced white father sought a custody modification because his wife (also white) was cohabiting with a black man, whom she subsequently married.[67] The court counselor recommended the change, claiming that the mother had chosen a lifestyle unacceptable to her former husband and to society.[68] The trial court accepted that recommendation, concluding that the best interests of the child would be served by the father's having custody.[69] The case was affirmed on appeal.[70]

When the Supreme Court decided the case, it made clear that the trial court had used the correct standard: "the child's welfare was the controlling factor."[71] Further, the Court recognized the "risk that a child living with a stepparent of a different race may be subject to a variety of pressures and stresses not present if the child were living with parents of the same racial or ethnic origin."[72] Nonetheless, the Court rejected that this possibility of teasing should even be considered, much less dispositive.[73] The Court wrote, "Private biases may be outside the reach of the law but the law cannot, directly or indirectly, give them effect."[74]

Studies indicate that children of gay and lesbian parents tend not to be teased on that account and, further, that the teasing which does occur is quite manageable by parent and child.[75] Courts should not allow their custodial policies to be determined by private bigotry. Doing so sends exactly the wrong messages both to the children themselves and to society as a whole.[76] Regrettably, children are teased for a variety of reasons.[77] As far as the child's interests are concerned, the most important element is not whether the child will be teased, since most children are teased in some way, but in how the teasing is handled.[78]

Moral Harm
While courts may limit the exposure of children to nonmarital partners out of a fear that the child will suffer emotional harm, they may also limit such visitation out of a fear that the child will suffer moral

harm, perhaps sometime in the future.[79] A Missouri appellate court argued that courts "cannot ignore the effect which the sexual conduct of a parent may have on a child's moral development."[80] The *Bottoms* appellate court pointed out that a "parent's behavior and conduct in the presence of a child influences and affects the child's values and views as to the type of behavior and conduct that the child will find acceptable."[81] Yet, the relevant question is whether or how those changes to views and values might constitute harm.

In general, courts will require detriment to the child before depriving the parent of custody, whether the "illicit" relationship involves a same-sex or an opposite-sex unmarried couple.[82] Certainly, were there reason to think that something terrible would occur in the future, courts would not feel constrained to wait until the harm had actually occurred. However, there is ample evidence that children of gay or lesbian parents are as healthy as those with heterosexual parents.[83] Thus, it simply will not do to say that even if there is no particular evidence of harm currently, it is fair to assume that there will be a detrimental effect sometime in the future. Further, even were there empirical evidence to that effect, courts are wary of using statistical evidence in determining custody cases, precisely because the court is supposed to determine which of the *particular* individuals seeking custody in *this* case would best promote the interests of the *particular* children before the court.

Housing

Historically, courts have imposed numerous visitation restrictions when a parent has cohabited with a nonmarital partner. For example, courts may prevent the partner from staying overnight while the children are visiting, even though the partner lives there. Sometimes, courts have required not only that the person not be there during visitation, but that the person move out entirely. Further, the court may additionally require that the parent not live with any adult of a particular sex.

It is important to remember, however, that the reason that the partner is prevented from living in the same house as the child is that the parent and his or her partner are not married.[84] If same-sex couples were permitted to marry, courts still might impose these housing limitations on couples living together *without benefit of marriage*. However, these limitations would *not* be imposed on individuals who had in fact married. Just as married interracial couples cannot be denied custody on that account, married same-sex couples could not be denied custody on that account.

APPLICATION

While the law is clear that parents have a fundamental interest in the care and companionship of their children and, at least in most states, that the nexus test must be used before a parent is to be deprived of custody, courts are not always evenhanded when applying the law in cases involving lesbian, bisexual, or gay parents. This may be due to a need for further education[85] or because some judges manifest bias from the bench.[86]

Courts express fears that any number of possible harms will occur when a child is raised by a gay or lesbian parent, *empirical evidence notwithstanding*. For example, courts may fear that allowing the child to be raised by a gay or lesbian parent will increase the likelihood that the child will grow up to be gay or lesbian. There is nothing wrong with being gay or lesbian, and the court should not be making a decision on that basis. In any event, children of gay or lesbian parents are no more likely to be gay or lesbian than are children of heterosexual parents.[87] Indeed, children raised by lesbian or gay parents cannot be distinguished from children raised by heterosexual parents with respect to their gender identity.[88]

Many of the fears that courts seem to have are simply unfounded. Children of gay or lesbian parents are not more likely to be molested than are children raised by heterosexual parents.[89] Nor are such children more likely to be harmed psychologically.[90] Nor are such children any less morally mature than are children of heterosexual parents.[91] Indeed, there is every reason to believe that the children of gay and lesbian parents will develop as successfully as will the children of heterosexual parents.[92]

Courts may realize that the children themselves are no more likely to be gay or lesbian if raised by a gay or lesbian parent. They may fear, however, that such children will be taught the "wrong" values, for example, that tolerance toward gays and lesbians is appropriate. But, tolerance of individuals of different races, religions, nationalities, sexual orientations, and so on, is an important value which should be taught to all children.

For current purposes, the point is not to discuss the numerous instances in which courts have allowed bias to affect their judgment,[93] but to emphasize that most states have recognized that gays, lesbians, and bisexuals can be good parents who of course should be allowed to have custody and visitation. An even clearer indication of the understanding that same-sex orientation is not incompatible with parenthood can be found in state policies regarding whether lesbians, bisexuals, or gays can adopt.

ADOPTION

In most states, individuals are permitted to adopt regardless of sexual orientation. Indeed, in some states, each member of a same-sex couple may be recognized as the legal parent of the child whom they are both raising. That a state will allow both members of a same-sex couple to be legal parents of the same child completely undermines the rationale often articulated for refusing to recognize same-sex unions.

Ironically, adoption is important to consider in the current context precisely because there is *no* fundamental right to adopt. Adoption is a state-created practice,[94] whereas the right to the custody and care of one's (biological) children involves rights that are not mere creations of the state.[95] Thus, a state has less of a burden insofar as it wants to regulate adoption, although of course its statutes must still be rationally related to legitimate state ends.[96] Despite this lighter burden, most states allow gays and lesbians to adopt, presumably out of a recognition that allowing such adoptions promotes the interests of all concerned.

FAMILY-LIKE ASSOCIATIONS

While the right to adopt is not fundamental, the Court has indicated its appreciation of the interests implicated in relationships which have many of the features of parent-child relationships, even if neither biology nor adoption is implicated. For example, in *Smith v. Organization of Foster Families for Equality and Reform (OFFER)*, the Court implied that "individuals may acquire a liberty interest against arbitrary governmental interference in the family-like associations into which they have freely entered, even in the absence of biological connection or state-law recognition of the relationship."[97] However, the Court held that the liberty interest in family-like associations was less weighty than the "constitutionally recognized liberty interest that derives from blood relationship, state-law sanction, and basic human right."[98] The Court ruled that whatever "liberty interest might otherwise exist in the foster family as an institution, that interest must be substantially attenuated where the proposed removal from the foster family is to return the child to his natural parents."[99]

The difficulty for the *OFFER* Court was that the rights of the foster parents were being pitted against the rights of the biological parents. Whereas "ordinarily procedural protection may be afforded to a liberty interest of one person without derogating from the substantive liberty of another," this description is inapt where there is a custody dispute between the foster and biological parents.[100] Where they are at odds over custody, "a tension is virtually unavoidable."[101]

At least two features of the *OFFER* opinion should be noted. First, the Court made clear that the rights of biological parents who have an actual relationship with their child are weightier than the rights of the foster parents. Second, foster parents do have a legally cognizable liberty interest in maintaining a relationship with "their" children, even if such interests may be outweighed by the interests of the biological parents. The Court would never have discussed a "tension" between these divergent interests if the foster parents did not have interests of which the Court had to take account.

The Supreme Court has both recognized that foster parents have an interest in their relationships with the children for whom they are responsible and has accorded that interest relative weight. In doing so, the Court balanced a number of considerations. On the one hand, children and foster parents may develop deep emotional ties.[102] On the other hand, the foster parents may have been afforded the opportunity to develop relationships with their foster children contingent on an agreement that those children might be removed[103] and, further, the natural parents may have placed the children in foster care precisely because they knew that the children would be returned upon request.[104]

Merely because the rights of foster parents may be outweighed by the rights of biological parents on fairness[105] grounds does not mean that foster parent rights are nonexistent. It is precisely because some courts have failed to appreciate that the nonbiological, nonadoptive parents have liberty interests in their relationships with the children in their care which may sometimes be asserted, in the words of the *OFFER* Court, "without derogating from the substantive liberty of another"[106] that courts have sometimes erred when discussing the rights of nonbiological, nonadoptive parents. Although the interest of the nonbiological, nonadoptive parent in maintaining the parent-child relationship may not be fundamental, it nonetheless should be accorded weight and should not be treated as if any legitimate state interest, no matter how unimportant, would justify overriding that parental interest.[107]

The Court's treatment of foster families has implications for adoption, whether by a single adult or a couple. When the relationship between a child and an adult has many of the characteristics of a parent-child relationship, that relationship may have constitutional significance. The point here should not be misunderstood. It is not argued that the nonbiological, nonadoptive parent's interest in parenting outweighs the biological or adoptive parent's interest or even the state's interest in assuring that children are well cared for. On the contrary, since the biological parent's rights can be terminated if that person's continuing to care for his or her child would be detrimental to that child's interests, the nonadoptive, nonbiological parent's interest is of course outweighed if that person would not be a fit parent. Indeed, it is important to emphasize that regardless of the parent's orientation, he or she will not be awarded custody if his or her having custody would be detrimental to the child.

CO-PARENTING

Sometimes, a gay or lesbian partner of the biological/adoptive parent[108] also wants to be the legal parent of that child. Such a child might benefit in a number of ways from such an adoption. There may be financial benefits.[109] There would be emotional benefits as well.[110] Further, such an arrangement may assure the continued relationship with the would-be adoptive parent, even should that adult and his or her partner separate or should the legal parent predecease the partner.[111] Otherwise, the child and the would-be adoptive parent might be separated, even if doing so would run counter to the best interests of the child.[112]

STEPPARENT ADOPTIONS

Before seeing how courts have handled cases in which the partner of a gay or lesbian parent wants to adopt the partner's child, it would be helpful to examine how courts handle a situation which is analogous in many respects: stepparent adoptions.[113] In both kinds of cases, the partner of the parent has a relationship with the child of the legally recognized parent. In both kinds of cases, the partner seeks to adopt the child so that the partner's relationship with the child will be formally and legally recognized.[114] In both kinds of cases, the bests interests of the child are thought to be of paramount concern,[115] especially if all interested parties consent to the adoption. While there are differences between a scenario involving a lesbian or gay couple and a scenario involving a stepparent, at least some of those differences militate in *favor* of allowing lesbian or gay adoptions. In any event, it is important to understand issues surrounding stepparent adoptions to understand the issues surrounding adoptions by gay and lesbian couples.

Suppose that an adult with minor children marries someone who is not biologically related to those children. One issue concerns the parental rights of the other biological parent. As suggested above, the noncustodial parent will have those rights respected, as long as unusual circumstances are not present.[116] However, unusual circumstances might be spelled out in terms of unfitness or "abandonment, persistent neglect of parental responsibilities, extended disruption of parental custody, or other similar extraordinary circumstances that would drastically affect the welfare of the child."[117]

Where the partner of a lesbian or gay parent seeks to adopt and the other parent objects, the situation should be treated in the same way as it would be were the partner of the custodial parent of a different sex. Certainly, terminating parental rights should not be done cavalierly. When a stepparent adoption is recognized, the non-custodial parent becomes a legal stranger to the child.[118] Given this severe result, courts should be reluctant to terminate parental rights regardless of the sex or sexual orientation of the would-be parent seeking adoption.[119]

While it is quite sensible for courts to be extremely reluctant to terminate a noncustodial parent's rights so that a stepparent or other partner can adopt, those same concerns are not implicated if no parental rights would thereby be terminated, assuming that the interests of the child would be promoted by the adoption. Legislatures have recognized that a stepparent and his or her spouse's children may become quite attached, and have enacted statutes making it easier for stepparents to adopt.[120] For example, legislatures have statutorily removed the requirement that the stepparent establish his or her spouse's unfitness before being able to adopt.[121] This approach is sensible. If the stepparent and the biological/adoptive parent are *vying* for custody, e.g., where the stepparent and noncustodial spouse each seek legal custody, then one might require that the biological/adoptive parent's unfitness be established before the stepparent could gain custody.[122] If the stepparent and biological/adoptive parent want to raise the child together, however, then not only would there be no need to establish the unfitness of one before allowing the other to adopt, but imposing such a requirement would be directly contrary to the best interests of all concerned.[123] Of course, in the latter scenario in which the biological/adoptive parent and his or her partner wish to raise the child together, the noncustodial biological/adoptive parent will either have to consent to the adoption or be shown to be unfit.

It would not be difficult to apply this paradigm to a same-sex couple. In order for the partner to be allowed to adopt, the noncustodial parent would have to either consent or be shown to be unfit.[124] Of course, if conception occurred as a result of an anonymous sperm donation, there would be no consent to obtain.[125]

The stepparent exception allows the custodial parent's marital partner to adopt without terminating that parent's rights.[126] However, some courts have viewed the stepparent exception quite narrowly. For example, in *In re Angel Lace M.*, the Wisconsin Supreme Court recognized that the father had consented to the termination of his parental rights.[127] However, because the mother and her lesbian partner could not marry,[128] the court was unwilling to allow the partner to adopt the child without also terminating the rights of the mother.[129] The court claimed to be bound by the relevant statute, although petitioners had offered an interpretation based on the stepparent exception which would have allowed the adoption, namely, that the rights of one (rather than both) of the biological parents would have to be terminated in order for the partner to be allowed to adopt.[130]

The Wisconsin Supreme Court rejected this interpretation because it allegedly would have allowed complete strangers to adopt.[131] Yet, there is reason to believe the court's reasoning disingenuous, since the best interests of the child would have been promoted had the partner adopted[132] and would not have been promoted had a complete stranger adopted the child.[133] Ironically, the concurring judge in *Angel Lace* encouraged the legislature to rewrite the adoption law in light of current societal conditions,[134] claiming that the court "can only interpret the law, not rewrite it,"[135] despite the court's having chosen to reject a plausible interpretation of the statute which would have led to a good result for all concerned.[136]

There are several reasons to believe that the *Angel Lace* court was not as constrained by the statute as it had claimed. First, the adoption statute did not expressly address whether a same-sex partner of a parent could adopt without that parent's rights having to be terminated.[137] Second, the legislature itself had mandated that the adoption statutes be liberally construed.[138] Third, it is not as if it would have been unprecedented for a court to liberally construe an adoption statute to promote the best interests of the child.[139] For example, several courts have allowed biological parents to adopt their own children, a use of the statute which, although presumably not intended, might nonetheless promote the interests of both the parents and the children.[140] Further, several courts when faced with statutes and facts similar[141] to those in *Angel Lace* have recognized the absurdity of requiring the biological/adoptive parent's rights to be terminated before the partner could adopt.[142] The supreme courts of Massachusetts,[143] Vermont,[144] and New York[145] have each allowed *both* members of same-sex couples to be legal parents of the same child. In each case, the individuals had a long committed relationship with their respective partners[146] and allowing the adoption was clearly in the best interest of the child.[147] As the Vermont Supreme Court suggested, when courts consider the language of and purpose behind adoption statutes, they realize that "it would be against common sense to terminate the biological parent's rights when that parent will continue to raise and be responsible for the child, albeit in a family unit with a partner who is biologically unrelated to the child."[148] The Vermont court made clear that the "paramount concern should be with the effect of our laws on the reality of children's lives."[149]

STEPPARENT VERSUS SAME-SEX PARTNER

Although there are some noteworthy similarities between cases involving adoption by a same-sex partner and cases involving adoption by a stepparent—for example, in both the adults may have had a longterm, committed relationship—there are some noteworthy differences as well. An important difference between the stepparent scenario and the one involving a lesbian or gay life partner is that in the latter case both adults might have agreed to raise the child together and thus both might have taken part in the planning to have and raise that child.[150] All else equal, this would indicate a greater investment in and commitment to the welfare of the child by the partner than the stepparent, since the child's very existence would not be contingent on something that the latter had done.

Certainly, there are other differences as well. The stepparent is married to the child's parent whereas the lesbian or gay partner is not. Here, as in a variety of other contexts, some courts suggest that the lesbian or gay partner is most appropriately analogized to a parent's nonmarital companion.[151] Yet, there is an important difference. In the latter case, the couple has chosen not to marry whereas in the former case the couple has been prevented by the State from marrying.[152] In many cases, the couple would be married were that a possibility.[153] It seems the height of bad faith to deny parental rights because of a failure to marry when the individuals would have married had the State afforded them that option.[154]

Lesbian and gay adoptions are important to consider for a number of reasons. First, that states allow such adoptions makes clear that lesbians and gays are fit parents. Second, when states are considering whether to allow both members of a same-sex couple to be the legal parents of the same child, the question is not whether the best interests of the child would thereby be promoted, since the courts would never allow such an adoption were it detrimental to the child's interests. Rather, the questions have been whether the statutory language would allow the court to promote the child's best interests by granting the adoption or, if not, whether the court would ignore the statutory language in order to avoid an absurd result. Here, the alleged reason that same-sex marriages should not be recognized—that gays and lesbians do not have and raise children—is a nonissue. The only question is whether both of the child's parents will be legally recognized as such.

There is another important issue which seems underappreciated by the courts. Adoptive parents have the same rights and responsibilities as do biological parents. The claimed importance of the biological tie between both parents and the child which is relied on by the courts to deny same-sex partners the right to marry is completely undermined by the case law which treats biological and adoptive parents as indistinguishable as a matter of law. If courts actually took the interests of parents and children seriously and considered the relevant case law, they would see that their positions against lesbian and gay families are unsupportable as a matter of law.

V   FULL FAITH AND CREDIT

▼

Marriage serves various functions and implicates a variety of interests, all of which apply to all couples regardless of sexual orientation. Many of the reasons offered to support same-sex marriage bans are most plausibly explained as pretexts for disadvantaging a disfavored group. Insofar as the marriage ban involves an invidious abridgement of the fundamental right to marry, all states will have to recognize same-sex marriages.

Suppose, however, that the Supreme Court were to rule that states had discretion with respect to whether to recognize same-sex marriages. Suppose further that Hawaii comes to recognize such marriages. A separate question is whether states will have to recognize those same-sex marriages validly celebrated in Hawaii.

At least facially, the Full Faith and Credit Clause would seem to require that if a same-sex marriage is validly celebrated in one state, all states must legally recognize that marital union. However, that appearance is deceptive both because the Full Faith and Credit Clause includes an exception which allows states in certain circumstances not to give credit to the statutes, judgments, or records of other states and because, as most courts and commentators agree, the interstate recognition of marriages implicates a choice-of-law rather than a full faith and credit question.

Choice of law is a notoriously murky area in which courts have wide discretion. Yet, courts have much *less* discretion than might first appear insofar as they must decide whether to validate a marriage validly celebrated in another state. Although state legislatures can explicitly declare that they will not recognize same-sex marriages that have been celebrated in other states, courts acting in good faith will be unable to refuse to recognize such marriages in their respective states, absent an explicit legislative declaration to that effect.

FULL FAITH AND CREDIT

The controversies surrounding whether states must recognize same-sex marriages validly celebrated in another state and whether Congress has the power to change the existing system cannot be understood without analyzing the Full Faith and Credit Clause itself, which reads: "Full Faith and Credit shall be given in each State to the public Acts, Records, and judicial Proceedings of every other State."[1] This brief sentence does not adequately explain the force or the breadth of the clause. For example, it does not specify the conditions under which a state might *refuse* to credit a public act, record, or judicial proceeding of another state. The Clause itself, however, delegates to Congress the authority to pass *general* laws to fill in some of the gaps.[2] The clause, in light of the relevant congressional enactment,[3] has been interpreted to mean that each state must treat the judgment of another state as it would be treated in the state in which the judgment was rendered.[4] If the judgment is not subject to modification in the state rendering it, then the judgment is not subject to modification in other states either.[5]

THE CLAUSE'S PURPOSES

In *Magnolia Petroleum Co. v. White*, the Supreme Court explained that the Full Faith and Credit Clause is a "nationally unifying force."[6] The Court had already made clear that the clause was designed to make the several states "integral parts of a single nation."[7] However, states cannot be integral parts of a single nation without surrendering some of their autonomy. As the *Sherrer* Court recognized, states may be required by the Full Faith and Credit Clause to sacrifice particular local policies as part of the price of membership in a federal system.[8]

Yet, there are limits to the extent to which the Full Faith and Credit Clause can bind state courts. For example, as Justice Felix Frankfurter noted in his *Vanderbilt* dissent, "*exceptional* circumstances may relieve a State from giving full faith and credit to the judgment of a sister State because 'obnoxious' to an overriding policy of its own."[9] This obnoxiousness exception is read quite narrowly, however. States are not permitted to ignore foreign judgments whenever they happen to disagree with the policies underlying those judgments; as the *Estin* Court explained, the Full Faith and Credit Clause may require "submission by one State even to hostile policies reflected in the judgment of another state."[10] Thus, merely because the policy of one state conflicts with the policy of another does not establish that a statute of the former would, in the words of the *Clapper* Court, "be obnoxious to the latter's public policy."[11]

Full Faith and Credit must be distinguished from comity. A court giving effect to the laws or judicial decisions of another jurisdiction because of the Full Faith and Credit Clause does so as a matter of obligation whereas a court doing the same thing out of comity does so out of deference. Thus, although each case involves one court's giving credit to a judgment rendered outside the state, the former involves a constitutionally imposed obligation while the latter does not,[12] since the Full Faith and Credit Clause does not apply to the judgments of foreign countries.[13] Indeed, as far as the Constitution is concerned, United States courts are free to ignore the judgments of other countries,[14] although there is a general trend in the direction of giving them effect nonetheless.

Courts respecting foreign judgments out of comity do not do so as a mere act of courtesy or good will,[15] but out of deference and respect.[16] Nonetheless, an attitude of deference or respect is more easily overcome than a constitutionally imposed obligation. The difference between comity and full faith and credit is important to consider in precisely those cases in which the court is tempted *not* to recognize a judgment rendered elsewhere. If the judgment of another state court is at issue, the Constitution may preclude a court from refusing to credit that judgment.

POLICY

Where a judgment contravenes and, indeed, is obnoxious to an important state policy, a court may ignore that judgment whether the judgment comes from the court of another state or of another country.[17] However, precisely because the Full Faith and Credit Clause is supposed to act as a unifying force and precisely because the clause does not apply to foreign countries, the standard for when other *states'* judgments may be ignored is more difficult to meet than the analogous standard for other *countries'* judgments. The Constitution informs the former but not the latter standard.

There are at least two issues implicated in analyses of whether full faith and credit must be given to a judgment rendered in another state. One is whether an important rather than a merely legitimate state interest is involved. Another is whether a particular judgment is in fact obnoxious to public policy. One state will be required to enforce another state's judgment, *either* because the former state's implicated interests are not particularly important *or* because the latter state's judgment is not particularly offensive to the former state's public policy.[18]

In *Estin v. Estin*, the Court noted that the "Full Faith and Credit Clause is not to be applied, accordion-like, to accommodate [judges'] personal predilections."[19] The clause requires "submission by one State even to hostile policies reflected in the judgment of another State, because the practical operation of the federal system, which the Constitution designed, demand[s] it."[20] Nonetheless, if the obligation clearly violates the settled public policy of the state, the judgment will not be enforced. For example, courts differ about whether gambling debts validly incurred in another jurisdiction may be enforced in a state where such debts could not validly be incurred.[21]

It bears emphasis that the relevant question for full faith and credit purposes is *not* whether application of either state's statutes would have led to the same outcome. An obligation enforcible in one jurisdiction and unenforcible in another may not be so offensive to public policy that a court in the latter jurisdiction should refuse to credit a judgment enforcing that obligation, even if the obligation would have been held unenforceable had that same court originally heard the case. As the Supreme Court pointed out in *Union National Bank v. Lamb*, "It is when a clash of policies between two states emerges that the need of the Clause is the greatest."[22] The mere fact that two state statutes differ does not entail that the statute of the former would be obnoxious to the latter's public policy.

DOMESTIC RELATIONS

In the context of domestic relations, full faith and credit issues tend to arise in contexts in which either a divorce secured in one state is challenged in another or in which the incidents of marriage—spousal support, inheritance rights, etc.—are at issue. Very important interests are at stake when courts decide these issues. For example, an individual who secures a divorce and then remarries may be charged with bigamy if the first divorce is not given full faith and credit in the state in which the charge has been brought.[23]

In order for a court to grant a divorce, it must have personal jurisdiction over at least one of the parties and subject matter jurisdiction. The state court will have subject matter jurisdiction over the dissolution of the marriage if at least one of the parties is domiciled in the state. Often, the issue to be litigated is whether the court has subject matter jurisdiction (because the court will have personal jurisdiction over one of the parties by virtue of that party's voluntary personal appearance when seeking the divorce).

When the domiciliary status of an individual seeking a divorce is itself at issue, the objecting spouse can challenge the divorce directly by appearing and presenting evidence that the person seeking a divorce is not domiciled in that state. Or, the challenging spouse can attack the decree in his or her home state by asserting that the person granted the divorce had not been domiciled there and thus that the state had not had jurisdiction to grant that decree.

For example, if Mr. and Mrs. Jones are domiciled in State A, Mr. Jones goes to State B and stays long enough to meet the residency requirement, gives notice of his intention to get a divorce and then does so,[24] that decree will be subject to attack. Mrs. Jones could have appeared in the original proceeding in State B to present evidence establishing that her husband had had no intention of becoming domiciled there. Or, she could choose to wait and attack the decree in her home state A. Further, if Mr. Jones moves back to State A to live before Mrs. Jones has attacked the decree, his moving back would be admissible to help establish that he had not in fact intended to make State B his domicile and thus that State B had not had jurisdiction to grant the divorce.

When a divorce decree is issued, there is a presumption that the decree-granting court has both personal and subject matter jurisdiction,[25] although that presumption is rebuttable. A court in a different jurisdiction can decide for itself whether the first court had subject matter jurisdiction, as long as that matter has not already been litigated.[26] In *Williams v. North Carolina*, the Supreme Court made it clear that it understood that one state court's being allowed to decide for itself whether another state court's determination of domicile is correct will itself cause uncertainty about marital status, but characterized this as "merely one of those untoward results inevitable in a federal system in which regulation of domestic relations has been left with the States and not given to the national authority."[27]

The Court has offered some protection for the person who wants certainty regarding his or her marital status. As long as each spouse participates in the divorce proceeding and each has been given an opportunity to contest the jurisdictional issues, the Full Faith and Credit Clause will bar either from later attacking the decree elsewhere as long as the decree is not susceptible to such attack in the courts of the decree-granting state.[28]

Although the current system regarding the interstate recognition of divorce decrees may allow a court in State X to decide for itself whether the person seeking a divorce was in fact domiciled in State Y (notwithstanding a court in State Y having already made a judgment to that effect), the system does not allow the court in State X to address whether it (or the state) approves of State Y's criteria for divorce. Otherwise, the resulting appeals process would put the Supreme Court in the position of having to weigh the relative merits of the different states' policies with respect to divorce and related matters, something which the Court clearly does not want to do.[29] According to the current system, the states must give full faith and credit to divorce decrees granted by the courts of other states as long as those latter courts have personal and subject matter jurisdiction.

CHOICE OF LAW

When the court of one state has to determine whether a divorce decree from another state should be given full faith and credit, the court does not have to decide which law is to be applied; it will merely make sure that the court had jurisdiction to grant the decree. Courts and commentators agree, however, that the recognition of marriages validly celebrated in other states involves a choice-of-law question.[30] Thus, because the law of more than one state is potentially applicable—the law of the state where the marriage is celebrated and the law of the state where the individuals are domiciled—a decision must be made with respect to which state's law will govern the validity of the marriage.

CHOICE-OF-LAW RULES

Choice of law is a notoriously murky area.[31] There may be difficulties in determining which states' laws even potentially apply in a particular case. As a general matter there are some constitutional limits on which states' laws are applicable to a particular occurrence or transaction. The *Hague* Court explained that "if a state has only an insignificant contact with the parties and the occurrence or transaction, application of its law is unconstitutional."[32] However, those limits are minimal and are controversial in application.[33] Further, even once it is clear which states' laws potentially apply, it may not be clear which state's law should in fact be used to determine the relevant rights and responsibilities. Indeed, the Court recognized in *Sun Oil v. Wortman* that "it is frequently the case under the Full Faith and Credit Clause that a court can lawfully apply either the law of one State or the contrary law of another."[34]

In *Alaska Packers Ass'n v. Industrial Accident Commission of California*, the Court explained the ramification of its position on Full Faith and Credit:

> It follows that not every statute of another state will override a conflicting statute of the forum by virtue of the full faith and credit clause, that the statute of a state may sometimes override the conflicting statute of another, both at home and abroad; and, again, that the two conflicting statutes may each prevail over the other at home, although given no extraterritorial effect in the state of the other.[35]

Given all of these possibilities, one might expect that the Supreme Court would issue explicit guidelines to lower courts so that they would know when forum law is appropriate to apply. The Court has refused to do so, believing it "unavoidable" that the Court "determine for itself the extent to which the statute of one state may qualify or deny rights asserted under the statute of another."[36] Although such an approach cannot help but create difficulties, the Court has presumably decided that the alternatives are even worse.

CHOICE OF LAW IN THE MARRIAGE CONTEXT

Happily, choice of law is much less murky in the context of the interstate recognition of marriages than it is in other contexts. For example, there are fewer difficulties in determining whose law potentially applies when one must determine the validity of a marriage. If a marriage is celebrated in the home (domiciliary) state, only that state's marriage law may be applied to determine the validity of the marriage. In a case involving a marriage celebrated outside of the domicile, the laws of the states of celebration and domicile potentially apply, *but no other states' laws are even potentially applicable.* Further, there is general agreement about whether the substantive law of the state of celebration or the state of domicile should apply. Basically, the law of the place of celebration will apply unless the marriage violates an important public policy of the domicile, in which case the domicile's law will apply and the marriage will be invalid.

When the issue is whether a *divorce* decree granted in one state must be recognized by another state, determining where the parties are domiciled will be quite important, since that will help determine whether the decree-granting court had jurisdiction to grant the divorce. If the decree-granting state was not the domicile of either party, the divorce will not be valid. However, when the issue is whether a *marriage* validly celebrated in one state must be recognized by another, the marriage may be valid even if the celebratory state was not the domicile of *either* party, as long as the marriage does not violate an important public policy of the domicile. Thus, the processes by which a state decides whether to recognize a marriage celebrated elsewhere and a divorce secured elsewhere differ in an important respect; in the former case, the domicile's substantive law is examined whereas in the latter case the relevant issue is whether the decree-granting state was in fact the domicile of one of the parties. While this may seem to be a trivial technicality, the difference between how marriages and divorces are treated in the interstate context has important implications, as will be made clear in the next chapter in the discussion of the Defense of Marriage Act.

Suppose that Robin Roberts and Kim Kennedy wish to marry. They are domiciliaries of State X but, regrettably, are prohibited by the state from marrying. Fortunately, State Y does not preclude them from marrying. They go to State Y, marry, and then return to State X to live.

After several years, Robin and Kim decide to separate. Kim files for divorce in State X. To avoid having to pay spousal support, Robin claims that the two were never legally married. As long as the marriage was valid in State Y, however, the court in State X would recognize that Kim and Robin had been legally married, unless certain fairly narrow conditions had been met,[37] for example, unless the marriage was obnoxious to an important public policy of State X.[38] Precisely because marriages which are not obnoxious to an important state policy might nonetheless be prohibited, the mere fact that domiciliaries could not have married in their home state will not entail that their marriage, validly contracted in another state, should not be recognized in their place of domicile.

The rule for when marriages validly contracted in one state must be recognized by the domiciliary state is quite similar to the rule for when states must enforce a foreign judgment—a (domiciliary) state may refuse to credit a marriage validly contracted in another state *only* when recognition of that marriage would be obnoxious to an important public policy. Yet, the similarity of this rule to the full faith and credit rule should not be thought to establish that choice of law plays no role in determining when or whether states must recognize marriages validly contracted in other states. On the contrary, choice of law plays two important roles in that context. First, the choice-of-law rule will be used to establish *which* state's public policy will be examined to determine if indeed the marriage is obnoxious to an important public policy.[39] Second, if indeed the marriage is obnoxious to an important public policy of the domicile, then the marriage will not be valid anywhere.[40]

The *First Restatement of the Conflicts of Laws* suggests that "a marriage is valid everywhere if the requirements of the marriage law of the state where the contract of marriage takes place are complied with."[41] However, the *Restatement* lists some exceptions. Section 132 reads:

Marriage Declared Void by Law of Domicil

A marriage which is against the law of the state of domicil of either party, though the requirements of the law of the state of celebration have been complied with, will be invalid everywhere in the following cases:

(a) polygamous marriage,

(b) incestuous marriage between persons so closely related that their marriage is contrary to a strong public policy of the domicil,

(c) marriage between persons of different races where such marriages are at the domicil regarded as odious,

(d) marriage of a domiciliary which a statute at the domicil makes void even though celebrated in another state.

Comment b to the section suggests that although clauses (a), (b), and (c) "state respects in which a marriage may offend a strong policy of the domiciliary state," these are not intended to be exclusive.[42] If a "marriage offends a strong public policy of the domicil in any other respect, such marriage will be invalid everywhere."[43] *Comment c* to the section describes how the term "odious" is to be understood in clause c. In order for a marriage to be odious, it must "not only be prohibited by statute but must offend a deep-rooted sense of morality in the state."[44]

The *Second Restatement of the Conflicts of Laws* suggests a similar policy: a "marriage which satisfies the requirements of the state where the marriage was contracted will everywhere be recognized as valid unless it violates the strong public policy of another state which had the most significant relationship to the spouses and the marriage at the time of the marriage."[45] Both *Restatements* suggest that a marriage that is valid where celebrated will be valid everywhere unless the marriage would be treated as *void* in the domicile; in the *First Restatement*, the chapter is entitled "Marriage Declared *Void* by Law of Domicil"[46] and the characterization of the exception in the *Second Restatement* is the classic description of a marriage that would be made void by statute.[47]

VOID MARRIAGES

Arguably, when a legislature declares a marriage void rather than merely prohibited, the state demonstrates that there is a strong public policy against such marriages and that such marriages, even if validly contracted elsewhere, should not be recognized by the state.[48] As a New York court explained, a state that declares a marriage void will treat the marriage as "void from its inception without any decree of the court and for all purposes."[49] It is an overstatement, however, to claim that all void marriages that are offensive to important public policies will be treated as void for all purposes. Numerous validly celebrated marriages including some allegedly extremely offensive to the domicile's public policy have been recognized by courts for certain purposes.

Historically, a variety of types of marriages have been declared void, running the gamut from incestuous or polygamous marriages to those which have been contracted too soon after a divorce. However, as the Supreme Court of Minnesota explains, precisely because there are important ramifications of treating a marriage as null and void, courts tend not to declare a marriage void unless there is an express declaration by statute to that effect.[50]

The general rule with respect to marriages is that if the marriage is valid where contracted, it is valid everywhere. However, there are exceptions to that rule: (1) incestuous or polygamous marriages, or (2) marriages prohibited because they violate public policy.[51]

Incestuous Marriages

Although no state recognizes incestuous marriages between individuals who are brother and sister by consanguinity, states disagree about what constitutes an incestuous marriage. For example, some states allow first cousins to marry while others do not. A state that holds marriages between first cousins *void* must decide whether to recognize such a marriage if validly celebrated in another state.

Courts in states declaring marriages between first cousins void have been far from unanimous when deciding whether to recognize such marriages if validly celebrated elsewhere.[52] Those courts recognizing the union of first cousins *despite the forum state's having declared such unions void* looked at additional factors such as whether sexual relations between the parties would be a criminal act.[53] This suggests that a state's having declared a marriage void may not suffice to justify such a marriage's not being recognized if validly contracted elsewhere. Indeed, perhaps surprisingly, several types of marriages, validly contracted in another state but void and allegedly offensive to an important public policy of the domicile, have not been deemed sufficiently offensive to justify refusing to recognize them for all purposes.

Polygamous Marriages

Even if there is a lack of consensus regarding whether all void, incestuous marriages will nonetheless be recognized if validly contracted elsewhere, it might seem that there certainly would be no lack of consensus with respect to whether polygamous marriages should be recognized. Over a hundred years ago, the Court made clear that Congress could prohibit such marriages.[54] Further, in 1985, the Tenth Circuit Court of Appeals upheld the state's right to maintain such a ban.[55] Yet, it bears repeating that the relevant question is not whether such marriages may be prohibited, but whether such marriages must be credited if validly celebrated elsewhere.

Currently, no state recognizes plural marriages and thus courts have not had to address the choice-of-law question that would be implicated by a different *state's* having recognized a polygamous marriage. *Perhaps* it would not be difficult to imagine how courts would rule, given their *relatively* consistent refusal to recognize such marriages when validly celebrated in other countries. Yet, courts have not been unanimous in this respect; courts have recognized plural marriages for certain purposes out of *comity*.

Several courts have recognized Native American polygamous marriages for purposes of succession.[56] These cases were complicated by court uncertainty about how to categorize the tribes. Some likened the tribes to foreign nations, while others discussed them as if they were independent political units within this country. Yet, at least for purposes here, it is not necessary to offer the correct legal categorization of tribes, as long as it is clear who does *not* have jurisdiction over Native American tribes and their practices.

There is general agreement that the tribes are not subject to state law.[57] In *Jones v. Meehan*, the Supreme Court made clear that the "Indian tribes within the limits of the United States are not foreign nations," although they are "distinct political communities."[58] Over a decade before *Jones*, the Court had already established in *United States v. Kagama* that the tribes have a "semi-independent position . . . as a separate people, with the power of regulating their internal and social relations."[59] Had the courts refusing to invalidate tribal marriages merely been refusing to regulate tribal internal affairs, their refusal would have been appropriate on *jurisdictional* grounds.

Yet, the courts who recognized the polygamous marriages out of comity had not been asked to regulate tribal "internal and social relations," which would have been beyond their jurisdiction, but instead to decide issues *within* their jurisdiction which implicated important state interests. In these cases, the *jurisdiction* of the courts was not in question. The only issue was whether the plural marriages would be recognized out of comity.

An analogy would be helpful to illustrate the point. It is of course true that a state would never try to tell India or Turkey what marriages they should or should not recognize.[60] Doing so would exceed the state's authority. However, states would be well within their authority to decide whether to recognize out of comity a marriage celebrated in either of those countries which was declared void by state law.[61]

Often, the issue of plural marriages came up in state courts to determine title to land located in the state.[62] It should be clear both that the courts had jurisdiction and that a state would not be required to recognize a tribal plural marriage out of comity.[63] Indeed, that is true by definition,[64] since a recognition out of comity is done out of deference or respect rather than because it must be done.[65] Nonetheless, most state courts recognized Native American plural marriages out of comity,[66] implying that marital unions which are void may nonetheless not be so obnoxious to public policy that they cannot be recognized, at least for certain purposes.

Perhaps it will be thought that so many complicated issues are implicated because the above cases involve Native American tribes that they should be treated as *sui generis* and thus as having no relevance to other cases. Yet, this claim is unpersuasive, both because plural marriages were recognized for certain purposes even when Native Americans were not involved,[67] and because the Native American cases were instrumental in securing that recognition (implying that they should not be treated as *sui generis*).[68] Despite having been described in the most unflattering terms, polygamous marriages have nonetheless been recognized for certain purposes, thus underscoring the tendency of some courts to refuse to hold legally celebrated marriages null and to no legal effect, even when declared void by the domicile.

MISCEGENATION

The *First Restatement* includes miscegenous marriages within those which need not be recognized, even if legally celebrated in another state. Courts need no longer address this issue directly because antimiscegenation laws were struck down in 1967 in *Loving*.[69] Nonetheless, it is illuminating to consider these cases because they help to illustrate the considerations which determine whether a marriage void in the domicile will nonetheless be recognized if valid in the state of celebration.

While most courts in states declaring interracial marriage void refused to recognize such marriages even if validly contracted in another state, some courts were willing to credit such marriages.[70] The *First Restatement* offers a possible explanation of this lack of uniformity. Section 132(c) explains that interracial marriages will be invalid if the domicile regards such marriages as odious.[71] *Comment (c)* to the section explains that for a marriage to be regarded as odious, it "must not only be prohibited by statute but must offend a deep-rooted sense of morality predominant in the state."[72] Insofar as an interracial marriage was void but did not offend a deep-rooted sense of morality predominant in the state, the marriage might be recognized if legally celebrated in another state, even if it could not be legally celebrated in the domicile. Thus, the deep-rooted sense of morality standard provided a check on which marriages would be refused interstate recognition.

Yet, it should not be thought that this criterion involving a deep-rooted sense of morality was somehow immune to abuse or gross misapplication. As a Vermont court made clear as far back as 1847, the views of "the most serious minded, earnest, and strenuously religious of our citizens"[73] cannot be inferred to represent the views of everyone. The court cautioned that when "making inquiry into the state of the moral feeling of the whole community, we must not forget that . . . it is almost infinitesimally divided."[74] The court suggested that before determining that "any given cause shocked the moral feeling of the community, we must be able to find but one pervading feeling upon that subject—so much so, that a contrary feeling, in an individual, would denominate him either insane, or diseased in his moral perceptions."[75] Thus, the test for whether a practice is odious is not simply whether the majority approves of it, but rather whether there is but one pervading feeling upon the subject.

When the issue is whether a marriage, validly celebrated in another state, should be recognized in the domicile, it is inappropriate to simply take a vote and see how many approve of such a marriage;

that *might* be the appropriate test for whether a particular practice should be *prohibited*, depending upon whether any individual fundamental interests were implicated. However, where the marriage has already been prohibited, the majority is presumed to disapprove of it. The relevant question is how strong and uniform that disapproval is.

One must be careful before accepting the claim that there is a universal abhorrence of a particular practice. As John Stuart Mill warns, universality is not established merely "because the writer or speaker is not only conscious of . . . [a particular view] in himself, but expects to find it in other people."[76] Mill notes that people claiming universality of agreement on particular issues "assume the utmost latitude of arbitrarily determining whose votes deserve to be counted. They either ignore the existence of dissentients, or leave them out of the account, on the pretext that they have the feeling which they deny having, or if not, that they ought to have it."[77] As Mill suggests, "The universal voice of mankind, so often appealed to, is universal only in its discordance. What passes for it is merely the voice of the majority, or, failing that, of any large number having a strong feeling on the subject; especially if it be a feeling of which they cannot give any account."[78]

The claim here is not that there *could not* be universal disapproval of same-sex marriages but merely that those who claim to represent this universal moral feeling are likely in error. Suppose however that same-sex marriages which were neither incestuous nor bigamous offended a deep-rooted sense of morality in the whole community. Even so, this still might not establish that courts should refuse to credit such marriages. If, for example, the state with the shocked community had incorporated within its code a view suggested in the Uniform Marriage and Divorce Act, namely, that only bigamous and incestuous marriages be prohibited,[79] or if that state has adopted a validation statute which said that all nonbigamous and nonincestuous marriages validly contracted in another state would be recognized in the domicile,[80] then the marriage would have to be recognized, notwithstanding the uniform reaction.

Suppose, for example, that marriages between individuals who had not yet reached the age of eighteen offended a deep-rooted sense of morality in the whole community of a particular state. Suppose, further, that they had adopted a law which said that any non-bigamous, nonincestuous marriage recognized in any state in the Union would be recognized by that state. Were two seventeen-year-olds to enter into a valid marriage in another state, that marriage would have to be recognized.

There are at least two difficulties with using the "shocked community" standard. First, as a Vermont court recognized long ago, the mere claim that something shocks the community does not make it so. Second, the positive law of a state might require that a marriage validly celebrated elsewhere be recognized, community outrage notwithstanding. Of course, were a marriage capable of eliciting a pervading feeling of moral shock within the whole community, the Legislature would amend the laws to make clear that the domicile would not recognize such marriages even if validly celebrated in another state. The history of choice of law in the context of the recognition of interracial marriages makes clear that states can assure that they will not have to recognize their domiciliaries' same-sex marriages, even if validly contracted in another state, as long as that intent is made explicit. Unless or until the Supreme Court rules that states may not preclude same-sex partners from marrying, states can take certain explicit measures to assure that they will not be forced to recognize same-sex marriages.

The history of antimiscegenation statutes is useful to consider for other reasons as well. Just as antimiscegenation laws wrongly denied a fundamental right, so too do laws denying individuals the right to marry a same-sex partner, since state prohibitions of same-sex marriages do not themselves pass constitutional muster.

The Supreme Court struck down antimiscegenation laws in 1967, and it is perhaps easy to forget just how offensive those marriages were thought to be. Most states banning such unions held that miscegenous marriages were sufficiently odious that they did not have to be recognized, even if they were validly celebrated in other states. The interracial marriage cases thus illustrate that merely because a "moral" aversion is uniform and deeply held does not establish that the aversion is appropriate, much less that it can or should overcome constitutional protections. Those who would argue that same-sex marriages offend the community's moral sense must remember that the same argument was used to prevent interracial marriage. The moral sense exception must be construed narrowly, if only to avoid invidious applications. The odiousness exception must be understood to mean that states may refuse to recognize marriages validly celebrated in another state, only if the moral aversion is not itself a mask for bigotry and prejudice.

Comment (b) to Section 132 of the *First Restatement* makes clear that polygamous, incestuous, and interracial marriages do not exhaust the categories of marriages which might be found to offend a strong policy of the domiciliary state. The context is important to note, however, since the comment is suggesting that there may be other *void* marriages that offend a strong policy of the state. The comment does not suggest that there are *nonvoid* marriages which nonetheless offend a strong public policy and thus should not be recognized even if legally celebrated elsewhere.

The Illinois Supreme Court articulated the rule for determining whether a marriage will be recognized. A "marriage valid where it is celebrated is valid everywhere, but there are two well-recognized exceptions, viz., marriages which are contrary to the *law of nature,* as generally recognized by *Christian nations,* and those which are declared by positive law to have no validity."[81] The law of nature criterion is generally regarded to preclude incest and polygamy,[82] although some commentators argue that it also might be used to preclude recognition of same-sex marriages.

NATURAL LAW

Commentators suggest that same-sex marriage is against Natural Law and thus obviously need not be credited, even if recognized in another state. Yet, there are numerous difficulties with attempting to invoke Natural Law to justify such a refusal. First, it is difficult to argue that the notion of a same-sex marriage is recognized by "Christian nations" to be contrary to Natural Law, given the practices of some of the Scandinavian countries.[83] Further, thousands of same-sex couples have been joined in religious ceremonies. Thus, it is not clear that Natural Law forbids such a union.

Suppose, however, that it were clear that such unions were precluded by Natural Law. Even so, this would hardly establish that the state should refuse to perform same-sex marriages, much less refuse to recognize them when performed in another state. Interracial marriages were once thought to violate Natural Law[84] and states must nonetheless allow interracial couples to marry.

Natural Law theorists seem not to appreciate the difficulties posed for their position on same-sex marriage by previous claims that interracial marriages contravene Natural Law. They might say that such marriages have always been acceptable and that those who said differently were wrong, although that would invite the response that individuals who believe same-sex marriages against Natural Law may also be wrong. Such theorists might say that interracial marriages did and still do violate Natural Law, although that would imply that Natural Law incorporates bigotry and, further, would undercut the assertion that our civil law is or should be based on Natural Law. Or, they might claim that interracial marriages were a violation of Natural Law but no longer are. However, this response would undercut the consistency and permanency associated with Natural Law.

Indeed, the alleged timelessness and constancy of Natural Law is one of the features which may make it poorly suited to inform public policy, since the latter is constantly changing. As a Maryland appellate court explained, "The public policy of our fathers may not have been the same as their predecessors, nor is the public policy of our fathers necessarily that of ours. Societal changes are constantly taking place."[85]

Natural Law itself has not been given much weight by the Court,[86] although a position *in accord* with Natural Law (assuming that a determinative content can be derived),[87] which has a secular justification may be adopted by the State.[88] Consider prohibitions against murder. The State promotes numerous interests by prohibiting murder, a crime which also contravenes Natural Law. While state murder prohibitions of course pass constitutional muster, they do so because of the secular interests thereby promoted rather than because murder is precluded by Natural Law.

It might be argued that *Bowers v. Hardwick* establishes the permissibility of using Natural Law as a basis for legislation because the *Bowers* Court confirmed the constitutional permissibility of using morality as a basis for legislation.[89] However, merely because Natural Law is *a* system of morality does not imply that it is the *only* system of morality. There are a variety of moral theories, many of which do not condemn same-sex relations. Thus, merely because law may be based on morality does not entail that it can be based on Natural Law. Further, many who believe morality a legitimate basis for legislation do not claim that the promotion of morality is an important, much less a compelling, state interest.[90] Thus, even were same-sex marriages immoral rather than promoting exactly the kinds of values and interests that more traditional marriages promote, the state interest in promoting morality is not alone of sufficient magnitude to refuse to recognize a marriage validly celebrated in another state.

The Natural Law criterion is misleading because it is neither a necessary nor a sufficient condition for refusing to recognize a marriage validly celebrated in another state. It is not necessary because, as both the *First Restatement* and the *Second Restatement* suggest, a marriage which is void at the domicile is void everywhere. It is not sufficient, because a marriage allegedly contrary to Natural Law, for example, an interracial marriage, may nonetheless have to be recognized by a state. Bracketing constitutional constraints on the power of legislatures to prohibit certain marriages, the relevant criterion for whether a state must credit a marriage validly celebrated in another state is not whether the marriage is contrary to Natural Law but, rather, whether the domiciliary state had made the marriage void.

In general, a state must declare a marriage void if such a marriage, although validly celebrated in another state, is nonetheless to be treated as having no legal effect. There is one narrow exception to this rule, which has been narrowed even further by the courts.

However, before the exception is discussed, it is first important to see why marriages prohibited in the domicile may nonetheless be recognized there if validly celebrated in another state.

VOIDABLE AND PROHIBITED MARRIAGES

A state may decide to make certain marriages voidable rather than void. Such a marriage is only void after it has been so declared by decree.[91] Before such a decree, it is recognized as valid.[92] Voidable marriages are viewed as less odious to public policy than void marriages, precisely because the state has implicitly if not explicitly declared that there are some conditions under which such marriages will remain valid.[93] For example, marriages between underage individuals are voidable rather than void and may be ratified by cohabitation after the age of majority has been reached.[94]

Just as voidable marriages are not viewed as particularly odious and thus not the kinds of marriages which the state should refuse to recognize if validly celebrated elsewhere, so too prohibited (but not void) marriages are viewed as less odious to public policy than void marriages. A marriage which could not be contracted in the domicile because prohibited might nonetheless be recognized in the domicile if contracted in another state.[95] There are a number of reasons why courts are willing to recognize such marriages.

The Pennsylvania Supreme Court explains that because the refusal to recognize a valid foreign marriage involves "destroying the uniformity of result which is so desirable in a case concerning the recognition of a marriage that is valid in the state where it was contracted," the policy which would be violated by recognizing the marriage must be very important to justify that refusal.[96] It is for the above reason among others that courts invoking the public policy exception to justify a refusal to recognize a marriage celebrated in another state are referring to *important* public policies,[97] as might be indicated by the legislature's having made the marriage *void*.[98] In most circumstances, a marriage which is prohibited but not void in a state will be recognized if validly contracted in another state.[99]

Were courts to require that all of the domicile's statutory requirements be met before a marriage celebrated in another state would be recognized, many marriages celebrated in other states would not be recognized in the domicile for unimportant reasons. For example, a marriage might be invalidated because the marriage certificate itself did not conform to state specifications. Such an invalidation policy might undermine a whole host of justified expectations, especially if the individuals did not even know about these technical requirements.

If individuals know that their state will not recognize a particular kind of marriage celebrated in another state, they will not have a *justified* expectation that their marriage will be recognized. As long as states are very clear about their policies, individuals will not be surprised because they had falsely assumed that their marriages would be recognized. States make clear their intent not to recognize certain marriages even if validly contracted in another state either by making the marriage void or by passing an evasion statute.

EVASION STATUTES

Individuals who are domiciled in a state which will not allow them to marry have a variety of alternatives, none particularly attractive. They can find other partners, which is easier said than done. As the California Supreme Court pointed out when it declared the state's antimiscegenation statute unconstitutional, people are not "as interchangeable as trains."[100] The couple might choose to move to another state, which may mean giving up a job, moving far from family and friends, and so on. Or, the couple might go to a state where they could validly be married and then return home, hoping that their domicile would recognize the marriage.

Not wanting their domiciliaries to be able to avoid their marriage laws by simply getting married in a state with a different law, states have passed evasion statutes. Arguably, these statutes were unnecessary insofar as they were designed to justify the refusal to recognize a marriage void in the domicile but legally celebrated elsewhere. Many courts, however, have recognized marriages celebrated elsewhere, laws in the domicile making the marriage void notwithstanding. When an evasion statute has been passed, courts are much less able to argue that the legislature's intent is unclear and that therefore the marriage legally celebrated elsewhere should be recognized by the domicile. The statute specifies which marriages, legally celebrated elsewhere, should nonetheless not be recognized in the domicile.

An evasion statute might follow the Uniform Evasion Act[101] and declare that domiciliaries who attempt to evade a statute making their marriage *void* by going to another state that recognizes the union will not have their marriage recognized by the domicile.[102] Or, the statute might declare that domiciliaries who attempt to evade a statute *prohibiting* their marriage by going to another state which recognizes the union will not have their marriage recognized by the domicile.[103]

The latter evasion act is much more encompassing than the former, since the latter includes both void and prohibited marriages whereas the former only includes void ones. By making *all* marriages prohibited in the state subject to the evasion statute, the state implies that both important and unimportant rules and regulations must be followed in order for the domicile to recognize the marriage. Courts sometimes blunt the force of these broad evasion statutes by distinguishing among the prohibitions, claiming that some are meant to apply only if the marriage is to be celebrated in the domicile while others are meant to apply wherever the marriage is to be celebrated. Unless such a distinction is made, a literal reading of the statute would entail that all marriages prohibited in the state will not be recognized in the domicile even if validly celebrated elsewhere.

Several states have evasion statutes. Arguably, those states with evasion statutes which specify that *all* marriages prohibited in the domicile will not be recognized even if validly contracted in another state will not have to recognize a domiciliary's same-sex marriage as long as such a marriage would be prohibited in the domicile. However, if the evasion statute only applies to *void* marriages, then the state will have to declare same-sex marriages void and not merely prohibited if the state is not going to recognize them.

Precisely because of the numerous interests served by recognizing marriages wherever celebrated and precisely because there are very clear ways in which the state can manifest its intent not to recognize same-sex marriages even if validly contracted in another state, there are persuasive reasons for courts to recognize such marriages celebrated in another state, absent explicit legislative direction to the contrary. A further reason is provided by the courts' having required that the domicile make very clear which marriages validly celebrated in another state will nonetheless not be recognized by the domicile.[104] States have been put on notice that they must make their intent very clear and thus the courts have even more reason to recognize marriages celebrated in other states when legislatures remain silent on this issue.

THE EFFECT OF STATUTES

The majority of states do not have an evasion statute. Further, the Uniform Evasion Act has been withdrawn, at least in part, because its purpose conflicts with that of the Uniform Marriage and Divorce Act, namely, to promote the recognition of all nonincestuous, non-bigamous marriages recognized in any of the states.[105]

Courts in states without an evasion statute may have to decide which marriages, void in the domicile, should nonetheless be recognized if celebrated in another state. To help them distinguish among the void marriages, courts will sometimes look at other statutes, for example, whether sexual relations between the parties is criminalized or whether the marriage itself is criminalized.[106]

Commentators disagree about how the presence of a sodomy statute would impact the recognition of a same-sex marriage celebrated in another state. Some seem to believe that such a statute poses an obstacle. However, there are at least two reasons that this obstacle does not seem great. First, laws prohibiting sodomy generally are allegedly not directed specifically against gay, lesbian, and bisexual people. Thus, the statute should not be inferred to indicate strong disapproval of same-sex marriages. Second, it is not at all clear that sodomy laws may constitutionally be applied to individuals who are married to each other. Sodomy laws that apply to opposite-sex partners and do not have an explicit exception for married couples are nonetheless understood not to apply to them. Presumably, the same would be true for same-sex partners.

Arguably, laws that protect gays, lesbians, and bisexuals indicate some public acceptance of or tolerance towards them. Certainly, such statutes do not entail that same-sex marriages are permissible.[107] Presumably, if the populace wanted to allow same-sex couples to marry, the Legislature would enact a statute to that effect. However, the point is not that the society prohibiting orientation discrimination therefore approves of same-sex marriages, but merely that the populace may thereby have indicated that such marriages would not be thought sufficiently odious that they should not be recognized if validly celebrated in another state.

STATE INTERESTS

Numerous interests are implicated in the recognition of marriages legally celebrated in other states. States have an interest in preserving the integrity of marriages and in safeguarding family relationships. The state has an interest in protecting the predictability of marriages, and the security and stability in marriages. Not only would all of these general interests support the recognition of same-sex marriages validly celebrated elsewhere, but the state may have an especially strong interest in promoting stable, long-term, monogamous relationships among same-sex couples if the spread of HIV might thereby be reduced. Further, the state also has nondomestic interests in recognizing foreign marriages, for example, thus promoting comity, facilitating multistate activity, and increasing uniformity and predictability.[108]

Indeed, a state would promote its own interests by allowing such marriages to be celebrated *within* the state, both because doing so would respect individual rights and because the state might thereby earn tourist dollars.[109] In any event, because there is a strong public policy for upholding marriages wherever possible,[110] courts should recognize same-sex marriages celebrated in other states absent express manifestation of legislative intent to the contrary. Not to do so would seem to be yet another instance of bad faith in which the rules applied to heterosexuals are suddenly suspended or nonexistent when lesbian, bisexual, or gay people are involved.

When Congress considered whether to pass the Defense of Marriage Act, it was clear in the debates that there was no understanding of how the current system regulating the interstate recognition of marriage works. Many representatives and senators worried that if same-sex marriages were validly celebrated in Hawaii, other states would be forced by the Full Faith and Credit Clause to recognize those unions. These members of Congress apparently forgot that before the antimiscegenation laws had been declared unconstitutional, states had not been required to recognize interracial marriages validly celebrated in other states. Thus, Congress set out to prevent the Full Faith and Credit Clause from having an effect which it does not have even without the Defense of Marriage Act. Ironically, precisely because Congress apparently did not understand the current system, the new law *will not* increase the number of states entitled to refuse to recognize a *marriage* validly celebrated in another state but will increase the number of states entitled to refuse to recognize a *divorce* decree validly secured in another state. The constitutionality and effects of the Defense of Marriage Act are examined in the next chapter.

VI THE DEFENSE OF MARRIAGE ACT

▼

The Defense of Marriage Act (DOMA), signed into law on September 21, 1996,[1] is designed to do two things: (1) prevent states from being forced by the Full Faith and Credit Clause to recognize same-sex marriages validly celebrated in other states, and (2) define marriages for federal purposes as the union of one man and one woman. The Act is unconstitutional because it is the antithesis of a full faith and credit measure which lacks sufficient generality and, without adequate justification, encroaches upon an area traditionally reserved for state regulation. Further, the act unreasonably restricts interstate travel and is motivated by a desire to impose an undeserved burden on a disfavored group.

Bracketing the unconstitutionality of the law, it is a public policy disaster. The act will undermine the unity among the states which the Full Faith and Credit Clause was designed to secure and will likely result in the destabilization of familial relations as well as the disappointment of the justified expectations of countless innocent individuals. That Congress would even consider passing such an act and that the president would even consider signing such a bill into law are testaments to the willingness of many to codify the stigmatization of a disfavored group in exchange for votes.

MARRIAGE

As a general matter *even after DOMA became law*, if two individuals living in one state decide to marry in another, that marriage is recognized in the home state. As long as the marriage is neither polygamous nor incestuous and does not violate a strong public policy of the domicile, it will be valid everywhere. However, if the marriage does violate a strong public policy of the domicile, as might be indicated by that state's having declared the marriage void, the marriage will not be valid anywhere.

Suppose that Kim Kennedy and Jan Jones are prevented from marrying in their home state, A, but are permitted to marry in the neighboring state, M. They marry and honeymoon in State M and then move back to State A to live. Suppose further that after a few years, Jan and Kim decide to divorce. To avoid paying spousal support, Jan claims that they were never validly married.

If at the time of their union their marriage was declared null and void by State A's law, Jan will probably win. A divorce would probably not be necessary or even possible, since they had never had a valid marriage, notwithstanding their having met all of State M's requirements.[2] If, however, the marriage between Kim and Jan was merely prohibited but not void according to State A's law, the marriage would likely be recognized by State A (prohibition notwithstanding) and a divorce would be necessary.[3]

Suppose that the above scenario is slightly modified. Jan and Kim marry in State M and then live in State A. A few years after they have been married, however, Jan gets a very attractive job offer in State O. Jan and Kim move there. A few years later Jan and Kim decide to divorce. Hoping to avoid paying spousal support, Jan claims that they were never validly married.

The analysis to determine the validity of Jan's and Kim's marriage when they have lived in State O for a few years mirrors the analysis determining the marriage's validity when they have always lived in State A. If *at the time of the marriage* State A's law declared the marriage void, then the marriage would be void everywhere. If State A recognized the marriage, then the marriage would be valid everywhere. Thus, according to current choice-of-law jurisprudence, if at the time of the marriage State A recognized Kim's and Jan's marriage as valid, their marriage would be valid in State O when they later moved there, *even if State O's domestic relations law made such marriages void*.[4] Because State O would have had no contacts with the parties or the marriage itself at the time of the union, State O's domestic relations law would simply be inapplicable to determine the validity of this marriage. As will be explained below, because DOMA did not address choice-of-law issues, this analysis holds true even when DOMA is the law of the land.

To understand this perhaps counterintuitive result, one should remember that there is a very strong presumption in favor of recognizing marriages.[5] There is a marked tendency in the law to "sustain marriages, not to upset them."[6] The *Madewell* court explained that "the law favors marriage and its continuance and frowns upon dissolution of the status by annulment or divorce."[7] The state has an interest in protecting the predictability of marriages,[8] and the security and stability in marriages.[9] Thus, the law will tend to be set up in ways that will favor the recognition and continuation of marriage and will disfavor its dissolution.

Even the ability to divorce has been characterized as connected in an important way to the *promotion* of marriage, e.g., because it may only be through getting a divorce that one will be able to meet someone else and eventually have an enduring, fulfilling, successful marriage.[10] Although this does not mean that states are precluded from imposing any limits on divorce,[11] it does mean that states cannot irretrievably foreclose the opportunity to divorce.[12]

The strong state interest in marriage is served in at least two different ways. First, states will tend to recognize those marriages validly celebrated in another state, even if they would be prohibited in the domicile.[13] As the *Loughran* Court made clear, "Marriages not polygamous or incestuous or otherwise declared void by statute will, if valid by the law of the state where entered into, be recognized as valid in every other jurisdiction."[14] Second, the validity of the marriage can be negated only by applying the laws of the states of celebration or domicile at the time of the marriage.[15] This adds certainty and stability to the marital status and prevents the marriage from being subject to invalidation by laws which, at the time of the marriage, could not reasonably have been anticipated would apply to the union.

The reason that each state will recognize a marriage recognized in both the states of celebration and domicile is *not* that the Full Faith and Credit Clause requires that recognition. Rather, it is because each state as a matter of its *own* law recognizes that the only states whose law might potentially be applicable to determine the validity of the marriage are the states of celebration and domicile at the time of the marriage.

Suppose that the system had been set up differently. Suppose that marriages validly celebrated in one state had to be recognized in each of the other states by virtue of the Full Faith and Credit Clause, assuming that the marriage was not obnoxious to an important public policy of the state where the court deciding the case was located. In such a system, the validity of any marriage would be at least potentially dependent upon its not being obnoxious to *any* state's law. Otherwise, someone who wanted to avoid the responsibilities of a marriage could simply move to a state where such marriages were considered obnoxious to an important public policy, confident that the state would refuse to recognize the marriage based on the obnoxiousness exception to the Full Faith and Credit Clause.

The current system does not allow forum shopping to defeat the responsibilities of marriage.[16] Because the interstate recognition of marriages involves choice of law and because of how each state's choice-of-law rules operate, only the exception involving obnoxiousness to the *domiciliary* state's law may invalidate a marriage.[17] This way, one of the parties to the marriage will not find out several years later that her marriage was void and *had never existed* because of the laws of a state with which she neither ever had had nor ever would have any contact.

SECTION 2 OF THE DEFENSE OF MARRIAGE ACT

Ironically, although the Defense of Marriage Act (as written) does not increase the number of states entitled to refuse to recognize a same-sex marriage validly celebrated in another state, it nonetheless is likely to destabilize the certainty and status of marriage and is almost an open invitation for states to pressure Congress for more exceptions regarding which marriages and divorces the states must recognize.[18] Further, the act creates the possibility that a heavy burden will be imposed on those same-sex couples considering migrating to or even traveling through certain states, and is clearly designed to insult and stigmatize a disfavored group. Section 2 of the Defense of Marriage Act reads:

> No state, territory or possession of the United States, or Indian tribe, shall be required to give effect to any public act, record, or judicial proceeding of any other State, territory, possession, or tribe respecting a relationship between persons of the same sex that is treated as a marriage under the laws of such *other* State, territory, possession, or tribe, or a right or claim arising from such relationship.[19]

Although this section of the act may seem extremely straightforward, there are some ambiguities and omissions which make it surprisingly difficult to interpret. Ironically, the co-sponsors' public statements have only added to the confusion rather than clarified the issues. Because the co-sponsors indicated that they did not understand the existing system when they tried to "fix" a problem which was not a problem in the first place, it is difficult to discern their intentions with respect to some of the areas of the law that were not discussed in the congressional debates but are nonetheless affected by the act as it is written. For example, the act affects which divorces will be recognized by other states.

MODIFYING FULL FAITH AND CREDIT

The Defense of Marriage Act is deceptively simple, at least in part, because there has been a failure to specify whether it is intended to modify choice-of-law rules.[20] Consider Section 2 of DOMA, which basically states that no state shall be required to give effect to a same-sex marriage merely because it is treated as a marriage under the laws of another state. Presumably, this does not mean that a state which recognizes such marriages under its *own* law is nonetheless not required to recognize such a marriage because other states also recognize that marriage. Yet, if the act is not intended to permit states to ignore their own laws (including their own choice-of-law rules) with respect to whether a same-sex marriage will be recognized,[21] it is unclear how this act changes anything with respect to which marriages are recognized; those states given the option by DOMA to refuse to recognize same-sex marriages already have that option, and those states not having that option will not have suddenly acquired it through DOMA.[22]

Suppose that a same-sex couple domiciled in State Z goes to State Y to marry, where they are permitted to do so. Suppose further that such a marriage does not violate a strong public policy of State Z and that State Z has adopted the *Second Restatement of the Conflicts of Law*. According to State Z's choice-of-law rules, the law of the state of celebration governs the validity of the marriage. Even with DOMA as the law of the land, a court in State Z could not in good faith refuse to give credit to the marriage, given that State Z's law requires that the marriage be recognized.[23]

Section 2 of the act will allow State Z to refuse to recognize its domiciliaries' same-sex marriages which have been validly celebrated in another state if, for example, State Z has declared such marriages void. However, that is a power which State Z has even without DOMA.[24] Section 2 of DOMA will *not* allow a state, N, to refuse to recognize, two years later, a marriage that was legally valid at the time of celebration according to the laws of the states of celebration and domicile. State N's *own* choice-of-law rule would require that it look to the other states' substantive domestic relations law to determine the validity of the marriage. Thus, if the same-sex couple in State Z marries in State Y and then two years later moves to State N because of some unforeseen event, DOMA as written would not allow State N to refuse to recognize that marital union.

CHOICE OF LAW

States have two kinds of law which must be distinguished: their substantive domestic relations law and their choice-of-law rules. The domestic relations law will include, among other things, language specifying who may marry whom. Their choice-of-law rules will specify, among other things, which state's substantive domestic relations law should be used to determine whether a particular marriage validly celebrated in one state must be recognized by another.

State choice-of-law rules are double-edged, since they specify both when the domicile's domestic relations law will apply and when the law of the place of celebration will apply. Assuming that the act's co-sponsors are correct that DOMA does not change state law,[25] same-sex marriages validly celebrated in one state will have to be recognized by all states unless the domiciliary state (1) has declared such marriages void, thereby indicating that the marriage violates an important public policy of the state, or (2) has passed some sort of Evasion Statute. A domiciliary state that merely prohibits such marriages without in addition passing an evasion statute will have made such marriages valid in every state.

The point here should not be misunderstood. Bracketing constitutional constraints, every state has the option to declare same-sex marriages void and to no legal effect, thereby assuring that domiciliaries' same-sex marriages validly celebrated in another state will not have to recognized. This was true before DOMA and is true after DOMA. The point here is simply that the domiciliary state must express its desire not to recognize those marriages in certain ways, either by declaring them void or by making them subject to an evasion statute.

A different point was not even addressed at the DOMA hearings. Currently, *according to each state's law*, the only state laws potentially applicable to determine the validity of a marriage are the laws of the states of celebration and domicile. A state which is not the domicile at the time of the marriage will be forced by its own law to recognize a marriage validly celebrated in another state as long as the domicile at the time of marriage would recognize it. Thus, because DOMA does not affect state law, the act has *no* effect on which marriages are recognized by the various states, although the same cannot be said of divorce.

INTERSTATE RECOGNITION OF DIVORCE

Currently, the general rule is that if a court of general jurisdiction in one state issues a divorce decree, that decree will be unassailable in other states' courts except for fraud or lack of jurisdiction.[26] However, because DOMA states that no state shall be required to give effect to any judicial proceeding respecting a same-sex marriage under the laws of another state, the act entitles a state to refuse to recognize a divorce decree of another state, even without a claim of fraud or lack of jurisdiction.

The reason that DOMA does not affect which *marriages* must be recognized is that each state has its own choice-of-law rules which specify whose substantive law is to determine the validity of the marriage. In cases involving *divorce* decrees, however, no choice-of-law issue is implicated. Rather, states must decide whether to give effect to a judgment under *another* state's law. DOMA, then, has some surprising implications. A state whose choice-of-law rules require that the state recognize all nonincestuous, nonbigamous marriages which do not violate the important public policy of the domiciliary state at the time of the marriage *may have to recognize a same-sex marriage but will not have to recognize a same-sex divorce.*

A separate question involves the constitutionality of DOMA's permitting states to refuse to recognize nonfraudulent divorces where the decree-granting court had jurisdiction. It is not clear that Congress even has the power to create an exception with respect to which divorces shall be given full faith and credit. In *Williams I*, the Court suggested that "the considerable interests involved and the substantial and far-reaching effects which the allowance of an exception [for divorce] would have on innocent persons indicate that the purpose of the full faith and credit clause and of the supporting legislation would [thereby] be thwarted to a substantial degree" were such an exception made.[27] Nonetheless, the *Williams I* Court refused to express its view concerning whether Congress has the power to create an exception for divorce, and that issue remains unresolved.[28]

CONGRESSIONAL POWER

The Full Faith and Credit Clause of the Constitution reads: "Full Faith and Credit shall be given in each State to the public Acts, Records, and Judicial Proceedings of every other state. And the Congress may by general laws prescribe the manner in which . . . [the] Acts, Records, and Proceedings [of other states] shall be proved and the Effect thereof."[29] In passing DOMA under the power granted by the clause, Congress passed the antithesis of a full faith and credit measure which lacks sufficient generality and invidiously discriminates against a disfavored group. Further, the act will have a chilling effect on interstate travel.

To see why the act lacks sufficient generality, one must examine the language of the Full Faith and Credit Clause. When the Constitution gives Congress the power to pass *general* laws by which to prescribe the manner and effect of the acts, records, and proceedings, it is unclear how general those laws must be. For example, one interpretation of the above is that the laws must be sufficiently general that they do not merely prescribe the effects of acts or of records but, instead, must prescribe the manner and effect of other states' acts *and* records *and* judicial proceedings. On this interpretation, Congress could not prescribe one rule for acts and a different rule for records, since the statute would then not be sufficiently general.

A less restrictive interpretation of the sentence is that Congress can prescribe one rule for acts and another for records but, for example, cannot distinguish between the effects of different kinds of acts for full faith and credit purposes. On this interpretation, Congress cannot make distinctions within a category, e.g., Congress could not mandate that certain judgments be treated in one way and other judgments in a different way.

It is clear that Congress does not believe that it must treat everything within the same category in the same way. For example, Congress passed the Parental Kidnapping Prevention Act (PKPA).[30] That act specifies the full faith and credit implications of a specific type of judgment, namely, one involving a child custody determination. Although the Supreme Court has not explicitly upheld the constitutionality of the PKPA, probably because that issue was not even raised,[31] there is reason to believe that the Court would uphold Congress's power to pass such an act.[32] Thus, it seems likely that the Court would uphold the constitutionality of Congress's differentiating among different types of judgments for full faith and credit purposes. Even so, however, it is not at all clear that Congress is therefore constitutionally empowered to pass DOMA. Arguably, DOMA is the antithesis of a full faith and credit measure which not only fails the generality test but attempts to invidiously discriminate against a disfavored group.

Regulating Subjudgments

For an analysis of whether Congress exceeds its constitutionally prescribed power by passing DOMA,[33] the issue is not whether Congress has the power to pass a general law regarding a particular type of judgment, e.g. which state has jurisdiction in cases involving child custody[34] or support[35] but, instead, whether Congress has the power to make a full faith and credit exception for a particular *subtype* of judgment. The PKPA is not analogous to DOMA because the PKPA involves a higher level of generality.[36] An analogue of DOMA within the context of determining which state has jurisdiction in custody determinations would involve Congress's adding another section to the Full Faith and Credit Clause, section 1738(D), which specified that states could ignore the PKPA jurisdictional rules when *certain* custody decisions were at issue, e.g., custody decisions of sister states where the child and the adoptive parent awarded custody were of different races.

Were Congress to pass section 1738(D), it would be objectionable on a number of grounds, not the least of which is that it would involve invidious racial discrimination. The point here, however, is merely that the permissibility of Congress's passing a law requiring that full faith and credit be afforded to a particular type of judgment does not entail that subtypes may also be subjected to differential treatment without offending the Constitution. The term "general" has no force if DOMA is sufficiently general to meet the relevant standard.

Prescribing versus Proscribing

The PKPA is not analogous to DOMA in another respect. The former *requires* states to afford full faith and credit to a particular type of judgment, whereas the latter involves a congressional authorization of the *refusal* to afford full faith and credit to a particular (subtype of) judgment. When passing DOMA, Congress is *proscribing* rather than *prescribing* full faith and credit, i.e., Congress is *undermining* the force and effect of the Full Faith and Credit Clause.

The DOMA sponsors suggest that DOMA will allow states to recognize out-of-state decrees should they so desire.[37] However, states could recognize out-of-state decrees out of comity *even were there no Full Faith and Credit Clause.* As the *Estin* Court made clear, "The Full Faith and Credit Clause . . . substituted a command for the earlier principles of comity and thus basically altered the status of the States as independent sovereigns."[38] DOMA does the exact opposite and substitutes the principles of comity for the earlier command to recognize sister state decrees.

Suppose that the difficulty posed by Congress's proscribing rather than prescribing full faith and credit is viewed as unproblematic. Presumably, Congress could pass more general laws with respect to the power of the states to refuse to recognize divorce decrees issued in other states.[39] Indeed, in *Haddock v. Haddock*,[40] the Court held that the Full Faith and Credit Clause did not require one state to recognize another state's divorce decree. When *Haddock* was overruled in *Williams v. North Carolina*, however, the Court pointed out that "the purpose of the full faith and credit clause . . . would be thwarted to a substantial degree if the rule of *Haddock v. Haddock* were perpetuated,"[41] at least suggesting that such an exception for divorce might be barred by the Constitution.

There is an additional theoretical difficulty posed here. If Congress has the power to pass a law excepting divorce from Full Faith and Credit requirements, it arguably has the power to pass an even more general exception to the Full Faith and Credit Clause, e.g., all judgments, or, perhaps, an even more general exception such as a law excepting all judgments, records, and judicial proceedings from full faith and credit requirements. Yet, to say that Article IV, Section 1 of the Constitution gives Congress the power to nullify the Full Faith and Credit Clause seems absurd.[42]

In *Hogan*, the Court analyzed whether Section 5 of the Fourteenth Amendment of the Constitution permitted Congress to exempt the Mississippi University for Women from Equal Protection requirements. Section 5 reads: "The Congress shall have power to enforce, by appropriate legislation, the provisions of this article."[43]

The Court recognized that "Section 5 of the Fourteenth Amendment gives Congress broad power indeed to enforce the command of the Amendment and 'to secure to all persons the enjoyment of perfect equality of civil rights and the equal protection of the laws against State denial or invasion.'"[44] Nonetheless, the Court suggested that "Congress' power under section 5 . . . 'is limited to adopting measures to enforce the guarantees of the Amendment; section 5 grants Congress no power to restrict, abrogate, or dilute these guarantees.'"[45] The Court held that "neither Congress nor a State can validate a law that denies the rights guaranteed by the Fourteenth Amendment."[46] Just as the explicit provision of power to Congress in the Fourteenth Amendment does not entitle Congress to "restrict, abrogate, or dilute" the protections of the amendment, the explicit provision of power to Congress in the Full Faith and Credit Clause does not entitle Congress to "restrict, abrogate, or dilute" the effects of the Full Faith and Credit Clause.

Invidious Distinctions

Perhaps it will be thought that Congress has the constitutional power to pass DOMA precisely because it is exempting only a subtype of judgments from full faith and credit. Yet, even if Congress as a general matter has the power to prescribe that a subtype of judgment would not be entitled to full faith and credit, a separate question is whether DOMA involves an attempt by Congress to invidiously discriminate against a disfavored group. Congress could not pass the hypothesized section 1738(D) allowing states to refuse to recognize other states' interracial custodial arrangements because such an act would involve an invidious racial distinction. As the Court made clear in *Palmore*, the "Constitution cannot control [such] prejudices but neither can it tolerate them."[47]

Suppose that Congress were to consider a different act amending the Full Faith and Credit Clause, namely, section 1738(E), which would allow any state to refuse to recognize an interracial marriage validly performed in another state. Just as *Palmore* would establish the impermissibility of Congress's passing section 1738(D), *Loving*[48] would establish the unconstitutionality of section 1738(E).

Loving is important to examine for a number of reasons when considering the constitutionality of DOMA. First, although *Loving* is an Equal Protection case,[49] it is also a Due Process case. The *Loving* Court held that antimiscegenation laws violate the Due Process Clause of the Fourteenth Amendment because the freedom to marry is "one of the vital personal rights essential to the orderly pursuit of happiness by free men."[50] Arguably, the denial by *any* state of the right of same-sex couples to marry involves a violation of the Due Process Clause of the Fourteenth Amendment.[51]

Suppose, however, that one brackets whether denying same-sex couples the right to marry abridges a vital personal right and instead concentrates on the Equal Protection issues suggested by DOMA. Although the Supreme Court has not addressed whether gays, lesbians, and bisexuals constitute a suspect or quasi-suspect class[52] and expressly avoided that issue in *Bowers*,[53] the Court has made clear that states have not been given *carte blanche* to discriminate on the basis of orientation. In *Romer*, the Court struck down Colorado's Amendment 2 as constitutionally offensive, at least in part, because it withdrew "from homosexuals but no others specific legal protection from the injuries caused by discrimination."[54] The Court suggested that Colorado's amendment raised "the inevitable inference that the disadvantage imposed is born of animosity toward the class of persons affected."[55] It is difficult to imagine what explanation could be offered for DOMA other than that of animus.[56]

A co-sponsor of DOMA states, "When we prefer traditional marriage and family in our laws it is not intolerance."[57] One could easily imagine a supporter of antimiscegenation statutes having made the same claim. Indeed, one could easily imagine a DOMA supporter claiming that the act is designed to "prevent breaches of the basic concepts of decency," which is exactly the argument offered by the State of Florida when trying to justify its punishing interracial fornication more severely than intraracial fornication.[58] The Court saw through Florida's argument and invalidated the statute.[59]

DOMA supporters suggest that this amendment is merely designed to "preserve the long-time tradition of marriage between one man and one woman,"[60] and to make clear that it is not a matter of indifference whether individuals establish families with opposite-sex rather than same-sex partners.[61] Yet, these are exactly the kinds of arguments that might have been offered to support a denial of recognition to interracial marriage; the goal would allegedly not have been to make an invidious distinction but, rather, to have preserved a longstanding tradition of reserving marriage for individuals of the same race and, perhaps, of having made clear that it was not a matter of indifference whether individuals established families with members of the same race rather than members of a different race.

CONGRESSIONAL INTENT

When considering DOMA's constitutionality, a court would have to decide whether Congress was thereby intending to invidiously discriminate against a disfavored class.[62] The court would also have to decide what Congress intended the act to include. For example, while it seems fairly clear how the act would apply to divorce, it is unclear whether the act would change anything with respect to the interstate recognition of marriage.

A court might be tempted to read into Section 2 a congressional imposition of a choice-of-law rule which would change the existing choice-of-law rules operative in the various states. However, such a temptation should be resisted. An examination of the language of DOMA reveals that no choice-of-law rules are suggested.[63] Further, the (alleged) problem that Congress seems to believe that it is rectifying is that posed by individuals marrying in Hawaii and then going back to their domiciles and demanding that their home states recognize the marriage.[64] Thus, were a court truly interested in interpreting DOMA, it would have to conclude that no choice-of-law rules are incorporated therein, either by basing that interpretation on a plain language reading[65] or by attempting to reflect the legislative understanding of what in fact was being passed. On its face, DOMA applies only to *other* states' laws.

DOMA is championed as an example of federalism at work.[66] However, if it were understood as the federal government's imposing choice-of-law rules on the states, it would not be considered a paradigmatic example of returning rights to the states. Although an argument can be made for mandating federal choice-of-law rules in certain kinds of cases,[67] the argument would *not* be that one thereby promotes federalism but rather, for example, that the diversity of state rules has unfortunate effects.[68]

It is not at all clear that Congress would have been so willing to pass DOMA if it had been made clear to the voters that Congress was thereby be changing each state's law. The voters might then have wondered about what the next federally imposed choice-of-law rule would be, for example, whether Congress would claim that states need not recognize the second marriages of individuals whose first marriages had ended in no-fault divorce.[69]

An additional difficulty is that it is simply unclear what this new choice-of-law rule would be were a court tempted to infer that one existed. One possibility would be that a same-sex marriage would not have to be recognized in any state which made such unions void. Another possibility would be that such marriages would not have to be recognized in any state prohibiting such unions. Yet another possibility would be that any state which became the domicile of a same-sex couple would have the option of refusing to recognize that union. A court would simply have to invent the choice-of-law rule allegedly intended by Congress.

Each of these possibilities would be constitutionally infirm. Bracketing their unconstitutionality, however, it is unclear how a court could even pretend to support its claim that congressional intent clearly mandated one rather than another. Further, precisely because there would be important differences depending upon which rule was chosen and because the choice of one over another would normally involve a careful balancing of different public goods,[70] the court would seem ill-suited to make the relevant choice.

INTERSTATE TRAVEL

DOMA has another serious difficulty, namely, its effect on interstate travel. The Supreme Court has made clear that the "constitutional right to travel from one state to another . . . occupies a position fundamental to the concept of our Federal Union."[71] The *Shapiro* Court explained that "the nature of our Federal Union and our constitutional concepts of personal liberty unite to require that all citizens be free to travel throughout the length and breadth of our land uninhibited by statutes, rules, or regulations which unreasonably burden or restrict this movement."[72] The Court has clearly indicated the great importance of the right to interstate travel, having suggested that the "constitutional right of interstate travel is virtually unqualified."[73] The right to pass freely from state to state is "among the rights and privileges of national citizenship,"[74] and is a "basic constitutional freedom."[75]

In *Crandall v. Nevada*, the Court addressed "the right of a State to levy a tax upon persons residing in the State who may wish to get out of it, and upon persons not residing in it who may have occasion to pass through it."[76] The Court considered the argument that "a tax of one dollar for passing through the State of Nevada . . . cannot sensibly . . . deprive a citizen of any valuable right."[77] Nonetheless, the Court struck the law as a violation of the right to interstate travel. It strains credibility to suggest that such a tax would implicate the right to interstate travel but that a threat to invalidate one's marriage would not.

In *Shapiro v. Thompson*,[78] the Court addressed the permissibility of a state's imposing a one-year waiting period for the receipt of government benefits. Although not doubting that "the one-year waiting period device is well suited to discourage the influx of poor families in need of assistance," the *Shapiro* Court struck down the law, because the "purpose of inhibiting migration by needy persons into the State is constitutionally impermissible."[79] So, too, the purpose of inhibiting same-sex, married couples from migrating to a state would be constitutionally impermissible.

The *Shapiro* Court reasoned that since the classification touched "on the fundamental right of interstate movement, its constitutionality must be judged by the stricter standard of whether it promotes a compelling state interest."[80] The Court did *not* impose strict scrutiny because poverty was a suspect classification; indeed, the *San Antonio* Court later refused to extend suspect status to indigents.[81]

Thus, even if in fact gays, lesbians, and bisexuals do not constitute a suspect or quasi-suspect class, DOMA would still be subject to strict scrutiny because of its effect on the fundamental right to interstate travel.

Perhaps it will be thought that DOMA will be treated differently because it is congressional legislation. However, the *Shapiro* Court made clear that "Congress may not authorize the States to violate the Equal Protection Clause."[82] Further, where Congress acts unconstitutionally, "the departure from the constitutional plan cannot be ratified by the 'consent' of state officials."[83]

The right to travel includes both the right to *travel through* a state and also the right to *migrate to* a state. DOMA would have a chilling effect on both.

DOMA entitles each state to refuse to give effect to any "right or claim arising from . . . [a same-sex] relationship."[84] Suppose that Sam Smith and John Jones, a same-sex married couple, were driving through State X to get to State Y. Unfortunately, a drunk driver ran into them. If John were severely hurt and had to spend time in the hospital, Sam might be denied rights normally afforded a spouse, for example, the right to have input concerning medical treatment decisions.[85] Further, the rights to sue for loss of consortium[86] or wrongful death might be lost,[87] even if spouses would normally have those rights in that state. The potential loss of these rights might induce same-sex couples not even to travel *though* the state. Such disparate treatment would clearly trigger right to interstate travel protections.

A seemingly more difficult question is whether the right to interstate travel is violated by the refusal to grant recognition to a marriage which had been recognized by both the states of celebration and domicile at the time of the marriage (assuming that the choice-of-law issue had somehow been resolved). If, indeed, there is no fundamental right to same-sex marriage,[88] then states have the right to refuse to recognize their domiciliaries' same-sex marriages, assuming that such a refusal promotes legitimate purposes and is not merely an attempt to invidiously discriminate against a disfavored minority.[89] If a state can prevent its domiciliaries from contracting same-sex marriages, then it might seem that a state could of course refuse to recognize nondomiciliaries' same-sex marriages without imposing an undue burden on interstate travel. The state would *appear* to be treating nondomiciliaries in the same way that it was treating its domiciliaries.

Yet, appearances notwithstanding, the state would not be treating domiciliaries and nondomiciliaries in the same way. When a state passes legislation declaring a particular marriage void, it prevents its domiciliaries from contracting a marriage of that type. A couple domiciled in a state where such marriages are void could not make plans and develop expectations based on the good faith belief that their marriage solemnized in another state would be treated as valid by the domicile. However, the situation is quite different where the domicile does recognize such a marriage, since couples living there would have a justified, good faith belief that they had a valid marriage. It would be both understandable and appropriate for them to make plans, develop expectations, and enter into binding legal agreements based on their being married.

Leaving aside choice-of-law difficulties, DOMA allows a state which was neither the place of celebration nor the place of domicile at the time of a same-sex marriage to refuse to recognize that marriage. Such a state would be in the position of invalidating a formerly valid marriage that neither member of the couple wanted dissolved.

Certainly, marriages are sometimes annulled or invalidated. However, that occurs when one of the parties asks for an annulment or, perhaps, when the marriage was never valid in the first place because the domicile considered such marriages void or, at least, voidable. Annulments do *not* occur in cases where the domicile at the time of the marriage considered the marriage valid (and not voidable) and neither of the married parties wishes the marriage to be dissolved.

Suppose that domiciliaries of State M marry, intending to spend their lives in State M. A few years after the marriage, however, the couple decides to move to State X, which treats such marriages as null and void. Notwithstanding State X's policy with respect to that marriage, the couple's marriage was valid in State X at the time of their union; according to current choice-of-law jurisprudence, a nonbigamous, nonincestuous marriage valid in the domicile is valid *everywhere.*

Current domestic relations law does not allow states to invalidate a previously valid marriage without the consent of at least one of the parties. Although a court can rule that a marriage was never valid, assuming that the relevant conditions have been met, a court cannot invalidate a marriage which *the state itself previously recognized as valid* if neither member of the couple wishes to have the marriage annulled. Thus, it is less surprising than might first appear that states are in a different position with respect to marriages validly celebrated in another state if the celebrants were domiciliaries rather than nondomiciliaries. The state can refuse to recognize the marriage of domiciliaries celebrated elsewhere if that union is treated as void in the domicile. In that case, the marriage was *never* valid. However, the state cannot refuse to recognize the marriage of current domiciliaries if their marriage was recognized by their domicile at the time of the marriage.

The analogue of a state's refusing to recognize a *valid* marriage of a couple domiciled in a different state at the time of their union would be the state's invalidating without the consent of either party a marriage of its domiciliaries *which the state had already recognized as valid.* Allowing states to invalidate previously valid marriages would be a public policy disaster: the justified and settled expectations of the parties would be disappointed,[90] the status of the children would be unclear, title to property would be clouded, and third party creditors would be in a tenuous position.[91]

The only exception to the rule above *might* be in the following case. Suppose that two individuals, living in State Z, marry in State M with the intention of moving to State X after the honeymoon. They *may* also be subject to State X's domestic relations law, since State X arguably would have the most significant contacts with the couple.[92] However, because a new domicile is not acquired until one actually moves there,[93] they would be nondomiciliaries until they had actually arrived in State X. Thus, State X, which was not the domicile at the time of the marriage, *might* nonetheless be viewed as the state with the most significant contacts at the time of marriage and thus might be constitutionally permitted to have its laws apply to determine the validity of the marriage.[94]

Even if the above is an exception, however, that would be because the couple would not have had a valid marriage according to the laws of State X, the state with the most significant contacts (the place where they planned to live).[95] If State Z were deemed the state with the most significant contacts (because that would have been their domicile until they had found a new home), then State X could not invalidate the marriage if the marriage were valid according to State Z's law.

Clearly, a state's implicitly threatening to invalidate a previously valid marriage as a cost of a couple's migrating to that state involves a strong disincentive to migrate there. Further, a state's refusing to recognize the rights or incidents of such a marriage would also be a strong disincentive to move there. However, the *Jones* Court recognized that "the right of a United State citizen to travel from one State to another and to take up residence in the State of his choice is protected by the Federal Constitution."[96] The *Dunn* Court recognized over twenty years ago that the "right to travel is an 'unconditional person right,' a right whose exercise may not be conditioned."[97] Indeed, as Justice Sandra Day O'Connor remarked in her *Zobel* concurrence, "It is hard to imagine a right more essential to the Nation as a whole than the right to establish residence in a new State."[98]

Marriage involves a very important interest. The Court has recognized that "even temporary deprivations of very important benefits and rights can operate to penalize migration."[99] State refusals to recognize valid same-sex marriages would implicate the fundamental right of interstate travel and would thus be unconstitutional.

Even if the burden on interstate travel were somehow viewed as unproblematic, a state could not refuse to recognize a marriage which its own choice-of-law rules determined to be valid. Realizing this, states might be tempted to change their own choice-of-law statutes to suggest that a same-sex marriage recognized as valid in the domicile would nonetheless not be recognized by that state. Such an approach would be ill-advised, however, both because the state would lack sufficient contact with the parties or the marriage to have a say in the matter anyway and because such a modification, if upheld, would invite other kinds of choice-of-law modifications by other states.[100] Permitting these kinds of modifications would do a great deal to undermine the purpose and force of the Full Faith and Credit Clause.

SECTION 3 OF THE DEFENSE OF MARRIAGE ACT

Section 2 of DOMA is a modification of the Full Faith and Credit Clause and thus is not envisioned as changing substantive domestic relations law. However, Section 3 of DOMA is envisioned as changing substantive domestic relations law, albeit for federal purposes. Because domestic relations law is usually left to the states, Congress must establish that it has a very important reason if it is justifiably to displace state law. Because Congress has not met its heavy burden of justification, Section 3 of DOMA involves an unconstitutional overreaching by Congress. Section 3 of DOMA reads:

> In determining the meaning of any Act of Congress, or of any ruling, regulation, or interpretation of the various administrative bureaus and agencies of the United States, the word 'marriage' means only a legal union between one man and one woman as husband and wife, and the word 'spouse' refers only to a person of the opposite sex who is a husband or a wife.[101]

Section 3 of DOMA is not plagued with some of the difficulties of Section 2, since its meaning is rather straightforward. The difficulty posed by Section 3 is that it involves Congress's overreaching without adequate justification. Indeed, it is difficult to believe that Congress's offering this amendment has any legitimate justification at all, since the goal of disadvantaging a disfavored minority is not viewed as a legitimate purpose. The Court has already made quite clear that "if the constitutional conception of 'equal protection of the laws' means anything, it must at the very least mean that a bare . . . desire to harm a politically unpopular group cannot constitute a *legitimate* governmental interest."[102] As the Supreme Court pointed out over one hundred years ago, if a statute purporting to protect the public morals "has no real or substantial relation to [that] object[. . .], or is a palpable invasion of the rights secured by the fundamental law, it is the duty of the courts to so adjudge, and thereby give effect to the constitution."[103] DOMA is a palpable invasion of rights.

Perhaps it will be argued that benefits acquired through marriage do not rise to the level of having constitutional significance. Yet, in *Turner v. Safley*, the Court recognized various aspects of marriage which make it a fundamental right.[104] Among those was that marriage is often a "precondition to the receipt of government benefits."[105] Indeed, it seems underappreciated that *all* of the aspects of marriage recognized by the *Turner* Court as significant apply to same-sex as well as opposite-sex couples.[106]

FEDERAL DOMESTIC RELATIONS LAW

The *Yazell* Court described family law as a "peculiarly state province."[107] Over one hundred years ago, the *Burrus* Court recognized that the "whole subject of domestic relations of husband and wife, parent and child, belongs to the laws of the states, and not to the law of the United States."[108] In his *McCarty* dissent, Justice William Rehnquist suggested that "[b]oth family law and property law have been recognized as a matter of peculiarly local concern and therefore governed by state and not federal law."[109]

There are at least two implications of family law being a matter of peculiarly local concern. One involves a presumption employed by the Court that Congress will not be trying to displace state law with respect to such matters and the other involves the heightened burden imposed on Congress if it is to justify its displacing state law.

PRESUMPTION OF NONDISPLACEMENT

The Court assumes that when Congress passes legislation, it is not trying to displace state law. As the *Mansell* Court explained, "Because domestic relations are preeminently matters of state law, we have consistently recognized that Congress, when it passes general legislation, rarely intends to displace state authority in this area."[110] However, the Court realizes that sometimes "Congress has directly and specifically legislated in the area of domestic relations."[111]

Compare Sections 2 and 3 of DOMA. On its face, Section 2 states that one state will not be required by the Full Faith and Credit Clause to recognize a marriage merely because it was valid under another state's law. Current choice-of-law jurisprudence dictates the same result. It is because of the state's *own* law that the state must recognize a marriage validly celebrated in another state which was not obnoxious to the public policy of the domicile at the time of the marriage.[112] Thus, Section 2 of DOMA does not change current law and does not involve Congress's displacing state authority.[113] The question at hand is whether Section 3 displaces state authority, since it defines who is married to whom, albeit for federal purposes only.

Section 3 of DOMA defines marriage for purposes of "determining the meaning of any Act of Congress, or of any ruling, regulation, or interpretation of the various administrative bureaus and agencies of the United States."[114] On its face, the act is regulating the definition of marriage for federal purposes only and thus might not seem to be displacing state law. However, such an interpretation would not account for the Court's jurisprudence in this area.

FEDERAL BENEFITS

The *De Sylva* Court suggested that the "scope of a federal right is, of course, a federal question, but that does not mean that its content is not to be determined by state, rather than federal law."[115] Indeed, the Court pointed out that state law should be applied especially "where a statute deals with a familial relationship; there is no federal law of domestic relations, which is primarily a matter of state concern."[116] Thus, merely because a statute concerns federal benefits does not entail that state law is inappropriate to consider. Especially because there is no federal domestic relations law, state laws regulating domestic relations will be used unless Congress clearly mandates otherwise.

There is no question but that Congress is clearly mandating otherwise in DOMA. The issue is not whether Congress intends to prevent same-sex couples from receiving federal benefits, since that is clearly the intention, but whether Congress can meet the requisite test to justify its displacing state law.

MAJOR DAMAGE TO FEDERAL INTERESTS

In *Rose v. Rose*, the Court made clear, "Before a state law governing domestic relations will be overridden, it 'must do "major damage" to "clear and substantial" federal interests'."[117] Thus, where there is a clear conflict between state and federal law, Congress has a heavy burden to bear to justify its displacing state law.

First, it should be clear that Congress is displacing state law. For example, suppose that according to state law retirement pay earned during marriage is to be treated as community property.[118] Suppose further that a same-sex couple is divorcing and that one of the members of the couple works for the federal government. Had the couple been composed of two members of opposite sexes, there would have been no question but that the retirement pay would be community property.[119] However, because the couple is composed of two members of the same sex, DOMA dictates that the retirement pay should not be so treated. Congress has clearly displaced state law.

The point here is not that Congress can never bear the relevant burden. Rather, the point, as the *Hisquierdo* Court explained, is that even in those cases in which the Court has upheld the congressional power to displace state domestic relations law, the Court has recognized that state family law "must do 'major damage' to 'clear and substantial' federal interests before the Supremacy Clause will demand that the state law be overridden."[120] For example, Congress may be able to displace state family law when national defense is at issue,[121] although even national defense should not be thought to give Congress *carte blanche* to act in any way that it chooses.[122] The Court has also upheld Congress's right to set up a scheme for allocating Railroad Retirement Act benefits.[123]

The important issue to be resolved is what qualifes as a sufficiently important interest for federal law to displace state law. The Court has made clear that it will not suffice to say that money will thereby be saved.[124] Otherwise, Congress could always justify its withdrawing benefits to particular types of families on the theory that doing so would save money.

When members of Congress discussed why Section 3 of DOMA is necessary, they made clear their fear that, otherwise, same-sex couples would be entitled to the relevant benefits.[125] However, that is simply to say that they did not want the couples to receive such benefits. The question is still why.

DOMA supporters claimed that DOMA helps confirm the tradition of marriage as a union between one man and one woman.[126] Indeed, one senator has suggested that "[t]he definition of marriage is not created by politicians and judges, and it cannot be changed by them. It is rooted in our history, our laws, our deepest moral and religious convictions, and our nature as human beings. It is the union of one man and one woman. This fact can be respected or it can be resented, but it cannot be altered."[127]

Yet, DOMA does not prevent states from recognizing same-sex marriages; it merely denies federal benefits to same-sex couples. If the purpose of DOMA is to protect the institution of marriage and if including same-sex couples really changes the institution, then DOMA is not rationally designed to meet its goal. DOMA does not prevent the definition and the institution from being changed; it merely allows Congress not to accord the federal benefits that go along with marriage.

Certainly, the act made clear that Congress did not believe that same-sex and opposite-sex unions are equally valuable. Yet, it is not at all clear that this suffices as a reason. Suppose, for example, that Congress had decided that it did not believe that interracial and intraracial marriages were equally valuable. Presumably, no one would claim that Congress could withdraw federal benefits from interracial or interreligious marriages because intraracial and intrareligious marriages were "preferred."[128]

Some members of Congress seem to have feared that their children would have received the wrong message if DOMA had not been passed.[129] Apparently, they believed it better for children to learn that bigotry is acceptable than that persons of the same sex can have loving, committed relationships.[130]

Congress is attempting to impose a stigma upon a class of individuals, a paradigmatic example of invidious discrimination. In his *Adarand* dissent, Justice John Paul Stevens described invidious discrimination as "an engine of oppression."[131] It is difficult to imagine how the Court that decided *Romer* could fail to make "the inevitable inference that the disadvantage imposed is born of animosity toward the class of persons affected."[132] On its face, DOMA is designed to burden a disfavored group. The legislative intent as manifested by the DOMA supporters only serves to bolster the inference of invidious intent.

A state's recognizing same-sex marriages would not only *not* do major damage to clear and substantial federal interests, it would not damage *legitimate* federal interests at all. For a court to hold otherwise would be an invitation for a whole host of federal enactments displacing state domestic relations law.

IMPLICATIONS OF DOMA

Suppose that DOMA is challenged in the courts and is upheld. A variety of effects are foreseeable, many of which even the supporters of DOMA presumably could not support. Consider Section 2, which allows states not to give effect to any right or claim arising from a same-sex marriage. It is important to consider which rights might be included.

In *Baehr v. Lewin*, the Hawaii Supreme Court listed some of the rights arising from marriage, including spousal support,[133] and child custody and support.[134] It is thus quite foreseeable that an individual wishing to avoid his or her marital responsibilities would move to a state which would refuse to give effect to such judgments.

It is unclear whether DOMA would be interpreted to allow a state to refuse to credit a judgment for child custody or support. Congress has passed other legislation related to these matters, such as the PKPA and the Full Faith and Credit for Child Support Orders Act. However, because they predate DOMA, it is unclear whether DOMA will be viewed as superseding or modifying those previous enactments. Insofar as the last-in-time rule governs,[135] the previous congressional enactments might be viewed as modified by DOMA.

Arguably, Congress did not intend DOMA to carve out an exception to the PKPA or the Child Support Act.[136] The *Wetmore* Court suggested, "Unless positively required by direct enactment the courts should not presume a design upon the part of Congress . . . to make the law a means of avoiding enforcement of the obligation, moral and legal, devolved upon the husband to support his wife and to maintain and educate his children."[137] Thus, it might be inferred that Congress did not intend to undermine these custody or support obligations, although the opposite inference might also be drawn.[138]

Ironically, those states taking advantage of DOMA to refuse to recognize the rights associated with marriage would induce same-sex couples to stay away but would also induce those wishing to avoid their marital responsibilities to come to the state. Even if DOMA were interpreted in such a way that it was held not to modify the PKPA or the Child Support Act, an individual still *might* avoid having to pay spousal support or having to honor a property settlement by going to a state which would not recognize the marriage. As a matter of public policy, it is at the very least surprising that states would want to encourage these types of behavior.

EFFECTS OF DOMA

If Congress has not exceeded its power by passing DOMA, then Congress presumably can pass other acts related to the recognition of marriage and divorce. Indeed, it would be surprising if states did not pressure Congress to create additional exceptions with respect to which divorces or marriages must be recognized. For example, were states to change their laws regarding no-fault divorce, it would not be surprising for them to demand that they not be forced to recognize no-fault divorces granted in other states and, perhaps, that federal benefits not be accorded to individuals who remarry after securing a no-fault divorce. The same arguments used to establish why DOMA must be passed, (e.g., federalism or a desire to teach that certain behaviors or people are not viewed as acceptable) might also be used to establish why a variety of other acts should be passed.

The decision in *Baehr v. Lewin* should lay to rest the argument that same-sex marriages are precluded by definition. Not only do some religions sanctify same-sex unions but Hawaii may actually come to recognize them. Courts must stop pretending that such unions are definitionally precluded and that legislative bodies are not responsible for their refusals to recognize such unions.

Same-sex marriage bans implicate a number of Equal Protection and Substantive Due Process issues which require careful analysis. Regrettably, courts have offered perfunctory treatments of the relevant issues, sometimes thereby changing the law in important ways. These changes put the privacy rights of all people at risk and undermine the consistency of and respect for the rule of law.

At first blush, the Equal Protection issues involving suspect and quasi-suspect classes might seem confined to a small group. Perhaps that would be so were the relevant criteria applied in a consistent and disinterested fashion. However, when the established criteria are misapplied, this creates a precedent which may have implications for a variety of groups. For example, it would not be surprising to see a court's pointing out that if the relatively powerless class of lesbians, bisexuals, and gays is nonetheless too powerful to merit special solicitude by the courts, then other groups either are too powerful to merit increased protection or are too powerful to merit *continued* increased protection.[139]

Even in cases involving no suspect or quasi-suspect classes, a statute will not pass constitutional muster unless it employs a rational means to promote a legitimate end. Statutes banning same-sex marriage because marriage is supposed to provide a setting for the production and raising of children are not using a rational means to promote that end, because gays, lesbians, and bisexuals also have children to raise. Statutes banning same-sex marriage to punish or penalize gays, lesbians, or bisexuals or even to express disapproval of that "lifestyle" are using a rational means to promote an illegitimate end, namely, disadvantaging a disfavored minority. Whether statutes employ irrational means to promote legitimate ends or rational means to promote illegitimate ends, they violate the guarantees of the Equal Protection Clause.

The fundamental rights jurisprudence which has been offered by the courts is disappointing both in the disingenuousness of the criteria chosen and in the disingenuousness of their application. Courts offer criteria for fundamental rights that do not even account for those rights already established. Indeed, there has been an attempt to reclassify rights already recognized as fundamental as (at most) mere liberty interests, in part by relying on badly reasoned decisions adversely affecting lesbians, gays, and bisexuals.[140]

Not only have courts used the wrong criteria to determine whether the right to marry a same-sex partner is fundamental, but they have failed to apply the purported criteria in a fair and disinterested way. Even if one ignores that the Supreme Court has articulated numerous interests served by the institution of marriage, all of which apply to same-sex as well as opposite-sex couples,[141] and even if one focuses on the claim that the purpose of marriage is to provide a setting for the production and raising of children, one sees that courts are misapplying the allegedly relevant criterion. Were that the correct criterion, lesbians, bisexuals, and gays would still have the right to marry. Indeed, those courts citing *Zablocki* to establish that same-sex marriage is not a fundamental right should reexamine the opinion and their analyses.

The *Zablocki* Court recognized that it "would make little sense to recognize a right of privacy with respect to other matters of family life and not with respect to the decision to enter the relationship that is the foundation of the family in our society."[142] This *does not* suggest that having a right to privacy with respect to other matters of family life is a *necessary* condition of having a right to marry, since as the *Turner* Court suggested there may be other implicated interests which justify finding the right to marry fundamental. However, this does suggest that having a right to privacy with respect to other matters of family life is a *sufficient* condition for one's having a fundamental right to marry. Gays, lesbians, and bisexuals do have rights of privacy with respect to other matters of family life, e.g., matters related to the production and raising of children, and thus *Zablocki* seems to *require* that such unions be recognized.

States will not be required to recognize same-sex marriages validly celebrated in other states as long as the state legislatures make clear that such unions will not be recognized. Thus, DOMA is unnecessary insofar as its purpose is to allow domiciliary states to refuse to recognize same-sex marriages validly celebrated in other states. Although the act does allow states to refuse to recognize same-sex divorces, it is not clear that Congress has the power to make this exception and, in any event, states not wanting to recognize same-sex marriages for public policy reasons would hardly relish the option of refusing to recognize a same-sex divorce, since they would thereby be implicitly if not explicitly recognizing the (continuation of the) same-sex marriage.

DOMA is the antithesis of a full faith and credit measure which will succeed only in causing further disunity among the states. It is not sufficiently general to meet the constitutional standard and, further, is clearly an attempt to invidiously discriminate against a disfavored group. Indeed, Congress does little to hide the animus that motivates the bill.

Neither Congress nor the states can impose undue burdens on the right to interstate travel. Even were there no other difficulties with the act, DOMA could not pass constitutional muster on this basis alone.

As a matter of public policy, DOMA is a disaster. It promotes bigotry, undermines the stability and certainty of marriage, hurts innocent individuals, and provides a relatively easy way for individuals to avoid their marital responsibilities.

All the difficulties posed by DOMA should not be allowed to obscure an important point. *Both* the Equal Protection and the Due Process Clauses are violated by state bans of same-sex marriages. As soon as the Supreme Court invalidates same-sex marriage bans because either or both of those clauses are violated, states will be forced not only to recognize those marriages validly celebrated in other states but also to allow domiciliaries to enter into such marriages at home.

It is clear that the real reason that same-sex marriages are not permitted is that some portion of the population does not approve of them. Yet, if that rationale suffices, a variety of marriages would seem to be at risk. The right to marry is simply too important to be determined by a popular vote. Indeed, if something as fundamental as who has the right to marry whom can be determined by popular vote, any allegedly fundamental right might also be so determined. Such a radical change in domestic relations jurisprudence poses risks for everyone.

The rights to marry and to have a family are fundamental. The state must have a compelling interest to justify the abridgment of fundamental rights, and there are no compelling interests that justify the prohibition of same-sex marriages. Indeed, since the compelling interests promoted by heterosexual marriages are also promoted by same-sex marriages and since the prohibition of same-sex marriages involves the abridgment of a fundamental right, same-sex marriage *must* rather than *should not* be recognized by the state.

Most of the arguments currently offered to justify the state refusal to recognize same-sex marriages were offered in the past to justify the state refusal to recognize interracial marriages. The Court rightly recognized that the arguments against allowing such marriages were specious and that the real reason that such marriages were not recognized involved irrational hatred and bigotry. The Court should recognize that the arguments supporting state refusals to recognize same-sex marriages are also specious and that hatred and bigotry really underlie that refusal.

As the Supreme Court has made clear, the right to marry is fundamental because marriages are expressions of emotional support and public commitment and, further, may involve strongly held religious beliefs. Marriage safeguards the ability to define oneself independently and serves as a buffer between the individual and the state. These interests are important for all people.

The children of gay and lesbian parents, like other children, have numerous financial and emotional needs, which include the needs for stability and for the assurance of continued contact between themelves and those that have raised them. All these needs would be served by allowing same-sex partners to marry.

Society is benefited by stable families providing healthy settings for children to be raised. The empirical data suggest that children do as well in gay and lesbian households as in heterosexual ones, and society is benefited when children are allowed to thrive. Further, society is benefited when the Supreme Court takes a stand against all forms of bigotry, Justice Scalia's view notwithstanding.[143] The failure to do so undermines tolerance and civility generally and thus undermines the very foundations of our society.

The Supreme Court must recognize that the right of same-sex partners to marry is fundamental, for the sake of those individuals whose rights are being abridged, for the sake of those individuals' children, and for the sake of society as a whole. That the courts seem willing to invoke allegedly compelling interests to penalize one group but to ignore those interests when other, relevantly similar groups are involved is itself cause for concern. The ideal of the rule of law, which is supposed to embody fairness and justice, becomes tainted when it is ignored or used in bad faith to promote prejudice and discrimination. If courts continue to uphold intrasexual marriage bans and continue to offer the kinds of analyses thus far offered to justify such policies, the implications for domestic relations jurisprudence specifically, and our legal system generally, are frightening to contemplate.

NOTES

I MARRIAGE BARRED BY DEFINITION

1 See *Loving v. Virginia,* 388 U.S. 1, 12 (1967).

2 See Gerald Gunther, *Constitutional Law,* 446 (12th ed., 1991).

3 478 U.S. 186, 199 (1986) (Blackmun, J., dissenting, quoting O. W. Holmes, "The Path of the Law," 10 *Harv. L. Rev.* 457, 469 [1897]).

4 See *Baker v. Nelson,* 191 N.W.2d 185, 185–86 n.1 (Minn. 1971) (citing dictionary to establish that marriage can only be between individuals of different sexes), appeal dismissed, 409 U.S. 810 (1972).

5 980 (2d ed., 1987).

6 Id. See also *Black's Law Dictionary,* 779 (6th ed., 1990) ("Information: An accusation exhibited against a person for some criminal offense, without an indictment. An accusation in the nature of an indictment, from which it differs only in being presented by a competent public officer on his oath of office, instead of a grand jury on their oath.").

7 See *Dean v. District of Columbia,* 653 A.2d 307, 315 (D.C. App. 1995) (Ferren, J., concurring in part and dissenting in part; "[T]he terms 'marriage' and 'gay marriage' are used colloquially today to refer to long-term same-sex relationships between gays and between lesbians.").

8 See, for example, William Safire, "Same-Sex Marriage Nears," *New York Times,* April 29, 1996, at A11.

9 972 (6th ed., 1990).

10 See id. at 972 (citing *Singer,* 522 P.2d 1187, 1193 (Wash. App. 1974)).

11 See *Singer,* 522 P.2d at 1192 n.6.

12 Id. at 1192 n.6.

13 See Mark Strasser, "Family, Definitions, and the Constitution: On the Antimiscegenation Analogy," 25 *Suffolk U. L. Rev.* 981, 986 (1991) (discussing use of dictionaries to establish legislative intent).

14 See Haw. Rev. Stat. Sec. 572–1 (Supp. 1995) ("[T]he marriage contract . . . shall be only between a man and a woman."); Ind. Code Sec. 31-7-1-2 (West 1996) ("Only a female may marry a male. Only a male may marry a

female."); Md. Code Ann., Fam. Law Sec. 2–201 (1991) ("Only a marriage between a man and a woman is valid in this State."); Minn. Stat. Ann. Sec. 517.01 (West 1990) ("Marriage, so far as its validity in law is concerned, is a civil contract between a man and a woman.").

15 Compare Ohio Rev. Code Sec. 3101.01 (Banks-Baldwin 1995) ("Male persons of the age of eighteen years, and female persons of the age of sixteen years, not nearer of kin than *second cousins*, and not having a husband or wife living, may be joined in marriage.") (italics added) with N.M. Stat. Ann. Sec. 40–1-7 (Michie 1994) ("All marriages between relations and children, including grandfathers and grandchildren of all degrees, between half brothers and sisters, as also of full blood; between uncles and nieces, aunts and nephews, are hereby declared incestuous and absolutely void. This section shall extend to illegitimate as well as to legitimate children.") The Compiler's notes to the New Mexico Statute read: "Prior to Comp. Laws 1884, this section contained the words 'and first cousins' following the word 'nephews'. Those words were deleted to accord with Laws 1880, Ch. 37, sec. 1, which repealed 'such parts of all laws as prohibit the marriage of cousins of any degree'."

16 See *Israel v. Allen*, 577 P.2d 762 (Colo. 1978) (en banc) (allowing brother to marry sister by adoption).

17 See Conn. Gen. Stat. Ann. Sec. 46b-21 (West 1995) ("No man may marry his . . . stepmother or stepdaughter, and no woman may marry her . . . stepfather or stepson. Any marriage within these degrees is void.").

18 *Stones v. Keeling*, 9 Va. (5 Call) 143, 148 (1804).

19 See *Loving v. Virginia*, 388 U.S. 1 (1967) (striking Virginia's antimiscegenation statute as unconstitutional).

20 Compare Va. Code Ann. Sec. 20–45.2 (Michie 1995) ("A marriage between persons of the same sex is prohibited") with Minn. Stat. Ann. Sec. 517.01 (West 1990) ("Marriage, so far as its validity in law is concerned, is a civil contract between a man and a woman.").

21 Cf. William N. Eskridge, Jr., *The Case for Same-Sex Marriage*, 76–77 (1996) ("After World War II, . . most Americans believed that a marriage between a black and a white person was literally not a marriage.").

22 *Foman v. Davis*, 371 U.S. 178, 181 (1962).

23 See Minn. Stat. Ann. Sec. 517.01 (West 1990) ("Marriage, so far as its validity in law is concerned, is a civil contract *between a man and a woman*, to which the consent of the parties, capable in law of contracting, is essential.") (italics added). The Minnesota legislature added the italicized words in 1977. In 1971, Richard Baker argued that the statute allowed two men to marry because of a lack of a specification to the contrary. See *Baker v. Nelson*, 191 N.W.2d 185, 185 (Minn. 1971), appeal dismissed, 409 U.S. 810 (1972).

24 See, for example, 142 *Cong. Rec.* S4947 (May 9, 1996) (Sen. Coats) ("The

definition of marriage is not created by politicians and judges, and it cannot be changed by them. It is rooted in our history, our laws, our deepest moral and religious convictions, and our nature as human beings. It is the union of one man and one woman. This fact can be respected or it can be resented, but it cannot be altered.").

25 501 S.W.2d 588, 589 (Ky. 1973).

26 See Andrew Sullivan, *Virtually Normal*, 99 (1995) (characterizing John Finnis's argument as involving the claim that "because homosexual sex cannot partake of the uniquely heterosexual union of procreation and emotional commitment that loving straight marital sex can partake in . . . [homosexual sex] *in itself is an assault on heterosexual union.*").

27 See id. at 23 ("There is no argument against . . . [a bigot], because an argument is not an appropriate response. And a liberal society can prevent that person from injuring another; but it cannot rationally engage him.").

28 John Stuart Mill, *On Liberty*, in *Collected Works of John Stuart Mill*, vol. 18, ed. John Robson (1977), Chap. 4, par. 12, at 283.

29 Id.

30 See, for example, *Shahar v. Bowers*, 70 F.3d 1218, 1223 (11th Cir. 1995) ("same-sex marriage is accepted within the Reconstructionist Movement of Judaism") vacated, reh'g granted en banc, 78 F.3d 499 (11th Cir. 1996) reh'g 114 F.3d 1097 (11th Cir. 1997) (en banc), aff'g 836 F. Supp. 859 (N.D. Ga. 1993); "Religion Briefs," *Arizona Republic/Phoenix Gazette*, July 22, 1995, at B4 ("Soka Gakkai International-USA, the largest Buddhist organization in America, has decided to permit wedding-like ceremonies for gay and lesbian couples, saying that nothing in Buddhist doctrine disallows the practice."); "Quakers Lead Way in Same-sex Marriage," *New York Times*, November 19, 1989, Sec. 4 at 22, col. 4 (Quakers have long recognized such unions); "Unitarians Endorse Homosexual Marriages," *New York Times*, June 29, 1984, Sec. A26, col. 4 (Unitarians countenance same-sex marriages).

31 See Haw. Rev. Stat. sec. 572–1.6 (Supp. 1995) ("Nothing in this chapter shall be construed to render unlawful, or otherwise affirmatively punishable at law, the solemnization of same-sex relationships by religious organizations.").

32 *Loving*, 388 U.S. at 3.

33 But see *Reynolds v. United States*, 98 U.S. 145 (1878) (polygamous unions may be outlawed).

34 852 P.2d 44 (Haw.) (plurality opinion), reconsideration granted in part, 875 P.2d 225 (Haw. 1993).

35 See *Adams v. Howerton*, 486 F. Supp. 1119, 1124 (C.D. Cal. 1980) (suggesting that the conceptual definition of marriage is logically prior to equal protection and due process analyses), aff'd, 673 F.2d 1036 (9th Cir.), cert. denied, 458 U.S. 1111 (1982).

36 653 A.2d 307, 361 (D.C. App. 1995) (Terry, J., concurring).

37 Id. at 362 (Terry, J., concurring).
38 See id. at 316 n.13 (Ferren, J., concurring in part and dissenting in part).
39 See Tex. Family Code Ann. sec. 1.01 (West 1993).
40 See Utah Code Ann. Sec. 30–1-2 (1995).
41 See id.
42 See Utah Code Ann. Sec. 30–1-9 (1995) (specifying the need for the consent of the parent or guardian and, possibly, the consent of a judge or court commissioner).
43 See Ga. Code Ann. 19–3-2(2) (1991).
44 See Md. Code Ann., Fam. Law Sec. 2–201 (1991).
45 Cf. Mark Strasser, "Family, Definitions, and the Constitution: On the Antimiscegenation Analogy," 25 *Suffolk U. L. Rev.* 981, 1020 (1991) (discussing how statutes barring interracial marriages could be used parasitically to justify statutes barring interracial coupling, and vice versa).
46 See *Moore v. City of East Cleveland*, 431 U.S. 494 (1977) (striking down zoning ordinance which limited occupancy to nuclear family).
47 See *Braschi v. Stahl Associates Co.*, 543 N.E.2d 49, 54 (N.Y. 1989).
48 *Borough of Glassboro v. Vallorosi*, 568 A.2d 888 (N.J. 1990).
49 *Robertson v. Western Baptist Hospital*, 267 S.W.2d 395 (Ky. 1954).
50 *Missionaries of Our Lady of La Salette v. Village of Whitefish Bay*, 66 N.W.2d 627 (Wis. 1954).
51 *Carroll v. City of Miami Beach*, 198 So.2d 643 (Fla. Dist. Ct. App. 1967).
52 543 N.E.2d 49 (N.Y. 1989).
53 Id. at 54.
54 See *Rovira v. AT&T*, 817 F. Supp. 1062 (S.D.N.Y. 1993).
55 *Braschi*, 543 N.E.2d at 54.
56 *Rovira*, 817 F. Supp. at 1064.
57 Id.
58 Id. at 1062.
59 *Hinman v. Dept. of Personnel Admin.*, 213 Cal.Rptr 410 (Ct. App. 1985).
60 *Phillips v. Wisconsin Personnel Comm'n*, 482 N.W.2d 121 (Wis. App. 1992).
61 *Ross v. Denver Dept. of Health and Hosps.*, 883 P.2d 516 (Colo. App. 1994).
62 *In re Estate of Cooper*, 564 N.Y.S.2d 684 (Sur. Ct. 1990).
63 See *In re Adoption of Adult Anonymous*, 435 N.Y.S.2d 527, 528 (Fam. Ct. 1981) ("[T]he adoptee testified that his family did not approve of the relationship, and he apparently feared that attempts might be made to set aside property arrangements between the parties if they were not legally adoptive father and adoptive son.").
64 See *In re Adult Anonymous II*, 452 N.Y.S.2d 198, 200 (App. Div. 1982) (suggesting that it may at first seem "a perversion of the adoption process for lovers to adopt one another").
65 See Ohio Rev. Code Ann. Sec. 3107.02 (Banks Baldwin 1995) (adult may be adopted only if totally and permanently disabled, mentally handicapped, or had child-parent relationship as minor).

66 *Anonymous II*, 452 N.Y.S.2d at 200.
67 Id. at 199.
68 435 N.Y.S.2d 527, 527 (Fam. Ct. 1981).
69 Id. at 528.
70 Id.
71 452 N.Y.S.2d at 201
72 Id.
73 Id.
74 471 N.E.2d 424, 425 (N.Y. 1984).
75 Id. at 427 (italics added).
76 Id. at 429 (Meyer, J., dissenting).
77 See *In re Adult Anonymous II*, 452 N.Y.S.2d 198 (App. Div. 1982); *In re Adoption of Adult Anonymous*, 435 N.Y.S.2d 527 (Fam. Ct. 1981).
78 *Robert Paul P.*, 471 N.E.2d at 426.
79 Id.
80 Id. at 427.
81 See Ohio Rev. Code Ann. Sec. 3107.02 (Banks Baldwin 1995).
82 *Robert Paul P.*, 471 N.E.2d at 428 (Meyer, J., dissenting).
83 503 N.Y.S.2d 752 (App. Div. 1986).
84 Id. at 754.
85 Id.
86 Id. at 755 (Kupferman, J.P., dissenting)
87 Id. at 755.
88 *Braschi*, 543 N.E.2d at 54.
89 See *Robert Paul P.*, 471 N.E.2d at 427 (Meyer, J., dissenting, suggesting that the court was being inconsistent, given *People v. Onofre*, 434 N.Y.S.2d 947 [N.Y. 1980] in which the state's sodomy law was struck down as unconstitutional), cert. denied, 451 U.S. 987 (1981).

II EQUAL PROTECTION

1 See Mark Strasser, "Suspect Classes and Suspect Classifications: On Discriminating, Unwittingly or Otherwise," 64 *Temple L. Rev.* 937, 941 (1991).
2 See Gerald Gunther, "The Supreme Court, 1971 Term—Forward: In Search of Evolving Doctrine on a Changing Court: A Model for a Newer Equal Protection," 86 *Harv. L. Rev.* 1, 8 (1972) (this level of scrutiny is "strict in theory and fatal in fact").
3 See *Michael M. v. Sonoma County Superior Court*, 450 U.S. 464 (1981) (gender-based classification upheld).
4 See *Steffan v. Perry*, 41 F.3d 677, 685 (D. C. Cir. 1994) ("It is hard to imagine a more deferential standard than rational basis."); Gerald Gunther, "The Supreme Court, 1971 Term—Forward: In Search of Evolving Doctrine on a Changing Court: A Model for a Newer Equal Protection," 86 *Harv. L. Rev.* 1, 8 (1972) (rational test involves "minimal scrutiny in theory, and virtually none in fact").

5   348 U.S. 483, 488 (1955).

6   473 U.S. 432 (1985).

7   See id. at 456 (Marshall, J., concurring in part and dissenting in part: "The Court holds the ordinance invalid on rational-basis grounds and disclaims that anything special, in the form of heightened scrutiny, is taking place. Yet, Cleburne's ordinance surely would be valid under the traditional rational-basis test applicable to economic and commercial regulation.").

8   See id. at 456 (Marshall, J., concurring in part and dissenting in part).

9   895 F.2d 563, 573 (9th Cir. 1990).

10   943 F.2d 989, 994 (9th Cir.), superseded, 963 F.2d 1160 (9th Cir. 1991), cert. denied, 506 U.S. 1020 (1992).

11   116 S. Ct. 1620, 1625 (1996).

12   Id. at 1627 (citing *Heller v. Doe*, 113 S. Ct. 2637, 2642 [1993]).

13   Id.

14   See id. at 1631 (Scalia, J., dissenting, suggesting that the amendment had a legitimate rational basis) and id. at 1629 (Scalia, J., dissenting, suggesting that the Court "places the prestige of this institution behind the proposition that opposition to homosexuality is as reprehensible as racial or religious bias").

15   See *San Antonio Indep. Sch. Dist. v. Rodriguez*, 411 U.S. 1, 28 (1973).

16   See *United States v. Carolene Products Co.*, 304 U.S. 144, 152 n.4 (1938) (prejudice against particular minorities may require judicial scrutiny due to potential failure of political process).

17   For further discussion of these and related points, see generally Mark Strasser, "Suspect Classes and Suspect Classifications: On Discrimination, Unwittingly or Otherwise," 64 *Temple L. Rev.* 937 (1991).

18   *Sugarman v. Dougall*, 413 U.S. 634, 642 (1973) (citing *Graham v. Richardson*, 403 U.S. 365, 372 (1971)).

19   See, for example, *Parham v. Hughes*, 441 U.S. 347, 353 (1979) (unjust to punish illegitimate child based on illegitimacy because child is not responsible for that condition).

20   See, for example, *Weber v. Aetna Casualty*, 406 U.S. 164, 172 (1972) (requiring classifications to bear a rational relationship to a legitimate state purpose).

21   *Massachusetts Bd. of Retirement v. Murgia*, 427 U.S. 307, 313 (1976) (citation omitted).

22   In listing the Supreme Court's criteria for suspect classes, the California Supreme Court wrote: "Another characteristic which underlies all suspect classifications is the stigma of inferiority and second class citizenship associated with them." *Sail'er Inn, Inc. v. Kirby*, 485 P.2d 529, 540 (Cal. 1971).

23   316 U.S. 535, 541 (1942).

24   100 U.S. 303, 306 (1879).

25 *Romer*, 116 S. Ct. at 1627.

26 *Loving v. Virginia*, 388 U.S. 1, 8 (1967).

27 *Korematsu v. United States*, 323 U.S. 214, 223–224 (1944) (suggesting that nationality is suspect).

28 See *City of New Orleans v. Dukes*, 427 U.S. 297, 303 (1976) (discussing "inherently suspect distinctions such as race, religion, or alienage"). See also *Burlington N. R.R. v. Ford*, 504 U.S. 648, 651 (1992) (discussing "suspect lines like race or religion").

29 See *Takahashi v. Fish and Game Comm'n*, 334 U.S. 410 (1948) (suggesting that alienage is suspect). However, the Court has suggested that not all limitations on aliens are suspect. See *Foley v. Connelie*, 435 U.S. 219, 294 (1978).

30 427 U.S. 307, 320 (1976) (Marshall, J., dissenting).

31 Id. at 318–19 (Marshall, J., dissenting).

32 See *Padula v. Webster*, 822 F.2d 97, 103 (D.C. Cir. 1987) (criminalization of sodomy in *Bowers v. Hardwick*, 478 U.S. 186 (1986) is not "invidious" discrimination because Supreme Court approved of it); *State v. Walsh*, 713 S.W.2d 508, 511 (Mo. 1986) (en banc) ("Homosexuals, as such, have never been denied the ability to engage in 'political give and take'."); Note, Doe and Dronenberg: "Sodomy Statutes Are Constitutional," 26 *Wm. & Mary L. Rev.* 645, 676–77 (1985) (Homosexuals do not constitute discrete and insular minority and do not have immutable characteristics).

33 Edward A. Fallone, Note, "Preserving the Public Health: A Proposal to Quarantine Recalcitrant AIDS Carriers," 68 *B. U. L. Rev.* 441, 493 (1988).

34 Note, "Homosexuals' Right to Marry: A Constitutional Test and a Legislative Solution," 128 *U. Pa. L. Rev.* 193, 206 (1979) (homosexuality is not a condition beyond individual's control).

35 See *Walsh*, 713 S.W.2d at 511; Patrick Devlin, *The Enforcement of Morals* (1959) (suggesting that homosexuality is immoral and should be criminalized).

36 See Chai R. Feldblum, "Sexual Orientation, Morality, and the Law: Devlin Revisited," 57 *U. Pitt. L. Rev.* 237, 256–262 (1996) (discussing the role of powerlessness in suspect class jurisprudence).

37 See *Dahl v. Secretary of the United States Navy*, 830 F. Supp. 1319, 1324 (E.D. Cal. 1993) (quoting *City of Cleburne v. Cleburne Living Center*, 473 U.S. 432, 445 (1985)).

38 See Alan Brownstein, "Harmonizing the Heavenly and Earthly Spheres: The Fragmentation and Synthesis of Religion, Equality, and Speech in the Constitution," 51 *Ohio St. L. J.* 89, 174 n.2 (comparing the political power of Catholics and Quakers).

39 Cf. *Collin v. Smith*, 578 F.2d 1197, 1199 (7th Cir. 1978) (describing the view of the National Socialist Party of America that Jews have inordinate political and financial power in the world), cert. denied, 439 U.S. 916 (1978).

40   *Dahl,* 830 F. Supp. at 1324 (citing *Cleburne,* 473 U.S. at 445).

41   See *Cleburne,* 473 U.S. at 467 (Marshall, J., concurring in part and dissenting in part, "The Court . . . has never suggested that race-based classifications became any less suspect once extensive legislation had been enacted on the subject.").

42   473 U.S. 432 (1985).

43   Id. at 442.

44   Id. at 445.

45   See *High Tech Gays v. Defense Indus. Sec. Clearance Office,* 895 F.2d 563, 574 (9th Cir. 1990); *Steffan v. Cheney,* 780 F. Supp. 1, 7–9 (D.D.C. 1991), aff'd sub nom. *Steffan v. Perry,* 41 F.3d 677 (D.C. Cir 1994).

46   *Cleburne,* 473 U.S. at 466 (Marshall, J., concurring in part and dissenting in part).

47   Some voting in favor may have feared that, otherwise, there would be affirmative action policies which would mandate that gays, lesbians, and bisexuals would have to be hired, although that is not what these initiatives said. For further discussion of these and related issues, see Mark Strasser, "Unconstitutional? Don't Ask; If It Is, Don't Tell: On Deference, Rationality, and the Constitution," 66 *U. Colo. L. Rev.* 375, 411–415.

48   See id.

49   *Romer,* 116 S. Ct. at 1626–27.

50   Id. at 1629 (Scalia, J., dissenting).

51   Id. at 1625.

52   54 F.3d 261, 263 (6th Cir. 1995), cert. granted, judgment vacated 116 S. Ct. 2519 (1996) on remand to 128 F.3d 289 (6th Cir. 1997).

53   See Andrew Sullivan, *Virtually Normal,* 68 (1995) ("There is overwhelming evidence . . . that at least part of homosexuality is determined so early as to be essentially involuntary.").

54   See *Equality Foundation,* 54 F.3d at 267 ("Because homosexuals generally are not identifiable 'on sight' unless they elect to be so identifiable by conduct (such as public displays of homosexual affection or self-proclamation of homosexual tendencies), they cannot constitute a suspect or quasi-suspect class . . . "), cert. granted, judgment vacated 116 S. Ct. 2519 (1996).

55   See id.

56   See *Mathews v. Lucas,* 427 U.S. 495, 523 (1976) (Stevens, J., dissenting, "The fact that illegitimacy is not as apparent to the observer as sex or race does not make this governmental classification any less odious.").

57   See *Walsh,* 713 S.W.2d at 510 ("The statute merely proscribes homosexual activity. It cannot be said in the usual circumstances that refraining from certain conduct is beyond control. Beyond prohibiting the specified conduct, the statute imposes no other burden.").

58   370 U.S. 660 (1962).

59   Id. at 666.

60   392 U.S. 514 (1968).

61   Id. at 543.

62   Id. at 532.

63   Justice Scalia does not seem to appreciate this point, since he seems to suggest that disapproval of sodomy would justify a whole host of laws directed against gays and lesbians, for example, Colorado's Amendment 2. See *Romer*, 116 S. Ct. at 1633 (Scalia, J., dissenting).

64   See *Bowers v. Hardwick*, 478 U.S. 186, 196 n.8.

65   822 F.2d 97, 103 (D.C. Cir. 1987).

66   871 F.2d 1068, 1076 (Fed. Cir. 1989), cert. denied, 494 U.S. 1003 (1990).

67   It is not maintained here that *Bowers v. Hardwick*, 478 U.S. 186 (1986) was decided correctly but merely that the decision does not have the implications that some courts seem to believe.

68   In *Bowers*, in which the Court held that sodomy may be criminalized, the Court explicitly refused to consider any Equal Protection issues, thus leaving open whether gays, lesbians, and bisexuals might constitute a suspect or quasi-suspect class, notwithstanding the Court's refusal to hold that homosexual sodomy was a fundamental right. See id. at 196 n.8.

69   But see Richard Posner, *Sex and Reason*, 308 (1992) (comparing Judaism with homosexuality); Sullivan, *Virtually Normal*, 119, 152 (comparing Judaism with homosexuality); David A. J. Richards, "Sexual Preference as a Suspect (Religious) Classification: An Alternative Perspective on the Unconstitutionality of Anti-Lesbian/Gay Initiatives," 55 *Ohio St. L. J.* 491 (1994) (comparing Judaism with sexual orientation).

70   See Posner, *Sex and Reason*, 296–97.

71   See *Bowers*, 478 U.S. at 197 (Burger, C.J., concurring: "To hold that the act of homosexual sodomy is somehow protected as a fundamental right would be to cast aside millennia of moral teaching.").

72   100 U.S. 303, 308 (1879).

73   347 U.S. 483, 494 (1954).

74   163 U.S. 537 (1896).

75   Id. at 551.

76   Id.

77   The *Loving* Court struck down Virginia's antimiscegenation statute precisely because of its white supremacist basis. See *Loving*, 388 U.S. at 11. Clearly, some courts have believed certain races morally inferior. In *Dallas v. State*, 79 So. 690, 691 (Fla. 1918), the Supreme Court of Florida included within its opinion a reference to a non-Caucasian "race that is largely immoral."

78   466 U.S. 429, 432 (1984).

79   See *Strauder*, 100 U.S. at 308.

80   Id. at 310.

81   443 U.S. 545, 557 (1979).

82   See Barry Parsons, Casenote, "*Bottoms v. Bottoms*: Erasing the Presumption Favoring a Natural Parent over Third Parties—What Makes This Mother Unfit?," 2 *Geo. Mason Independent L. Rev.* 457, 465 n.62 (suggest-

ing that 90 percent of American heterosexual couples engage in sodomitic relations).

83   See Harry V. Jaffa, " 'Our Ancient Faith': A Reply to Professor Anastaplo," in *Original Intent and the Framers of the Constitution*, 369, 383 (1994).

84   *Romer*, 116 S. Ct. at 1632–33.

85   See id. at 1633.

86   Id. at 1625.

87   See Tex. Penal Code Sec. 21.06 (West 1994).

88   852 P.2d 44 (Haw.) (plurality opinion), reconsideration granted in part, 875 P.2d 225 (Haw. 1993).

89   Id. at 67.

90   Id. at 60.

91   440 U.S. 268, 273 (1979).

92   Id. at 282–83.

93   Id. at 282.

94   See *Baehr*, 852 P.2d at 71 (Heen, J., dissenting).

95   See id. at 67–68.

96   *Loving*, 388 U.S. at 8.

97   Id.

98   See *Baehr*, 852 P.2d at 71 (Heen, J., dissenting: "The effect of the statute is to prohibit same sex marriages on the part of professed or nonprofessed heterosexuals, homosexuals, bisexuals or asexuals.").

99   See Craig Bradley, "The Right Not to Endorse Gay Rights: A Reply to Sunstein," 70 *Ind. L. J.* 29, 34 (1994).

100   442 U.S. 256, 273 (1979).

101   421 U.S. 7, 14–15 (1975).

102   *Bradwell v. Illinois*, 83 U.S. (16 Wall.) 130, 141 (1872) (Bradley, J., concurring).

103   411 U.S. 677, 684 (1973).

104   458 U.S. 718, 729 (1982).

105   Id. at 724–25.

106   *Orr*, 440 U.S. at 283.

107   *Hogan*, 458 U.S. at 725.

108   468 U.S. 609, 625 (1984).

109   429 U.S. 190, 199 (1976).

110   See *Baehr*, 852 P.2d at 67 n.33.

111   *Loving* involved discrimination against a suspect class *and* abridgement of a fundamental right. See *Loving*, 388 U.S. at 11–12.

112   *Romer*, 116 S. Ct. at 1627.

III   THE FUNDAMENTAL INTEREST IN MARRIAGE

1   See *Griswold v. Connecticut*, 381 U.S. 479 (1965) (striking law preventing married couples from having access to contraception as violation of the fundamental right to privacy).

2   See *Korematsu v. United States*, 323 U.S. 214, 218–19 (1944) (Japanese
    relocation camps during World War II constitutional because of pressing
    public necessity); *Hirabayashi v. United States*, 320 U.S. 81, 100 (1943)
    (danger of espionage and sabotage during time of war and threatened
    invasion compelling enough interests to warrant legislation affecting in-
    dividuals based on ancestry). But see Mark Strasser, "Unconstitutional?
    Don't Ask; If It Is, Don't Tell: On Deference, Rationality, and the Consti-
    tution," 66 *U. Colo. L. Rev.* 375, 380–382 (1995) (discussing why these cases
    in fact involved invidious discrimination).

3   *Planned Parenthood of Southeastern Pennsylvania v. Casey*, 505 U.S. 833,
    851 (1992) (plurality opinion).

4   381 U.S. 1, 12 (1967).

5   Id. (quoting *Skinner*, 316 U.S. at 541).

6   381 U.S. 479, 486 (1965).

7   455 U.S. 745, 753 (1982).

8   *Baehr*, 852 P.2d at 56.

9   434 U.S. 374 (1978).

10 Id. at 386.

11 Id.

12 *Baehr*, 852 P.2d at 56 (emphasis added).

13 See, for example, Thomas B. Edsall, "Disillusioned Rainbow Coalition
    Mulls Third-Party Bid," *Washington Post*, May 28, 1995, at A4 ("Jackson
    and prominent members of the black clergy voiced their anger over what
    they see as Republican efforts to turn concerns over out-of-wedlock
    births and families without fathers into minority issues."); Barbara Vobej-
    da, "The Debates over Welfare: Moynihan, Observing from the Wings,"
    Washington Post, June 4, 1995, at A1 (discussing Senator Moynihan's ef-
    forts to "get welfare recipients into the work force and to discourage out-
    of-wedlock births").

14 See Robert D. Reischauer, "The Blockbuster Inside the Republicans' Bud-
    get: In the Rush to Fiscal Devolution, Has Anyone Figured Out How to
    Divvy Up the Cash?" *Washington Post*, May 14, 1995, at C2 (stating that
    "out-of-wedlock births have soared").

15 See Mary McGrory, "No Legitimate Solution in Sight," *Washington Post*,
    March 16, 1995, at A2 ("Social scientists project a 50 percent illegitimacy
    rate by the turn of the century.").

16 See *Eisenstadt v. Baird*, 405 U.S. 438, 453 (1972) ("If the right of privacy
    means anything, it is the right of the individual, married or single, to be
    free from unwarranted governmental intrusion into matters so funda-
    mentally affecting a person as the decision whether to bear or beget a
    child.").

17 See *Stanley v. Illinois*, 405 U.S. 645 (1972).

18 486 F. Supp. 1119 (C.D. Cal. 1980), aff'd, 673 F.2d 1036 (9th Cir.), cert.
    denied, 458 U.S. 1111 (1982).

19 Id. at 1124.

20 Id. (emphasis added).

21 Id.

22 Id. at 1124–25.

23 Id. at 1125.

24 See John M. Finnis, "Law, Morality and 'Sexual Orientation,'" 69 *Notre Dame L. Rev.* 1049, 1066 (1994) (discussing exception for sterile couples).

25 Martha C. Nussbaum, "Platonic Love and Colorado Law: The Relevance of Ancient Greek Norms to Modern Sexual Controversies," 80 *Va. L. Rev.* 1515, 1529 (1994) (suggesting that the permissibility of unwillingly sterile couples' engaging in sexual relations "raises some deep questions about the consistency of [Finnis's] reasoning").

26 See Finnis, "Law, Morality, and 'Sexual Orientation,'" at 1068 (italics added).

27 Allowing same-sex female, but not male, couples to marry would trigger at least heightened scrutiny. Further, more complicated ways might be devised in which males' lovemaking might result in procreation.

28 See Finnis, "Law, Morality and 'Sexual Orientation,'" 1066 (discussing why individuals who "*happen* to be sterile" can partake of the intrinsic goodness of marriage) (italics added) and id. at 1068 (discussing conduct between husband and wife as "masturbatory" which involves sodomy or fellatio or coitus interruptus). See also Stephen Macedo, "Homosexuality and the Conservative Mind," 84 *Geo. L. J.* 261, 272 ("The new natural lawyers strikingly treat gay and lesbian sexual activity like most forms of heterosexual activity: like all sex outside of marriage and all contracepted sex, *including* all contracepted sex between married couples.").

29 For a discussion of some of the difficulties in delimiting actions, see Mark Strasser, *Agency, Free Will, and Moral Responsibility*, 37–78 (1992).

30 See *International Union, UAW v. Johnson Controls*, 499 U.S. 187 (1991) (involving jobs where exposure to lead increases likelihood of sterility). While one might appeal to the difference between intended and foreseen consequences (making use of the Principle of Double Effect), this distinction is more complicated for moral purposes than is often realized. See Strasser, *Agency, Free Will, and Moral Responsibility*, 203–210.

31 See Robert P. George and Gerard V. Bradley, "Marriage and the Liberal Imagination," 84 *Geo. L. J.* 301, 305 (1995).

32 See id. at 307.

33 John Stuart Mill, *Utilitarianism*, in *Collected Works of John Stuart Mill*, vol. 10, Chap. 2, par. 2, at 210 (1969).

34 Id.

35 380 U.S. 89, 93 (1965).

36 405 U.S. 438, 454 (1972).

37 *Singer*, 522 P.2d at 1195.

38 Id.

39 Id.

40 See Randolph E. Schmid, "Working Mom Is Now U.S. Norm," *Detroit Free Press*, June 16, 1988, at 8B ("The number of childless couples with both husband and wife employed and the wife of childbearing age increased from 3 million to 4.3 million over the 11-year period [1976–1987]."). The 4.3 million couples involved only a subset of all of the married, childless couples, because some couples might not have been of childbearing age and others might not have had both individuals working outside of the home.

41 See Tom Walker, "'Career Survival Kit' Offers Tips for Worried Workers," *Atlanta Constitution*, October 3, 1991, at B3 ("The share of U.S. households represented by two-parent families with children shrank 13 percent from 1970 to 1990.").

42 *Adams*, 486 F. Supp. at 1124.

43 See *State v. Jackson*, 80 Mo. 175, 179 (1883) ("It is stated as a well authenticated fact that if the issue of a black man and a white woman, and a white man and a black woman, intermarry, they cannot possibly have any progeny, and such a fact sufficiently justifies those laws which forbid the intermarriage of blacks and whites, laying out of view other sufficient grounds for such enactments.").

44 See *Naim v. Naim*, 87 S.E.2d 749, 756 (Va.) ("We find . . . no requirement that the State shall not legislate to prevent the obliteration of racial pride, but must permit the corruption of blood even though it weaken or destroy the quality of its citizenship."), vacated on procedural grounds, 350 U.S. 891 (1955).

45 See *Loving*, 388 U.S. at 8 ("[T]he State argues, the scientific evidence is substantially in doubt and, consequently, this Court should defer to the wisdom of the state legislature in adopting its policy of discouraging interracial marriages.").

46 *Skinner*, 316 U.S. at 541.

47 See *Pierce v. Society of the Sisters*, 268 U.S. 510, 535–36 (1925) (holding that parents and guardians have a fundamental right to direct the upbringing of their children and the children for whom they are responsible); *Meyer v. Nebraska*, 262 U.S. 390, 399 (1923) (holding that the guarantee of liberty in the 14th Amendment is "not merely freedom from bodily restraint, but also the right of the individual to . . . marry, establish a home and bring up children").

48 See *Dean*, 653 A.2d at 333 (Ferren, J., concurring in part and dissenting in part).

49 See id. at 345 (Ferren, J., concurring in part and dissenting in part, noting that between eight and ten million children are raised in gay and lesbian households).

50   See id. at 333.

51   431 U.S. 494 (1977).

52   Id. at 503–4.

53   Id. at 501.

54   *Roberts*, 468 U.S. at 618–19.

55   But see *Wisconsin v. Yoder*, 406 U.S. 205, 224 (1972) ("A way of life that is odd or even erratic but interferes with no rights or interests of others is not to be condemned because it is different.").

56   Cf. *Michael H. v. Gerald D.*, 491 U.S. 110, 141 (1989) (Brennan, J., dissenting: "We are not an assimilative, homogeneous society, but a facilitative, pluralistic one, in which we must be willing to abide someone else's unfamiliar or even repellent practice because the same tolerant impulse protects our own idiosyncracies.").

57   *Zablocki*, 434 U.S. at 386.

58   Id. at 383.

59   See *Eisenstadt*, 405 U.S. 453.

60   *Zablocki*, 434 U.S. at 384.

61   481 U.S. 537, 545 (1987).

62   Id.

63   Id. ("Of course, we have not held that constitutional protection is restricted to relationships among family members.").

64   482 U.S. 78 (1987).

65   Id. at 95.

66   Id.

67   Id. at 96.

68   Id.

69   Id. For a discussion of some of the benefits conferred by marriage, see William N. Eskridge, Jr., *The Case for Same-Sex Marriage*, 66–67 (1996).

70   See *Dean*, 653 A.2d at 336 (Ferren, J., concurring in part and dissenting in part: "Appellants proffer that, given the nature of homosexuality, *Turner*'s attributes of marriage—emotional support, religious or spiritual significance, physical consummation, and government and other benefits—are as relevant and important to same-sex couples as to heterosexual couples.").

71   See id. at 332 (Ferren, J., concurring in part and dissenting in part: "An historical survey of Supreme Court cases concerning the fundamental right to marry, however, demonstrates that the Court has called this right 'fundamental' because of its link to procreation." (citing *Baehr*, 852 P.2d at 55).

72   *Roberts*, 468 U.S. at 619.

73   Id.

74   Id.

75   Id.

76   Id. at 618.

77 See *Michael H. v. Gerald D.*, 491 U.S. 110, 141 (1989) (Brennan, J., dissenting, "In a community such as ours, 'liberty' must include the freedom not to conform."); *Coates v. City of Cincinnati*, 402 U.S. 611, 616 (1971) (discussing "discriminatory enforcement against those whose association together is 'annoying' because their ideas, their lifestyle, or their physical appearance is resented by the majority of their fellow citizens").

78 See Richard Epstein, "Caste and the Civil Rights Laws: From Jim Crow to Same-Sex Marriages," 92 *Mich. L. Rev.* 2456, 2460 (1994) ("[T]he current prohibitions against same-sex marriages are themselves a mistake—regardless of what one thinks of the wisdom or morality of these marriages—and should be rejected as inimical to the basic principle of freedom of association on which a liberal society should rest."); see also David A. J. Richards, "Constitutional Legitimacy and Constitutional Privacy," 61 *N. Y. U. L. Rev.* 800, 853 (1986) (arguing that a basic principle of equal rights is that they "must be fairly extended to the most despised minorities").

79 See *Bowers*, 478 U.S. at 205 (Blackmun, J., dissenting).

80 505 U.S. 833, 851 (1992) (plurality opinion).

81 *Loving*, 388 U.S. at 12.

82 *Zablocki*, 434 U.S. at 386.

83 Id. at 388.

84 See id. at 396 (Powell, J., concurring in the judgment).

85 See id. at 399 (Powell, J., concurring in the judgment: "A 'compelling state purpose' inquiry would cast doubt on the network of restrictions that the States have fashioned to govern marriage and divorce.").

86 Milton C. Regan, Jr., "Reason, Tradition, and Family Law: A Comment on Social Constructionism," 79 *Va. L. Rev.* 1515, 1525 (1993) (suggesting that "incest statutes are a crude form of regulation that sweeps both too broadly and too narrowly.").

87 *Wisconsin v. Yoder*, 406 U.S. 205, 247 (1972) (Douglas, J., dissenting, suggesting that the *Yoder* decision would eventuate an overruling of *Reynolds v. United States*, 98 U.S. 145 (1878), which upheld the state prohibition of polygamy). See also *Romer*, 116 S. Ct. at 1635 (Scalia, J., dissenting, suggesting that after *Romer* the constitutionality of polygamy statutes is now in doubt).

88 *Potter v. Murray City*, 760 F.2d 1065, 1070 (10th Cir.) ("[T]he State is justified, by a compelling interest, in upholding and enforcing its ban on plural marriage to protect the monogamous marriage relationship."), cert. denied, 474 U.S. 849 (1985); see also *Barlow v. Blackburn*, 798 P.2d 1360, 1366–67 (Ariz. App. 1990) (holding that the state has a compelling interest in maintaining monogamous marriage qualification for its peace officers).

89 See *State v. Jackson*, 80 Mo. 175, 177 (1883) (suggesting that recognizing a federal constitutional right to marry would undermine incest laws).

90   *Dean*, 653 A.2d at 313 (Ferren, J., concurring in part and dissenting in part) (discussing genetic concerns raised by incest); see also *In re Estate of Loughmiller*, 629 P.2d 156, 158 (Kan. 1981) (discussing reasons for preventing incestuous marriages).

91   *Bagnardi v. Hartnett*, 366 N.Y.S.2d 89 (Sup. Ct. 1975).

92   *Israel v. Allen*, 577 P.2d 762 (Colo. 1978) (en banc).

93   *Moe v. Dinkins*, 669 F.2d 67, 68 (2d Cir.), cert. denied, 459 U.S. 827 (1982).

94   See id. ("[T]he right of minors to marry has not been viewed as a fundamental right deserving strict scrutiny.").

95   *Sosna v. Iowa*, 419 U.S. 393 (1975).

96   See generally Mark Strasser, "Family, Definitions, and the Constitution: On the Antimiscegenation Analogy," 25 *Suffolk U. L. Rev.* 981 (1991).

97   198 P.2d 17, 19 (Cal. 1948).

98   Id. at 25.

99   Id. at 31 (Carter, J., concurring).

100 See *Baehr*, 852 P.2d at 70 (Heen, J., dissenting, "[T]he plaintiff in *Loving* was not claiming a right to a same sex marriage.").

101 *Baker*, 191 N.W.2d at 187 (emphasis added).

102 See Eskridge, *The Case for Same-Sex Marriage*, 77.

103 See *Naim*, 87 S.E.2d at 752 (discussing with approval a case holding that "the natural law which forbids their intermarriage and the social amalgamation which leads to a corruption of races is as clearly divine as that which imparted to them different natures"); see also *Loving*, 388 U.S. at 3 (discussing the trial court's view that God did not intend such marriages).

104 See *Baehr*, 852 P.2d at 57.

105 Id.

106 See *Jantz v. Muci*, 759 F. Supp. 1543, 1546 (D. Kan. 1991), ("[H]omosexuality is not considered a deeply-rooted part of our traditions precisely because homosexuals have historically been subjected to invidious discrimination." (citation omitted)), rev'd, 976 F.2d 623 (10th Cir. 1992), cert. denied, 508 U.S. 952 (1993); see also *Dean*, 653 A.2d at 345 (Ferren, J., concurring in part and dissenting in part: "[T]he discrimination faced by homosexuals is plainly no less pernicious or intense than the discrimination faced by other groups already treated as suspect classes.").

107 An analogous error might be found in *Bowers v. Hardwick*, 478 U.S. 186 (1986). See Laurence Tribe, *American Constitutional Law*, 1427 (2d ed., 1988) ("The Court's error in *Hardwick* was that it used the wrong level of generality to conceptualize the plaintiff's claim of liberty.").

108 *Bowers*, 478 U.S. at 194.

109 *Casey*, 505 S. Ct. at 980 (1992) (Scalia, J., concurring in part and dissenting in part).

110 410 U.S. 113, 168 (1973) (Stewart, J., concurring).

111 Id. at 116 ("The Texas statutes under attack here are typical of those that have been in effect in many States for approximately a century.").

112 See *Casey*, 505 U.S. at 983 (Scalia, J., concurring in part and dissenting in part); see also id. at 952 (Rehnquist, C.J., concurring in part and dissenting in part: "Nor do the historical traditions of the American people support the view that the right to terminate one's pregnancy is 'fundamental.'").

113 See *San Antonio Indep. Sch. Dist. v. Rodriguez*, 411 U.S. 1, 100 (1973) (Marshall, J., dissenting: "I would like to know where the Constitution guarantees the right to procreate.").

114 381 U.S. 479 (1965).

115 See *Poe v. Ullman*, 367 U.S. 497, 501 (1961) ("The Connecticut law prohibiting the use of contraceptives has been on the State's books since 1879.").

116 See 405 U.S. 438, 447 (1972) ("Section 21 stems from Mass. Stat. 1879, c. 159, s 1, which prohibited, without exception, distribution of articles intended to be used as contraceptives.").

117 *Casey*, 505 U.S. at 847–48 (noting that "[m]arriage is mentioned nowhere in the Bill of Rights and interracial marriage was illegal in most States in the 19th century").

118 Id. at 847.

119 Id. at 848.

120 Id. at 901.

121 Id.

122 Id. at 849.

123 *Griswold*, 381 U.S. at 495 (Goldberg, J., concurring).

124 *Michael H. v. Gerald D.*, 491 U.S. 110, 139 (1989) (Brennan, J., dissenting, suggesting that if the degree of specificity used in *Michael H.* had been used in *Eisenstadt* and *Griswold*, the results would have been much different).

125 Id. at 138 (Brennan, J., dissenting).

126 See id. at 132 (O'Connor, J., concurring in part, characterizing Scalia's approach as "inconsistent with our past decisions in this area" because "[o]n occasion the Court has characterized relevant traditions protecting asserted rights at levels of generality that might not be 'the most specific level' available").

127 *Bowers*, 478 U.S. at 195.

128 Id. at 196 (Burger, C.J., concurring).

129 *Baker v. Wade*, 553 F. Supp. 1121, 1125 (N.D. Tex. 1982) ("[F]or a period of 83 years, oral sodomy was not illegal in Texas—whether committed by man and wife, by unmarried male and female, or by homosexuals."), rev'd, 769 F.2d 289 (5th Cir. 1985), cert. denied, 478 U.S. 1022 (1986); *Commonwealth v. Wasson*, 842 S.W.2d 487, 491 (Ky. 1993) ("Unlike the present statute our common law tradition punished neither oral copulation nor any form of deviate sexual activity between women." [emphasis omitted]).

130 *Bowers*, 478 U.S. at 190.

131 See id. at 200 (Blackmun, J., dissenting); see also *High Tech Gays v. Defense Indus. Sec. Clearance Office*, 668 F. Supp. 1361, 1371 (N.D. Cal. 1987) ("It is important to note that, at present, it has not been established that anyone, heterosexual or homosexual, has a fundamental right to engage in sodomy. The United States Supreme Court has never held that heterosexuals have a fundamental right to engage in sodomy."), rev'd in part, vacated in part, 895 F.2d 563 (9th Cir. 1990); *State v. Santos*, 413 A.2d 58 (R.I. 1980) (holding that unmarried persons committing sodomy are unprotected); *State v. Poe*, 252 S.E.2d 843 (N.C. Ct. App. 1979) (holding that sodomy outside of marriage is not protected), review denied, appeal dismissed, 259 S.E.2d 304 (N.C. 1979), appeal dismissed sub nom. *Poe v. North Carolina*, 445 U.S. 947 (1980).

132 *Poe*, 252 S.E.2d at 845 ("[T]he state, consistent with the Fourteenth Amendment, can classify unmarried persons so as to prohibit fellatio between males and females without forbidding the same acts between married couples."); *State v. Santos*, 413 A.2d 58, 68 (R.I. 1980) ("[W]e hold that the right of privacy is inapplicable to the private unnatural copulation between *unmarried* adults." (emphasis added)).

133 See *Dean*, 653 A.2d at 343 (Ferren, J., concurring in part and dissenting in part).

134 *Bowers*, 478 U.S. at 191.

135 Id. at 203 (Blackmun, J., dissenting, quoting *Carey v. Population Services International*, 431 U.S. 678, 711 [1977]) (Powell J., concurring in part and concurring in the judgment).

136 See Richard A. Posner, *Sex and Reason*, 299 (1992); see also Arthur A. Murphy, "Homosexuality and the Law: Tolerance and Containment II," 97 *Dickinson L. Rev.* 693, 694 (1993) (offering a "containment" strategy so as not to encourage homosexuality).

137 *Baker*, 553 F. Supp. at 1130 ("In some countries (e.g., England, France, Holland, Finland), homosexual conduct has been decriminalized for years, and there is no greater incidence of homosexuality in those countries than in the United States. Moreover, there have been no adverse side effects in the 21 states that have now decriminalized consensual sodomy between adults in private."), Posner, *Sex and Reason*, 297 ("No one as far as I know has suggested, let alone presented evidence, that the removal of legal disabilities to homosexuality in countries such as Sweden and the Netherlands, and the growth of social tolerance to which that removal must in large part have been due, caused the number of homosexuals to increase."); David A. J. Richards, "Sexual Autonomy and the Constitutional Right to Privacy: A Case Study in Human Rights and the Unwritten Constitution," 30 *Hastings L. J.* 957, 993 (1979) ("The many countries which have legalized homosexual relations show no decline in the incidence of heterosexual marriage.").

138 See *Evans v. Romer*, 882 P.2d 1335, 1347 (Colo. 1994) (en banc) ("[W]e

reject defendants' suggestion that laws prohibiting discrimination against gay men, lesbians, and bisexuals will undermine marriages and heterosexual families because married heterosexuals will 'choose' to 'become homosexual' if discrimination against homosexuals is prohibited. This assertion flies in the face of the empirical evidence presented at trial on marriage and divorce rates."), aff'd, 116 S. Ct. 1620 (1996); *People v. Onofre*, 415 N.E.2d 936, 941 (N.Y. 1980) ("Certainly there is no . . . empirical data submitted which demonstrates that marriage is nothing more than a refuge for persons deprived by legislative fiat of the option of consensual sodomy outside the marital bond."), cert. denied, 451 U.S. 987 (1981).

139 See *Equality Found. of Greater Cincinnati, Inc. v. City of Cincinnati*, 860 F. Supp. 417, 442 (S.D. Ohio 1994) ("[T]estimony from both the Plaintiffs' and Defendants' witnesses established that heterosexual males are far more responsible than gays in this society for the breakdown of the family unit."), rev'd, 54 F.3d 261 (6th Cir. 1995), cert. granted, judgment vacated, 116 S. Ct. 2519 (1996) on remand to 128 F.3d 289 (6th Cir. 1997).

140 See *Dean v. District of Columbia*, Civ. A. No. 90-13892, 1992 WL 685364, at *4 (D.C. Super. Ct. June 2, 1992) ("[L]egislative authorization of homosexual, same-sex marriages would constitute tacit state approval or endorsement of the sexual conduct."), aff'd, 653 A.2d 307 (D.C. 1995).

141 James Trosino, Note, "American Wedding: Same-Sex Marriage and the Miscegenation Analogy," 73 *B. U. L. Rev.* 93, 93 (1993) ("The majority of Americans, however, disapprove of gay marriage."); Scott K. Kozuma, "*Baehr v. Lewin* and Same-Sex Marriage: The Continued Struggle for Social, Political and Human Legitimacy," 30 *Willamette L. Rev.* 891, 911 (1994) ("Currently, most Americans oppose the legal sanctioning of same-sex marriages.").

142 See *Evans v. Romer*, 882 P.2d 1335, 1347 (Colo. 1994) (en banc), aff'd., 116 S. Ct. 1620 (1996); Epstein, "Caste and the Civil Rights Laws," at 2470.

143 See *Commonwealth v. Bonadio*, 415 A.2d 47, 50 (Pa. 1980). The *Bonadio* court held that "[m]any issues that are considered to be matters of morals are subject to debate, and no sufficient state interest justifies legislation of norms simply because a particular belief is followed by a number of people, or even a majority. Indeed, what is considered to be 'moral' changes with the times and is dependent upon societal background."

144 See *Baker*, 553 F. Supp. at 1132; *Onofre*, 415 N.E.2d at 940–941.

145 See *Bowers*, 478 U.S. at 212 (Blackmun, J., dissenting).

146 Id. at 211–12 (Blackmun, J., dissenting: "A state can no more punish private behavior because of religious intolerance than it can punish such behavior because of racial animus.").

147 *Barnes v. Glen Theatre, Inc.*, 501 U.S. 560, 580 (1991) (Scalia, J., concurring in the judgment, suggesting that moral concerns are not "particularly 'important' or 'substantial,' or amount . . . to anything more than a

rational basis for regulation." (emphasis omitted)); See also David Caudill, "Legal Recognition of Unmarried Cohabitation: A Proposal to Update and Reconsider Common-Law Marriage," 49 *Tenn. L. Rev.* 537, 557
(1982) ("[L]aws that advance a particular view of morality bear a weaker
relationship to the public welfare than do laws to ensure the public's
security and safety." (footnote omitted)); J. Harvie Wilkinson III and G.
Edward White, "Constitutional Protection for Personal Lifestyles," 62
Cornell L. Rev. 563, 617 (1977) ("Least persuasive of the state's justifications
for restricting lifestyle freedoms is the general promotion of morality.").

148   *Casey*, 505 U.S. at 850 ("Men and women of good conscience can disagree,
and we suppose some always shall disagree, about the profound moral
and spiritual implications of terminating a pregnancy, even in its earliest
stage."); see also *Bowers*, 478 U.S. at 212 (Blackmun, J., dissenting: "Reasonable people may differ about whether particular sexual acts are moral
or immoral.").

149   *Casey*, 505 U.S. at 850.

150   *Dean*, 653 A.2d at 355 (Ferren, J., concurring in part and dissenting in
part).

151   *Coates v. City of Cincinnati*, 402 U.S. 611, 615 (1971).

152   *Perez*, 198 P.2d at 32 (Carter, J., concurring: "[I]t is not conceded that a
state may legislate to the detriment of a class—a minority who are unable
to protect themselves, when such legislation has no valid purpose behind
it. Nor may the police power be used as a guise to cloak prejudice and
intolerance. Prejudice and intolerance are the cancers of civilization.").

153   *Gay Rights Coalition of Georgetown Univ. Law Ctr. v. Georgetown Univ.*,
536 A.2d 1, 37 (D.C. App. 1987) (en banc).

154   Sue Nussbaum Averill, Comment, "Desperately Seeking Status: Same-Sex
Couples Battle for Employment-Linked Benefits," 27 *Akron L. Rev.* 253,
278 (1993) ("In 1988, U.S. census officials estimated that there were 1.6
million unmarried same-sex couples living in the United States."); see
also Evan Wolfson, "Crossing the Threshold: Equal Marriage Rights for
Lesbians and Gay Men and the Intra-Community Critique," 21 *N. Y. U.
Rev. L. & Soc. Change* 567, 583 (1994) (discussing two studies indicating
that a large percentage of gays and lesbians would marry if they were able
to marry someone of the same sex).

155   See *Missouri ex rel. Gaines v. Canada*, 305 U.S. 337, 351 (1938).

156   See id.

157   235 U.S. 151, 161–62 (1914).

IV   THE CUSTODY AND ADOPTION OF CHILDREN

1   *Santosky v. Kramer*, 455 U.S. 745, 753 (1982).

2   262 U.S. 390, 399 (1923).

3   505 U.S. at 851.

4   *In re J. P.*, 648 P.2d 1364, 1373 (Utah 1982).

5 Id. at 1373.
6 452 U.S. 18, 40 (1981) (Blackmun, J., dissenting).
7 Id. at 38 (Blackmun, J., dissenting).
8 *Bennett v. Jeffreys*, 356 N.E.2d 277, 283 (N.Y. 1976).
9 *In re Adoption of Syck*, 562 N.E.2d 174, 183 (Ill. 1990).
10 *Champagne v. Welfare Division of Nevada State Dept. of Human Resources*, 691 P.2d 849, 857 (Nev. 1984).
11 384 N.W.2d 222 (Minn. App. 1986).
12 Id. at 224.
13 Id. at 225.
14 Id.
15 406 F. Supp. 10 (S.D. Iowa 1975).
16 Id. at 22.
17 Id. ("even if all of the evidence harmful to the Alsagers is assumed to be true, their home situation did not justify permanent termination").
18 *Bellotti v. Baird*, 443 U.S. 622, 648 (1979).
19 Id. at 638.
20 *Alsager*, 406 F. Supp. at 22.
21 Id. at 18 ("Wary of what conduct is required and what conduct must be avoided to prevent termination, parents might fail to exercise their rights freely and fully.").
22 Id.
23 Id. at 638.
24 See *Franz v. United States*, 707 F.2d 582, 598 (D.C. Cir. 1983) (society is not well-equipped to be "sufficiently sensitive to the myriad, constantly fluctuating needs and drives of children to be able to provide them the combination of support and guidance necessary to prepare them for later life"), supplemented by 712 F.2d 1428 (D.C. Cir. 1983).
25 *J.P.*, 648 P.2d at 1376.
26 Id.
27 Id.
28 Id. at 1375–76.
29 *In re Marriage of Matzen*, 600 So.2d 487, 490 (Fla. App. 1992).
30 *Champagne*, 691 P.2d at 855.
31 Id.
32 562 N.E.2d 174, 183 (Ill. 1990).
33 *In re Adoption of Children by D.*, 293 A.2d 171, 175 (N.J. 1972).
34 *J.P.*, 648 P.2d at 1374 (parent's constitutionally protected rights violated when terminated "solely on the basis of a finding that 'such termination will be in the child's best interest'").
35 *S.E.G. v. R.A.G.*, 735 S.W.2d 164, 165 (Mo. App. 1987) ("Minor children's preference will be followed only if that preference is consistent with the best interests and welfare of the child.").
36 *S. v. J.*, 367 N.Y.S.2d 405, 410 (1975).

37 *Brown v. Brown*, 237 S.E.2d 89, 91 (Va. 1977).

38 443 U.S. 622, 638 (1979).

39 See generally *Capitol Square Review and Advisory Board v. Pinette*, 115 S. Ct. 2440 (1995) (discussing endorsement test).

40 *Casey*, 505 U.S. at 850 ("Men and women of good conscience can disagree, and we suppose some always shall disagree, about the profound moral and spiritual implications of terminating a pregnancy, even in its earliest stages.").

41 See *Bowers v. Hardwick*, 478 U.S. at 212 (Blackmun, J., dissenting: "Reasonable people may disagree about whether particular sexual acts are moral or immoral.").

42 *State Dept. of Health and Rehabilitative Services v. Cox*, 627 So.2d 1210, 1215 (Fla. App. 1993) ("At this time, the orientation/activity question is simply a matter upon which reasonable persons can and do disagree—as a matter of scientific fact and as a matter of moral, religious, and legal opinion."); approved in part, quashed in part, 656 So.2d 902 (Fla. 1995).

43 *Tucker v. Tucker*, 881 P.2d 948, 951 (Utah App.) (comparing same-sex cohabitation to "cohabitation with a member of the opposite sex without benefit of marriage"), rev'd, 910 P.2d 1209 (Utah 1996).

44 See Homer Clark, *The Law of Domestic Relations in the United States* (2d ed., 1988), 806 (discussing "the child's need for stability and continuity in his relationships with his parents").

45 See William N. Eskridge, Jr., *The Case for Same-Sex Marriage*, 59 (1996).

46 See id. at 78–80.

47 *Bowers*, 478 U.S. at 191.

48 See id. at 195–96 ("it would be difficult, except by fiat, to limit the claimed right to homosexual conduct while leaving exposed to prosecution adultery.").

49 Id. at 191.

50 Juliet Cox, Comment, "Judicial Enforcement of Moral Imperatives: Is the Best Interest of the Child Being Sacrificed to Maintain Societal Homogeneity?," 59 *Mo. L. Rev.* 775, 785 (1994) ("Forty-five percent of white Americans responding to a 1991 Gallup poll disapproved of interracial marriages and twenty percent believed such marriages should be illegal.").

51 See *Bowers*, 478 U.S. at 196 (discussing the "presumed belief of a majority of the electorate in Georgia that homosexual sodomy is immoral and unacceptable").

52 See *McLaughlin v. Florida*, 397 U.S. 184 (1964) (striking down Florida law punishing interracial coupling more severely than intraracial coupling). Presumably, the Florida populace believed the former worse than the latter. If the general views of the populace were dispositive in these matters, then the Florida law would have to have been upheld.

53 See *Loving v. Virginia*, 388 U.S. 1 (1967) (states cannot prohibit interracial marriage).

54 *Conkel v. Conkel*, 509 N.E.2d 983, 986 (Ohio App. 1987) ("before depriving the sexually active parent of his crucial and fundamental right of contact with his child, a court must find that the parent's conduct is having, or is probably having, a harmful effect on the child"); *Rowsey v. Rowsey*, 329 S.E.2d 57, 61 (W.V. 1985) ("A change of custody based on a speculative notion of potential harm is an impermissible exercise of discretion.").

55 See *Bottoms v. Bottoms*, 444 S.E.2d 276, 282 (Va. App. 1994) ("courts must not delay in granting a remedy until a parent's conduct or behavior has harmed the child; the rule of law does not require that the damage sought to be avoided must occur before a court may act to prevent injury or to remedy a harmful situation"), rev'd, 457 S.E.2d 102 (Va. 1995).

56 *DiStefano v. DiStefano*, 401 N.Y.S.2d 636, 637 (App. Div. 1978); *In re Marriage of P.I.M.*, 665 S.W.2d 670, 672 (Mo. App. 1984) ("It is more sensible to change a child's custody when there is a reasonable likelihood of an adverse effect on the child if he is kept in his present surroundings than to wait until damage is done and then attempt to repair that damage.").

57 See Marie Weston Evans, Note, "Parent and Child: *M.J.P. v. J.G.P.*: An Analysis of the Relevance of Parental Homosexuality in Child Custody Determinations," 35 Okla. L. Rev. 633, 649–50 (discussing judicial misconceptions including that gays or lesbians are more likely to molest children).

58 See David Flaks, "Gay and Lesbian Families: Judicial Assumptions, Scientific Realities," 3 Wm. & Mary Bill Rts. J. 345, 360 (1994).

59 See Shaista-Parveen Ali, Comment, "Homosexual Parenting: Child Custody and Adoption," 22 U. C. Davis L. Rev. 1009, 1019 (1989) ("courts should consider homosexuals as less likely to molest their children").

60 See *Whaley v. Whaley*, 399 N.E.2d 1270, 1275 (Ohio App. 1978) ("Where it is shown that a custodial parent is engaging in conduct of questionable morality, and where it is shown that the child is not doing well, there is a danger that a trial court may grant a change of custody without direct evidence of a cause and effect relationship between the two phenomena.").

61 *Thigpen v. Carpenter*, 730 S.W.2d 510, 513 (Ark. App. 1987).

62 628 N.E.2d 633, 642 (Ill. App. 1993).

63 See id.

64 See *Bottoms*, 444 S.E.2d at 279.

65 Current military policy on lesbians and gays may involve an analogous kind of conflation of categories. See Mark Strasser, "Unconstitutional? Don't Ask; If It Is, Don't Tell: On Deference, Rationality, and the Constitution," 66 U. Colo. L. Rev. 375, 448–53 (1995) (discussing some of the First Amendment implications of current military policy).

66 *Conkel*, 509 N.E.2d at 987 ("This court cannot take into consideration the unpopularity of homosexuals in society when its duty is to facilitate and guard a fundamental parent-child relationship.").

67   466 U.S. at 430.

68   Id. at 431.

69   Id.

70   Id.

71   Id. at 432.

72   Id. at 433. See also *In re R.M.G.*, 454 A.2d 776, 802 (D.C. App. 1982) (Newman, C.J., dissenting: "The racism experienced by blacks in this society may be encountered even more often by blacks in interracial families. Those with racist attitudes are undoubtedly opposed to interracial families.").

73   See *Palmore*, 466 U.S. at 434 ("The effects of racial prejudice, however real, cannot justify a racial classification removing an infant child from the custody of its natural mother found to be an appropriate person to have such custody.").

74   Id. at 433. See also *In re Custody of Temos*, 450 A.2d 111, 120 (Pa. Super. 1982) ("But a court must never *yield* to prejudice, because it cannot *prevent* prejudice.").

75   Marc Elovitz, "Adoption by Lesbian and Gay People: The Use and Misuse of Social Science Research," 2 *Duke J. Gender, L. & Pol.* 207, 215 (1995) ("One study shows that only about five percent of the children studied who had lived with an openly lesbian or gay parent experienced harassment by other children. Where children do experience harassment, the incidents generally are infrequent and consist of relatively minor verbal teasing, such as name-calling. Such experiences have not been shown to have any significant impact on the children involved."); Flaks, "Gay and Lesbian Families," at 363 ("Those studies that have addressed this issue have found only minimal amounts of teasing—which the children and parents were able to successfully manage."); Donald Stone, "The Moral Dilemma: Child Custody When One Parent is Homosexual or Lesbian—An Empirical Study," 23 *Suffolk U. L. Rev.* 711, 741 (1989) ("The children surveyed seldom experienced harassment, or merely shrugged it off when it did occur, while some children remained entirely oblivious to teasing by others.").

76   Barry Parsons, Casenote, "*Bottoms v. Bottoms,* Erasing the Presumption Favoring a Natural Parent over Third Parties—What Makes This Mother Unfit?," 2 *Geo. Mason Independent L. Rev.* 457, 471 (1994) (courts deciding custody on this basis would "only give credence to bigotry").

77   Elovitz, "Adoption by Lesbian and Gay People," at 215 ("Of course, many children are teased because of some way in which they or their families are different from the norm. Teasing may be based on a child's physical appearance, race, religion, economic status, or any number of other factors."); Nancy Polikoff, "This Child Does Have Two Mothers: Redefining Parenthood to Meet the Needs of Children in Lesbian-Mother and Other Nontraditional Families," 78 *Geo. L. J.* 459, 567–68 (1990) ("Chil-

dren whose families are in some way different from the norm may have to confront distressing reactions from others. These differences can include, among other things, the family's ethnic traits and practices, race, religious affiliation, the parents' country of origin, physical appearance, or occupation.").

78 Yvonne Tamayo, "Sexuality, Morality and the Law: The Custody Battle of a Non-Traditional Mother," 45 *Syracuse L. Rev.* 853, 861 (1994).

79 *Jarrett v. Jarrett*, 400 N.E.2d 421, 425 (Ill. 1980) ("To wait until later years to determine whether Jacqueline had inculcated her moral values in the children would be to await a demonstration that the very harm which the statute seeks to avoid had occurred."), cert. denied, 449 U.S. 927 (1980).

80 *G.A. v. D.A.*, 745 S.W.2d 726, 728 (Mo. App. 1987).

81 *Bottoms*, 444 S.E.2d at 281.

82 See, for example, *Bezio v. Patenaude*, 410 N.E.2d 1207, 1216 (Mass. 1980) (same-sex relationship does not make a parent unfit to further the welfare of the child unless the parental behavior "adversely affects the child"); *In re Burrell*, 388 N.E.2d 738, 739 (Ohio 1979) (opposite-sex relationship between unmarrieds does not warrant denial of custody in the "absence of evidence showing a detrimental impact upon the child of the relationship").

83 *In re Opinion of the Justices*, 530 A.2d 21, 28 (N.H. 1987) (Batchelder, J., dissenting: "the overwhelming weight of professional study on the subject concludes that no difference in psychological and psychosexual development can be discerned between children raised by heterosexual parents and children raised by homosexual parents"); Flaks, "Gay and Lesbian Families," at 355 ("there has been no evidence to suggest that these children are in any way inferior relative to their peers raised by heterosexual parents"); Stephen B. Pershing, "'Entreat Me Not to Leave Thee': *Bottoms v. Bottoms* and the Custody Rights of Gay and Lesbian Parents," 3 *Wm. & Mary Bill Rts. J.* 289, 309 (1994) ("the current social science research record conclusively demonstrates the factual untenability of any assumption that children are harmed by the experience of growing up in the custody of lesbian or gay rather than heterosexual adults").

84 See *In re Marriage of Diehl*, 582 N.E.2d 281, 292 (Ill. App. 1991) ("An intimate cohabitation relationship of a parent, be it heterosexual, homosexual or lesbian in nature is a proper factor to be considered by the trial court in making a custody determination."), cert. denied sub nom. *Diehl v. Diehl*, 591 N.E.2d 20 (Ill. 1992); *Tucker*, 881 P.2d at 951 (lesbian cohabitation "should be analyzed similarly to a situation involving cohabitation with a member of the opposite sex without benefit of marriage").

85 See generally Nancy Polikoff, "Educating Judges about Lesbian and Gay Parenting: A Simulation," 1 *L. & Sexuality* 173 (1991) (discussing issues related to educating judges about lesbian and gay parenting).

86 See, for example, *Pleasant v. Pleasant*, 628 N.E.2d 633 (Ill. App. 1993).

Writing for the court, Judge David Cerda wrote, "We are disturbed by the judge's numerous homophobic comments. His personal beliefs improperly clouded his judgment." Id. at 642.

87 *Conkel v. Conkel*, 509 N.E.2d 983, 986 (Ohio App. 1987) ("This court takes judicial notice that there is no consensus on what causes homosexuality, but there is substantial consensus among experts that being raised by a homosexual parent does not increase the likelihood that a child will become homosexual."); *Cox*, 627 So.2d at 1222 (Appendix - [*Seebol v. Farie*, Case No. 90–923-CA-18]) ("Mental health experts have found the incidence of same-sex orientation among the children of homosexual parents as randomly and in the same proportion as found among children in the general population"). See also Flaks, "Gay and Lesbian Families," at 369 ("researchers have found that gay and lesbian parents are no more likely to have gay or lesbian children than are heterosexual parents").

88 *Cabalquinto v. Cabalquinto*, 669 P.2d 886, 890 (Wash. 1983) (en banc) (Stafford, J., concurring in part and dissenting in part: "A psychologist specializing in gender identification testified that a child's sexual preference is developed early in life."); Elovitz, "Adoption by Lesbian and Gay People," at 212 ("With regard to gender role behavior, the research finds no significant influence exerted by a parent's sexual orientation.").

89 Flaks, "Gay and Lesbian Families," at 360 ("gay men and lesbians are no more likely to molest children or to commit crimes with children than are heterosexual men and women"); Ali, Comment, "Homosexual Parenting," at 1019 ("courts should consider homosexuals as less likely to molest their children"); Marilyn Riley, Note, "The Avowed Lesbian Mother and Her Right to Child Custody: A Constitutional Challenge That Can No Longer Be Denied," 12 *San Diego L. Rev.* 799, 853 (1975) ("The myth about child molestation has also been abandoned by experts.").

90 Flaks, "Gay and Lesbian Families," at 371 ("The social science literature reviewed here demonstrates clearly that lesbians and gay men can and do raise psychologically healthy children"); Parsons, Casenote, "*Bottoms v. Bottoms*," at 473 ("recent studies show that children of gay and lesbian parents are not harmed psychologically").

91 Flaks, "Gay and Lesbian Families," at 357 ("No significant differences between the children's moral maturity were found.").

92 Charlotte Patterson, "Adoption of Minor Children by Lesbian and Gay Adults: A Social Science Perspective," 2 *Duke J. Gender, L. & Pol.* 191, 191 (1995) ("there is every reason to believe, based on research findings, that children of lesbian and gay parents develop as successfully as do children of heterosexual parents"); Marla Hollandsworth, "Gay Men Creating Families Through Surro-Gay Arrangements: A Paradigm for Reproductive Freedom," 3 *Am. U. J. Gender & L.* 183, 189 (1995) ("Social science and medical studies have found that gay and lesbian parents are good parents

and that their children suffer no ill effects from being raised in gay households.").

93 For a discussion of numerous cases, including *Bottoms v. Bottoms*, 457 S.E.2d 102 (Va. 1995), in which courts have manifested bias in custody and visitation determinations, see Mark Strasser, "Fit To Be Tied, On Custody, Discretion, and Sexual Orientation," 46 *Am. U. L. Rev.* 841 (1997).

94 See *Cox*, 627 So.2d at 1221 (Appendix: [*Seebol*]) ("Adoption, unknown at common law, is statutory in nature.").

95 See *J. P.*, 648 P.2d at 1373.

96 Arguably, the states preventing adoption on the basis of orientation have adopted policies which are not rationally related to legitimate state ends. See generally Mark Strasser, "Legislative Presumptions and Judicial Assumptions: On Parenting, Adoption, and the Best Interests of the Child," 45 *U. Kan. L. Rev.* 49 (1996).

97 431 U.S. 816, 846 (1977).

98 Id.

99 Id. at 846–847.

100 Id. at 846.

101 Id.

102 Id. at 836 ("many children . . . develop deep emotional ties with their foster parents").

103 See id. at 826.

104 Id. at 846.

105 The biological parents might estop the foster parents from asserting any rights or might claim to have detrimentally relied on the foster parents' promise to relinquish control upon request. See *Black's Law Dictionary*, (6th ed., 1990) 551 (Estoppel "means that [a] party is prevented by his own acts from claiming a right to detriment of [the] other party who was entitled to rely on such conduct and has acted accordingly."). See also La. Civil Code Art. 1967 (West 1987) (defining detrimental reliance: "A party may be obligated by a promise when he knew or should have known that the promise would induce the other party to rely on it to his detriment and the other party was reasonable in so relying.").

106 *OFFER*, 431 U.S. at 846. As the D.C. Court of Appeals has suggested:
a parent's right to the preservation of his relationship with his child derives from the fact that the parent's achievement of a rich and rewarding life is likely to depend significantly on his ability to participate in the rearing of his offspring. A child's corresponding right to protection from interference in the relationship derives from the psychic importance to him of being raised by a loving, responsive, reliable adult.
Franz v. United States, 707 F.2d 582, 599 (D.C. Cir.) (footnotes omitted), supplemented by 712 F.2d 1428 (D.C. Cir. 1983).

107   *Opinion of the Justices*, 530 A.2d at 28 (Batchelder, J., dissenting: "While parenting an adopted or foster child is not a fundamental right, . . . parenting is so ingrained in our culture that to deny the opportunity to adopt or provide foster care is a deprivation of liberty only in a lesser degree.").

108   It does not matter whether the legal parent is biologically related to the child or instead has adopted that child. For legal purposes, these different kinds of parents are indistinguishable.

109   See *Adoption of Tammy*, 619 N.E.2d 315, 320 (Mass. 1993) ("adoption will entitle Tammy to inherit from Helen's family trusts and from Helen and her family under the law of intestate succession"); see also *In re M.M.D. & B.H.M.*, 662 A.2d 837, 858 (D.C. App. 1995) (outlining some of the financial benefits of an adoption); Elizabeth Zuckerman, Comment, "Second Parent Adoption for Lesbian-Parented Families: Legal Recognition of the Other Mother," 19 *U. C. Davis L. Rev.* 729, 741–42 (1986) (discussing some of the financial benefits accorded by an adoption).

110   *In re Adoption of a Child by J.M.G.*, 632 A.2d 550, 552 (N.J. Super. Ct. Ch. Div. 1993) ("The importance of the emotional benefit of formal recognition of the relationship between J.M.G. and the child must not be underestimated.").

111   *Tammy*, 619 N.E.2d at 320 ("Of equal, if not greater significance, adoption will enable Tammy to preserve her unique filial ties to Helen in the event that Helen and Susan separate, or Susan predeceases Helen.") *In re Adoption of Two Children by H.N.R.*, 666 A.2d 535, 537 (N.J. App. 1995) (adoption would "assure the continuity of the custodial . . . rights and responsibilities characterizing the parental relationship"); Julia Frost Davies, Note, "Two Moms and a Baby: Protecting the Nontraditional Family through Second Parent Adoptions," 29 *New Eng. L. Rev.* 1055, 1069–70 (1995) (adoption assures custodial contact).

112   *Tammy*, 619 N.E.2d at 320 ("children have been denied the affection of a functional parent who has been with them since birth, even when it is apparent that this outcome is contrary to the children's best interests"); *In re Jacob*, 660 N.E.2d 397, 399 (N.Y. 1995) ("in the event of the biological parent's death or disability, the other parent will have presumptive custody").

113   *Ex Parte in re Petition of L.S. and V.L. for the Adoption of a Minor*, 1991 WL 219598, *3 (D.C. Super.) ("The situation resembles a step-parent adoption"); *In re M.M.D. & B.H.M.*, 662 A.2d 837, 860 (D.C. App. 1995) ("we do not hesitate to hold that this stepparent exception applies here, even though the natural parent (by adoption), Bruce, is not the 'spouse of the adopter', Mark."); *J.M.G.*, 632 A.2d at 553 ("The court feels constrained by the state of the law from proclaiming J.M.G. an actual 'stepparent', given the fact that same-sex marriages are not legal in this state. However, I am convinced that in this adoption, J.M.G. should be treated as a stepparent

as a matter of common sense, and in order to protect the child's interests in maintaining her relationship with her biological mother."); Denise Glaser Malloy, Note, "Another Mother?: The Courts' Denial of Legal Status to the Non-Biological Parent upon Dissolution of Lesbian Families," 31 *U. Louisville J. Fam. L.* 981, 985 (1992) ("The status of the non-biological parent in a lesbian family is clearly analogous to that of the stepparent in this scenario.").

114 Zuckerman, Comment, "Second Parent Adoption," at 737 (stepparent adoption merely formalizes an existing relationship); Note, *Joint Adoption: A Queer Option?*, 15 Vt. L. Rev. 197, 201 (1990) ("in a stepparent adoption an existing relationship is merely formalized").

115 See *Adoptions of B.L.V.B. and E.L.V.B.*, 628 A.2d 1271, 1276 (Vt. 1993).

116 See *In re Clausen*, 502 N.W.2d 649, 668 (Mich. 1993) (discussing protection given to parent-child relationships).

117 *In re Interest of Z.J.H.*, 471 N.W.2d 202, 205 (Wis. 1991), overruled by *In re Custody of H.S.H.-K.*, 533 N.W.2d 419 (Wis. 1995).

118 See, for example, Wis. Stat. Ann. 48.92 (West 1995 Supp.) ("After the order of adoption is entered the relationship of parent and child between the adopted person and the adopted person's birth parents . . . shall be completely altered and all the rights, duties and other legal consequences of the relationship shall cease to exist."); Polikoff, "This Child Does Have Two Mothers," at 476–77 ("if a stepparent adoption is completed, the noncustodial biological parent becomes a legal stranger to the child").

119 See *Z.J.H.*, 471 N.W.2d at 205 ("a non-parent may not bring an action to obtain custody of a minor child unless the natural or adoptive parent is unfit or unable to care for the child, or there are compelling reasons for awarding custody to a third party").

120 See *In re A. J. J.*, 438 N.Y.S.2d 444, 446 (Sur. Ct. 1981) ("the Legislature has carved an exception to this section that provides for retention of responsibilities and rights so long as the natural parent having lawful custody of the child marries or remarries and consents that the stepfather or stepmother adopt the child").

121 See, for example, Wis. Stat. Ann. 48.835(3)(b) (West 1987) ("If the person filing the adoption petition is a stepparent with whom the child and the child's parent reside, the stepparent shall file only a petition to terminate the parental rights of the parent who does not have custody of the child.")

122 See *Simpson v. Simpson*, 586 S.W.2d 33, 35 (Ky. 1979) (must prove custodial parent unfit); see also *Zack v. Fiebert*, 563 A.2d 58, 63 (N.J. App. 1989)("normally, when a third party seeks custody as against a natural parent, the standard should be the termination standard of unfitness"); *In re Camilla*, 620 N.Y.S.2d 897, 901 (Fam. Ct. 1994) ("in the majority of adoptions, it is anticipated that children will be removed from the home of the biological parent(s)").

123 Davies, Note, "Two Moms and a Baby," at 1067 (stepparent exception

created precisely because parent and stepparent will live together with child).

124   *In re Custody of Menconi*, 453 N.E.2d 835, 837 (Ill. App. 1983) (nonconsenting parent must be shown to be unfit); *In re Adoption of Children by D.*, 293 A.2d 171, 172–73 (N.J. 1972) ("a court must act with great caution and circumspection when one natural parent does not consent to the proposed adoption").

125   *In re Interest of R.C.*, 775 P.2d 27, 28 (Colo. 1989) (en banc) ("Agreement is likewise not a relevant consideration when the semen donor is anonymous.").

126   See, for example, Wis. Stat. Ann. 48.835(3)(b) (West 1987).

127   516 N.W.2d 678, 682 (Wis. 1994).

128   Id. at 686.

129   Id. at 682.

130   Id. See also *J.M.G.*, 632 A.2d at 552 (construing stepparent statute liberally so that the rights of one of the biological parents did not have to be terminated).

131   *Angel Lace*, 516 N.W.2d at 682 ("a complete stranger could petition to adopt a minor who is a member of this stable family").

132   Id. at 689 (Heffernan, J., dissenting).

133   See id. at 693 (Heffernan, J., dissenting: "It seems highly unlikely that a court would find such an adoption to be in the best interests of the child.")

134   Id. at 687 (Wis. 1994) (Geske, J., concurring).

135   Id. (Geske, J., concurring).

136   Other courts have taken the tack which would promote the interests of all concerned parties. See, for example, *H.N.R.*, 666 A.2d at 538 (liberally construing statute to benefit all).

137   *Angel Lace*, 516 N.W.2d at 687 (Heffernan, J., dissenting: "The adoption statutes on their face do not address this issue.").

138   Id. at 693 (Heffernan, J., dissenting, discussing "the legislature's clear statement that the best interests of the child are paramount").

139   See *Adoption of Tammy*, 619 N.E.2d 315 (Mass. 1993); *Adoptions of B.L.V.B. and E.L.V.B.*, 628 A.2d 1271 (Vt. 1993). See also *Jacob*, 660 N.E.2d at 399 ("What is to be construed strictly and applied rigorously in this sensitive area of the law, however, is legislative purpose as well as legislative language. Thus, the adoption statute must be applied in harmony with the humanitarian principle that adoption is a means of securing the best possible home for a child.").

140   *Petition of Curran*, 49 N.E.2d 432 (Mass. 1943); Bridges v. Nicely, 497 A.2d 142 (Md. 1985); *In re Jessica W.*, 453 A.2d 1297 (N.H. 1982); *In re Adoption of a Child by A.R.*, 378 A.2d 87 (N.J. Super. 1977); *In re Anonymous Adoption*, 31 N.Y.S.2d 595 (Sur. Ct. 1941).

141   Other statutes were similar rather than identical. See *Angel Lace*, 516

N.W.2d at 692 (Heffernan, J., dissenting: "Although the statutes interpreted in [the Massachusetts and Vermont] cases are not identical to those of Wisconsin, they have congruent purposes and thus the interpretation by those courts is highly relevant.").

142 *Adoptions of B.L.V.B. and E.L.V.B.*, 628 A.2d 1271, 1272 (Vt. 1993) ("absurd result"); *In re Dana*, 624 N.Y.S.2d 634, 635 (N.Y. App. 1995) (result would be "ludicrous"), rev'd sub nom. *In re Jacob*, 660 N.E.2d 397 (N.Y. 1995); *Petition of L.S. and V.L.*, 1991 WL 219598 at *2 ("particularly counterproductive and even ludicrous result"); *H.N.R.*, 666 A.2d at 538 ("wholly absurd and untenable result").

143 *Adoption of Tammy*, 619 N.E.2d 315 (Mass. 1993).

144 *Adoptions of B.L.V.B. and E.L.V.B.*, 628 A.2d 1271 (Vt. 1993).

145 *In re Jacob*, 660 N.E.2d 397 (N.Y. 1995).

146 *B.L.V.B.*, 628 A.2d at 1272 (7 years); *Tammy*, 619 N.E.2d at 316 (10 years); *Jacob*, 660 N.E.2d at 398 (19 years). See also *Camilla*, 620 N.Y.S.2d at 899 (9 years); *J.M.G.*, 632 A.2d at 551 (10 years).

147 See *B.L.V.B.*, 628 A.2d at 1276 ("To deny legal protection of their relationship, as a matter of law, is inconsistent with the children's best interests and therefore with the public policy of this state, as expressed in our statutes affecting children."); *Tammy*, 619 N.E.2d at 320 (discussing benefits of adoption); *Jacob*, 660 N.E.2d at 399 (discussing benefits of that adoption).

148 *B.L.V.B.*, 628 A.2d at 1274. See also *J.M.G.*, 632 A.2d at 553 ("it would defeat the purpose of the adoption to cut off the parental rights of the biological mother, and it would be antithetical to the child's best interests. The point of this adoption is to give the child all of the benefits of having both 'parents' legally responsible for her well being.").

149 *B.L.V.B.*, 628 A.2d at 1276.

150 *A.C. v. C.B.*, 829 P.2d 660, 661 (N.M. App. 1992) (after living together for 7 years, "the parties, according to Petitioner, entered into an oral agreement to raise a child as coparents"), cert. denied, 827 P.2d 837 (N.M. 1992); *Alison D. v. Virginia M.*, 572 N.E.2d 27, 28 (N.Y. 1991) ("Together, they planned for the conception and birth of the child and agreed to share jointly all rights and responsibilities of child-rearing"); Malloy, Note, "Another Mother?," at 997 ("A stepparent enters the relationship with the children based solely on the marriage to the child's biological parent. However, in lesbian families, the women make a conscious decision to conceive a child by artificial insemination or adoption."); Paula Ettelbrick, "Who Is a Parent?: The Need to Develop a Lesbian Conscious Family Law," 10 *N. Y. L. Sch. J. Hum. Rts.* 513, 516–17 (1993) ("Typically, a lesbian couple will decide to have a child and agree that both will raise their child as co-equal parents, despite the fact that only one may be a biological or adoptive parent. Both women plan for the pregnancy, share in providing financial and emotional support for the child, and assume child care responsibilities.").

151 See *Angel Lace*, 516 N.W.2d at 686 ("Annette may not adopt Angel because Annette and Georgina are not married.") See also *Beatty v. Truck Ins. Exch.*, 8 Cal.Rptr.2d 593, 596 (Ct. App. 1992) ("To the extent plaintiffs were treated differently than a 'married couple', it is because they are not married and not because they are homosexuals."); *Hinman v. Dept. of Personnel Admin.*, 213 Cal.Rptr. 410, 416 (Ct. App. 1985) ("Homosexuals are simply a part of the larger class of unmarried persons"); *Phillips v. Wisconsin Personnel Comm'n*, 482 N.W.2d 121, 129 (Wis. App. 1992) (appellant is "in the same position as all unmarried heterosexual males and females").

152 *Jacob*, 660 N.E.2d at 405 (opposite-sex partners have option to marry whereas same-sex partners do not).

153 See *Shahar v. Bowers*, 70 F.3d 1218, 1223 (11th Cir. 1995) (describing religious same-sex ceremony), vacated, reh'g granted en banc, 78 F.3d 499 (11th Cir. 1996) reh'g 114 F.3d 1097 (11th Cir. 1997) (en banc), aff'g 836 F. Supp. 859 (N.D. Ga. 1993); *Nancy S. v. Michele G.*, 279 Cal.Rptr. 212, 214 (Ct. App. 1991) ("In August of 1969, appellant and respondent began living together, and in November of that year they had a private 'marriage' ceremony."); *Angel Lace*, 516 N.W.2d at 680 ("Georgina and Annette symbolically solemnized their commitment to each other by partaking in a marriage-like ceremony in Milwaukee.")

154 Joseph Arsenault, Comment, "'Family' but Not 'Parent': The Same-Sex Coupling Jurisprudence of the New York Court of Appeals," 58 *Alb. L. Rev.* 813, 835 (1995) ("If the law requires marriage for legal recognition and yet forbids same-sex partners to marry, it inherently discriminates against the members of such a union.").

V FULL FAITH AND CREDIT

1 U.S. Constitution, Art. IV, Sec. 1.

2 Id. ("And the Congress may by general laws prescribe the Manner in which such Acts, Records and Proceedings shall be proved, and the Effect thereof.").

3 1 U.S. Stat. at Large 122 (properly authenticated records and judicial proceedings "shall have such faith and credit given to them in every court within the United States, as they have by law or usage in the courts of the state from whence the said records are or shall be taken.").

4 See *Morris v. Jones*, 329 U.S. 545, 547 (1947).

5 Judgments subject to modification in the rendering state, e.g., judgments concerning child custody and support, would also be subject to modification elsewhere. This has led to abuse, forcing Congress to pass the Parental Kidnapping Prevention Act, 28 United States Code Annotated (U.S.C.A.) Sec. 1738A, and the Full Faith and Credit for Child Support Orders Act, 28 U.S.C.A. Sec. 1738B.

6 320 U.S. 430, 439 (1943).

7 *Milwaukee County v. M. E. White Co.*, 296 U.S. 268, 277 (1935).

8   *Sherrer v. Sherrer*, 334 U.S. 343, 355 (1948).

9   *Vanderbilt v. Vanderbilt*, 354 U.S. 416, 426 (1957) (Frankfurter, J., dissenting) (italics added).

10 *Estin v. Estin*, 334 U.S. 541, 546 (1948).

11 *Bradford Electric Light Co. Inc. v. Clapper*, 286 U.S. 145, 162 (1932).

12 *Estin*, 334 U.S. at 546 (Full Faith and Credit substitutes "a command for the earlier principles of comity").

13 *Golden v. Golden*, 68 P.2d 928, 932 (N.M. 1937) ("the 'full faith and credit' clause of the Constitution of the United States (Art. 4, Sec. 1), . . . is not applicable to the judgments of foreign countries.").

14 *Clapper*, 286 U.S. at 154.

15 *Hilton v. Guyot*, 159 U.S. 113, 163–164 (1895) ("'Comity', in the legal sense, is neither a matter of absolute obligation, on the one hand, nor of mere courtesy and good will, upon the other.").

16 *Bobala v. Bobala*, 33 N.E.2d 845, 849 (Ohio App. 1940).

17 *Rosenstiel v. Rosenstiel*, 209 N.E.2d 709, 715 (N.Y. 1965) (Desmond, C.J. concurring in part), cert. denied, 383 U.S. 943 (1966).

18 Id. (legitimate goal of administrative convenience not sufficient to overcome full faith and credit obligation); *Magnolia Petroleum*, 320 U.S. at 439 (discussing various legitimate interests not sufficiently compelling to overcome full faith and credit obligation); *Kenney v. Supreme Lodge of the World*, 252 U.S. 411, 414–15 (1920) (discussing policy not sufficiently contravened to justify refusal to credit a foreign judgment).

19 334 U.S. 541, 545–46 (1948).

20 Id. at 546.

21 Compare *Intercontinental Hotels Corporation v. Golden*, 254 N.Y.S.2d 527 (N.Y. 1964) (gambling debts enforcible under Puerto Rican law are enforcible in New York) with *Dorado Beach Hotel Corp. v. Jernigan*, 202 So.2d 830 (Fla. App. 1967) (gambling debt enforcible in Puerto Rico not enforcible in Florida), *appeal dismissed*, 209 So.2d 669 (Fla. 1968).

22 337 U.S. 38, 42 (1949).

23 *Williams v. North Carolina*, 317 U.S. 287, 289 (1942) (*Williams I*) ("Petitioners were tried and convicted of bigamous cohabitation under s 4342 of the North Carolina Code, 1939, and each was sentenced for a term of years to a state prison.").

24 If Mr. Jones knows of his wife's address, then he can give actual notice by sending her a letter, fax, or telegram informing her of his intention. If he does not know and cannot find out through reasonable efforts where she lives, for example, because she moved once he left to live in State B, Mr. Jones can give constructive notice by publication. See Homer Clark, *The Law of Domestic Relations in the United States*, 421–22 (2d ed., 1988).

25 *Cook v. Cook*, 342 U.S. 126, 128 (1951) ("A judgment presumes jurisdiction over the subject matter and over the persons.").

26 *Williams v. North Carolina*, 325 U.S. 226, 230 (1945) (*Williams II*).

27 Id. at 237.

28 *Sherrer*, 334 U.S. at 351.

29 Id. at 354.

30 C. W. Taintor, II, "What Law Governs the Ceremony Incidents and Status of Marriage," 19 *B. U. L. Rev.* 353, 367 (1939) ("Since the question of the creation of the marriage status must be referred to the law of some state or to the laws of two states acting together, the problem is one of choice of law. "); Robert Cordell II, "Same-Sex Marriage: The Fundamental Right of Marriage and an Examination of Conflict of Laws and the Full Faith and Credit Clause," 26 *Colum. Hum. Rts. L. Rev.* 247, 265 (1994) ("the decision to honor a marriage from another state, especially a marriage which conflicts with the laws in the state deciding, involves a choice of laws question").

31 See Stewart Sterk, "The Marginal Relevance of Choice of Law Theory," 142 *U. Pa. L. Rev.* 949, 951 (1994).

32 *Allstate Insurance Co. v. Hague*, 449 U.S. 302, 310–11 (1981).

33 See id. at 334–38 (Powell, J., dissenting, describing the insignificant contacts which the Court nonetheless held were sufficient).

34 486 U.S. 717, 727 (1988).

35 294 U.S. 532, 548 (1935).

36 Id. at 547.

37 *Vandever v. Industrial Commission of Arizona*, 714 P.2d 866, 869 (Ariz. App. 1986) ("The exceptions to this general rule are extremely limited and include only the strongest of public policy considerations."); Eugene Scoles and Peter Hay, *Conflict of Laws*, Sec. 13.5, (2d ed., 1992) ("a marriage is valid everywhere if valid under the law of the state where the marriage takes place, except in rare instances").

38 *Barrons v. United States*, 191 F.2d 92, 95 (9th Cir. 1951) ("A marriage is generally recognized as valid in any state if it was valid in the state where it was celebrated, at least unless it collides with some strong public policy of the state of residence.").

39 *In re Estate of Lenherr*, 314 A.2d 255, 258 (Pa. 1974) (discussing the *Second Restatement*'s specification that a marriage valid in the place of celebration is valid everywhere "unless it violates the strong public policy of another state which had the most significant relationship to the spouses and the marriage at the time of the marriage [quoting *Second Restatement*, Sec. 283]").

40 See *First Restatement*, Sec. 132 and *Second Restatement*, Sec. 283.

41 *First Restatement*, Sec. 121. The American Law Institute (comprised of lawyers, judges, and law professors) puts out the Restatements, which offer a (re)statement of the law as it develops in the United States. The Restatements are highly influential but are not binding on an individual state unless the state itself decides to adopt the position offered in the Restatement.

42 Id. Sec. 132, Cmt. b.

43 Id. Sec. 132, Cmt. b.

44 Id. Sec. 132, Cmt. c.

45 *Second Restatement,* Sec. 283.

46 *First Restatement,* Sec. 132 (italics added).

47 Compare id. Sec. 132 Cmt. b (describing void marriage as one which offends strong policy) with *Second Restatement,* Sec. 283 (suggesting that marriages need not be recognized if they violate the strong public policy of the state).

48 *Laikola v. Engineered Concrete,* 277 N.W.2d 653, 656 (Minn. 1979) ("marriages declared void by the Minnesota Legislature demonstrate a strong public policy. Therefore, out-of-state marriages by Minnesota residents that would be void under Minnesota law should not be recognized by the Minnesota court.").

49 *People, on Complaint of Kay v. Kay,* 252 N.Y.S. 518, 523 (Mag. Ct. 1931). See also *Succession of Gabisso,* 44 So. 438, 441 (La. 1907) ("The marriage here relied on, being an absolute nullity in contravention of public policy and good morals, was not susceptible of ratification, acquired no validity by the lapse of time, remains open to attack, and cannot serve as the basis of an action; in short, in legal contemplation, it never existed.").

50 *In re Kinkead's Estate,* 57 N.W.2d 628, 633 (Minn. 1953) ("the far-reaching ramifications of treating a marriage as a nullity forbid that it should be held invalid without a decree of dissolution unless it is expressly declared void by statute").

51 *In re Estate of Loughmiller,* 629 P.2d 156, 158 (Kan. 1981).

52 Compare *In re Estate of Mortenson,* 316 P.2d 1106 (Ariz., 1957) (holding marriage void) with *In re Estate of Loughmiller,* 629 P.2d 156 (Kan. 1981) (recognizing marriage).

53 See *Loughmiller,* 629 P.2d at 161 ("The reason for the inclusion of first cousins in K.S.A. 23–102 has become less compelling in recent years as evidenced by the legislature's omission of sexual intercourse between first cousins in the definition of incest."); *Mazzolini,* 155 N.E.2d at 209 ("by Section 2905.07, Revised Code, sexual relations between cousins are not incestuous").

54 See *Reynolds v. United States,* 98 U.S. 145, 165 (1878). This was up to Congress rather than a state legislature because it involved a territory of the United States. See id. at 166 ("It is constitutional and valid as prescribing a rule of action for all those residing in the Territories, and in places over which the United States have conclusive control.").

55 See *Potter v. Murray City,* 760 F.2d 1065, 1070 (10th Cir.) ("the State is justified, by a compelling interest, in upholding and enforcing its ban on plural marriage"), cert. denied, 474 U.S. 849 (1985).

56 *Hallowell v. Commons,* 210 F. 793, 800 (8th Cir. 1914); *Wall v. Williams,* 11

Ala. 826, 837–838 (1847); *Kobogum v. Jackson Iron Co.*, 43 N.W. 602, 603 (Mich. 1889); *Compo v. Jackson Iron Co.*, 6 N.W. 295, 296 (Mich. 1883); *United States ex rel. Davis v. Shanks*, 15 Minn. 302 (Minn. 1870); *Boyer v. Dively*, 58 Mo. 510 (1875); *Ortley v. Ross*, 110 N.W. 982, 982–83 (Neb. 1907); *Hastings v. Farmer*, 4 N.Y. 293, 294 (1850); *Morgan v. M'Ghee*, 24 Tenn. 5, 6–7 (5 Humph. 13, 14) (1844).

57   *Hallowell*, 210 F. at 800; *Kobogum*, 43 N.W. at 605 ("The United States supreme court and the state courts have recognized as law that no state laws have any force over Indians in their tribal relations."); *Shanks*, 15 Minn. at 304 ("The Indians within our territory have always been considered and recognized by the United States as distinct political communities; and so far as is essential to constitute them separate nations, the rights of sovereignty have been conceded to them.").

58   175 U.S. 1, 10 (1899).

59   118 U.S. 375, 381–82 (1886).

60   See *Kobogum*, 43 N.W. at 605 (The tribes "were placed by the constitution of the United States beyond our jurisdiction, and we had no more right to control their domestic usages than those of Turkey or India.").

61   See *People v. Ezeonu*, 588 N.Y.S.2d 116 (Crim. Ct. 1992).

62   *Kobogum*, 43 N.W. at 603; *Ortley v. Ross*, 110 N.W. 982 (Neb. 1907).

63   Cf. *Stevens v. United States*, 146 F.2d 120, 122 (10th Cir., 1944).

64   See *Black's Law Dictionary*, (6th ed., 1990) 267 ("Comity: Courtesy, complaisance; respect; a willingness to grant a privilege, not as a matter of right, but one of deference and good will.").

65   For example, the recognition of tribal marriages might be thought required were this construed as a supremacy issue, given that Congress has authority over the tribes. See *Shanks*, 15 Minn. at 304 ("If it were necessary to find a jurisdiction, we might find it in the United States government, which has under the constitution power to regulate commerce with these Indian tribes."). Cf. *Hallowell*, 210 F. at 800 ("The Indians were subject, while their tribal relations existed, to the laws only of Congress, and in the absence of such laws were left to be governed by their own laws and customs as to domestic and social practices including marriage, and whether they should practice monogamy or polygamy was left wholly to them."). Were this a supremacy issue, the recognition would not be extended out of comity, but out of constitutional mandate.

66   See, for example, *Morgan*, 24 Tenn. at 6 (5 Humph. at 14) ("Our courts of justice recognize as valid all marriages of a foreign country, if made in pursuance of the forms and usages of that country; and there is no reason why a marriage made and celebrated in an Indian Nation should be subject to a different rule of action.").

67   See *Gibson v. Hughes*, 192 F. Supp. 564 (S.D.N.Y. 1961); *In re Dalip Singh Bir's Estate*, 188 P.2d 499, 501 (Cal. App. 1948).

68   See *Dalip Singh*, 188 P.2d at 501 (citing cases in which Native American

polygamous marriages have been recognized for certain purposes). *Dalip Singh* has itself been cited with approval by other courts. See *Gibson*, 192 F. Supp. at 569; *Lenherr*, 314 A.2d at 258 n.4.

69 388 U.S. 1 (1967).

70 See, for example, *Medway v. Needham*, 16 Mass. 157 (1819).

71 *First Restatement*, Sec. 132(c).

72 Id. Sec. 132, Cmt. c.

73 *Adams v. Gay*, 19 Vt. 358, 367 (1847).

74 Id.

75 Id.

76 John Stuart Mill, "Whewell on Moral Philosophy," in *Collected Works of John Stuart Mill*, vol. 10, ed. John Robson (1969), 167, 179.

77 Id.

78 Id. at 194.

79 Uniform Laws Annotated (U.L.A.) Marr. & Divorce Sec. 207 (1970) (amended 1973). The National Conference of Commissioners on Uniform State Laws (composed of lawyers, judges, legislators, and law school professors) proposes Uniform Laws which, it is hoped, each state will adopt. The Uniform Laws are influential but are not binding on a state until that state officially adopts the Uniform Law (possibly amended in light of state concerns) as its own.

80 See *Vandever*, 714 P.2d at 869 ("The only marriages validly contracted in another jurisdiction that are denied recognition in Arizona are those involving the marriage of persons with a certain degree of consanguinity."); *Spencer v. People in Interest of Spencer*, 292 P.2d 971, 973 (Colo. 1956) (en banc) (discussing Colorado statute which reads "All marriages contracted without this state, which shall be valid by the laws of the country in which the same were contracted, shall be valid in all courts within this state. This section shall not be construed so as to allow bigamy or polygamy in this state.").

81 *Wilson v. Cook*, 100 N.E. 222, 222 (Ill. 1912) (italics added); see also *Lanham v. Lanham*, 117 N.W. 787, 788 (Wis. 1908).

82 See *Lanham*, 117 N.W. at 788 (The exception—"Marriages which are deemed contrary to the law of nature as generally recognized by Christian civilized states . . . covers polygamous and incestuous marriages."). See also *Bronislawa K. v. Tadeusz K.*, 393 N.Y.S.2d 534, 535 (1977); *Spencer*, 292 P.2d at 973; *Pearson v. Pearson*, 51 Cal. 120, 125 (Cal. 1875); *McDonald v. McDonald*, 58 P.2d 163, 164 (Cal. 1936) (in bank)("An exception, of course, arises when the marriage is regarded as odious by common consent of nations; e. g., where it is polygamous or incestuous by the laws of nature.").

83 See *In re Custody of H.S.H.-K.*, 533 N.W.2d 419, 439 (Wis. 1995) (Day, J., concurring and dissenting: "Sweden, Denmark and Norway have all legalized same-sex marriages"); Martha Nussbaum, "Platonic Love and Colo-

rado Law: The Relevance of Ancient Greek Norms to Modern Sexual Controversies," 80 *Va. L. Rev.* 1515, 1524 (1994) ("four of the five Scandinavian countries, having already protected homosexuals from discrimination, have also adopted some form of domestic partnership registration for same-sex couples in order to give these couples the tax, inheritance, and other civic benefits of marriage."); Jorge Martin, "English Polygamy Law and the Danish Registered Partnership Act: A Case for the Consistent Treatment of Foreign Polygamous Marriages and Danish Same-Sex Marriages in England," 27 *Cornell Int'l L. J.* 419, 419 (1994) ("Denmark became the first country in modern Western civilization legally to recognize same-sex marriages, officially calling these unions 'registered partnerships'."); Michael L. Closen and Joan E. Maloney, "The Health Care Surrogate Act in Illinois: Another Rejection of Domestic Partners' Rights," 19 *Southern Illinois Univ. L. J.* 479, 513–14 (1995) ("Denmark, Finland and Sweden have adopted legislation effectively sanctioning same-sex marriages, and Greenland is about to do so as well.").

84 See *Naim v. Naim*, 87 S.E.2d 749, 752 (Va. 1955) (discussing with approval a case holding that "the natural law which forbids their intermarriage and the social amalgamation which leads to a corruption of races is as clearly divine as that which imparted to them different natures."). See also *Loving*, 388 U.S. at 3 (discussing the trial court's view that God did not intend such marriages).

85 *Linton v. Linton*, 420 A.2d 1249, 1251 (1980) (Md. App. 1980).

86 See *Rochin v. California*, 342 U.S. 165, 171 (1952) (suggesting that due process of law "is not to be derided as resort to a revival of 'natural law'"); *Adamson v. California*, 332 U.S. 46, 74 (1947) (Black, J., dissenting, suggesting that the "natural law formula . . . should be abandoned as an incongruous excrescence on our Constitution").

87 See *Sniadach v. Family Finance Corp. of Bay View*, 395 U.S. 337, 351 (1969) (Black, J., dissenting, describing the "Natural Law concept which under our system leaves to judges alone the power to decide what the Natural Law means. These so-called standards do not bind judges within any boundaries that can be precisely marked or defined by words for holding laws unconstitutional.").

88 See *Bowers*, 478 U.S. at 211 (Blackmun, J., dissenting, "The legitimacy of secular legislation depends . . . on whether the State can advance some justification for its law beyond its conformity to religious doctrine.").

89 Id. at 196.

90 *Barnes v. Glen Theatre, Inc.*, 501 U.S. 560, 580 (1991) (Scalia, J., concurring in the judgment); David S. Caudill, "Legal Recognition of Unmarried Cohabitation: A Proposal to Update and Reconsider Common-Law Marriage," 49 *Tenn. L. Rev.* 537, 557 (1982); J. Harvie Wilkinson III and G. Edward White, "Constitutional Protection for Personal Lifestyles," 62 *Cornell L. Rev.* 563, 617 (1977).

91   *Kinney v. Commonwealth*, 71 Va. 858, 860 (1878) ("other marriages . . . are voidable only—that is, declared to be void only from the time they shall be so declared by decree of divorce or nullity").

92   *In re Interest of S.I.*, 173 A.2d 457, 460 (1961) ("Until so annulled, however, this court is required to recognize the marriage as valid.").

93   See *Wilkins v. Zelichowski*, 129 A.2d 459, 462 (N.J. App. 1957), rev'd, 140 A.2d 65 (N.J. 1958).

94   *Mangrum v. Mangrum*, 220 S.W.2d 406, 408 (Ky. 1949) ("a marriage under age may be ratified by later cohabitation").

95   *Loughran v. Loughran*, 292 U.S. 216, 223 (1934); *Kinkead's Estate*, 57 N.W.2d at 632.

96   *In re Estate of Lenherr*, 314 A.2d 255, 258 (Penn. 1974).

97   *Kinkead's Estate*, 57 N.W.2d at 631.

98   *Cf. Mangrum*, 220 S.W.2d at 408 ("If the Legislature had intended to declare such a marriage against the public policy of the state, it would have made it absolutely void regardless of the place where the marriage ceremony was performed."). But see *Johnson v. Lincoln Square Properties*, 571 So.2d 541, 542 (Fla. App. 1990) (marriage void according to Florida law nonetheless recognized).

99   See, for example, *Mazzolini*, 155 N.E.2d at 208 (upholding the marriage, noting that the Legislature had not explicitly made marriages between first cousins void).

100   *Perez*, 198 P.2d at 25.

101   *Schwartz v. Schwartz*, 236 Ill. App. 336, 338 (1925) (emphasis added) ("The only marriages which by [the Uniform Evasion Act] are made null and void are marriages which are contracted in a foreign state or country by residents of this state and which could not be contracted in this state because they are *prohibited and declared void* by the laws of this state.") Approval for the Uniform Evasion Act has been withdrawn by the National Conference of Commissioners on Uniform State Laws. See Unif. Marr. & Divorce Act, Sec. 210 Cmt.; Scoles and Hay, *Conflict of Laws*, Sec. 15.16 (2d ed., 1992).

102   Ill. Ann. Stat. Chap. 750, Sec. 5/216 (West 1993) (italics added):
      if any person residing and intending to continue to reside in this state and who is disabled or prohibited from contracting marriage under the laws of this state, shall go into another state or country and there contract a marriage *prohibited and declared void* by the laws of this state, such marriage shall be null and void for all purposes in this state with the same effect as though such prohibited marriage had been entered into in this state.
      Vt. Stat. Ann. Tit. 15, Sec. 5 (1989) (italics added):
      If a person residing and intending to continue to reside in this state is prohibited from contracting marriage under the laws of this state and such person goes into another state or country and there contracts a

marriage *prohibited and declared void* by the laws of this state, such marriage shall be null and void for all purposes in this state.

Mass. Gen. Laws. Ann. Chap. 207, Sec. 10 (West 1987) (italics added):

If any person residing and intending to continue to reside in this commonwealth is disabled or prohibited from contracting marriage under the laws of this commonwealth and goes into another jurisdiction and there contracts a marriage *prohibited and declared void* by the laws of this commonwealth, such marriage shall be null and void for all purposes in this commonwealth with the same effect as though such prohibited marriage had been entered into in this commonwealth.

Miss. Code Ann. Sec. 93–1-3 (1994) ("Any attempt to evade section 93–1-1 [incestuous and void marriages] by marrying out of this state and returning to it shall be within the prohibitions of said section."). Me. Rev. Stat. Ann. tit. 19, Sec. 91 (West 1981) ("When residents of this State, with intent to evade subchapter II [void marriages] and to return and reside here, go into another state or country and there have their marriage solemnized and afterwards return and reside here, such marriage is void in this State.").

103   Wis. Stat. Ann. 765.04 (West 1993) (italics added):

If any person residing and intending to continue to reside in this state who is disabled or prohibited from contracting marriage under the laws of this state goes into another state or country and there contracts a marriage *prohibited or declared void* under the laws of this state, such marriage shall be void for all purposes in this state with the same effect as though it had been entered into in this state.

See also *Johnson v. Johnson*, 104 N.W.2d 8, 13 (N.D. 1960) ("the validity of marriages prohibited by the laws of this state when contracted outside of North Dakota by residents of this state will be determined according to our laws").

104   *In re May's Estate*, 114 N.E.2d 4, 7 (N.Y. 1953); *Leefeld v. Leefeld*, 166 P. 953, 954 (Or. 1917).

105   See Unif. Marr. & Divorce Act, Sec. 210 Cmt. ("This section . . . codifies the emerging conflicts principle that marriages valid by the laws of the state where contracted should be valid everywhere, even if the parties to the marriage would not have been permitted to marry in the state of their domicil. . . . [T]he section expressly fails to incorporate the 'strong public policy' exception of the *Restatement* and hence may change the law in come jurisdictions."); see also *Leszinske v. Poole*, 798 P.2d 1049, 1054 (N.M. App.), cert. denied, 797 P.2d 983 (N.M. 1990).

106   Compare *Loughmiller*, 629 P.2d at 161 ("Although our statutes prohibit first cousin marriages and impose criminal penalties where such marriages are contracted in Kansas, we cannot find that a first cousin marriage validly contracted elsewhere is odious to the public policy of this state. The reason for the inclusion of first cousins in K.S.A. 23–102 has

become less compelling in recent years as evidenced by the legislature's omission of sexual intercourse between first cousins in the definition of incest.") with *Catalano v. Catalano*, 170 A.2d 726, 728 (Conn. 1961) ("To determine whether the marriage in the instant case is contrary to the public policy of this state, it is only necessary to consider that marriages between uncle and niece have been interdicted and declared void continuously since 1702 and that ever since then it has been a crime for such kindred to either marry or carnally know each other."). See also *United States ex rel. Devine v. Rodgers*, 109 F. 886, 888 (E.D. Pa. 1901) ("it seems to me to be impossible to recognize this marriage as valid in Pennsylvania, since a continuance of the relation here would at once expose the parties to indictment in the criminal courts, and to punishment by fine and imprisonment in the penitentiary."); *Toler v. Oakwood Smokeless Coal Corporation*, 4 S.E.2d 364, 368 (Va. 1939) ("The statutes and public policy of Virginia as reflected by legislative pronouncement and judicial construction, are emphatically opposed to the recognition of the validity of a bigamous union. . . . The punishment in this State for bigamy is not less than three nor more than eight years in the penitentiary.").

107   See, for example, Mass. Gen. Laws Ann. Chap. 151B, Sec. 4, notes on Section 19 (West 1996) (employment discrimination act including orientation should not "be construed so as to legitimize or validate a 'homosexual marriage'").

108   Larry Kramer, "Return of the Renvoi," 66 *N. Y. U. L. Rev.* 979, 1016–17 (1991).

109   See generally Jennifer Gerarda Brown, "Competitive Federalism and the Legislative Incentives to Recognize Same-Sex Marriage," 68 *S. Cal. L. Rev.* 745 (1995).

110   Scoles and Hay, *Conflict of Laws*, Sec. 13.8, (2d ed., 1992) (discussing the "strong public policy . . . for upholding the validity of marriage wherever possible").

VI   THE DEFENSE OF MARRIAGE ACT

1   See Associated Press, "Clinton Draws Criticism from Gay Activists," *Chicago Tribune*, September 23, 1996 at 6 ("Clinton signed the Defense of Marriage Act into law early Saturday" [September 21]).

2   Sometimes, states will recognize marriages validly celebrated elsewhere, even if they are void in the domicile. See, e.g., *In re May's Estate*, 114 N.E.2d 4 (N.Y. 1953) and *Horton v. Horton*, 198 P. 1105 (Ariz. 1921).

3   For further discussion of these and related issues, see Mark Strasser, "Judicial Good Faith and the *Baehr* Essentials; On Giving Credit Where It's Due," 28 *Rutgers L. J.* 313 (1997).

4   See *Restatement (Second) of the Conflicts of Laws*, Sec. 283 (a "marriage which satisfies the requirements of the state where the marriage was

contracted will everywhere be recognized as valid unless it violates the strong public policy of another state which had the most significant relationship to the spouses and the marriage at the time of the marriage.").

5 See Russell Weintraub, *Commentary on the Conflict of Laws* (2d ed., 1980), Sec. 5.1C ("A marriage should be upheld whenever valid to avoid upsetting the expectations of the parties and to legitimate children.").

6 *Madewell v. United States*, 84 F. Supp. 329, 332 (E.D. Tenn. 1949).

7 *Wilkins v. Zelichowski*, 129 A.2d 459, 461 (N.J. App. 1957), *rev'd*, 140 A.2d 65 (N.J. 1958).

8 *Vandever v. Industrial Commission of Arizona*, 714 P.2d 866, 869 (Ariz. App. 1986).

9 See Thomas Keane, Note, "Aloha, Marriage? Constitutional and Choice of Law Arguments for Recognition of Same-Sex Marriages," 47 *Stan. L. Rev.* 499, 516 (1995) ("Clarity of marital status gives the married couple security in their relationship and also benefits third parties, notably children and creditors."). See also Joseph Hovermill, "A Conflict of Laws and Morals: The Choice of Law Implications of Hawaii's Recognition of Same-Sex Marriages," 53 *Md. L. Rev.* 450, 455 (1994) ("A choice of law rule that validates out-of-state marriages provides stability and predictability in questions of marriage, ensures the legitimization of children, protects party expectations, and promotes interstate comity.").

10 See *Boddie v. Connecticut*, 401 U.S. 371, 373 (1971) (italics added) ("given the basic position of the *marriage relationship* in this society's hierarchy of values . . . , due process does prohibit a State from denying, solely because of inability to pay, access to its courts to individuals who seek judicial dissolution of their marriages").

11 See *Sosna v. Iowa*, 419 U.S. 393, 406 (1975) (upholding Iowa's residency requirement for divorce).

12 See id. at 406.

13 See *Kinkead's Estate*, 57 N.W.2d at 632.

14 *Loughran*, 292 U.S. at 223.

15 See, for example, *Second Restatement*, Sec. 283.

16 See *Black's Law Dictionary*, 655 (6th ed., 1990) (Forum shopping: "Such occurs when a party attempts to have his action tried in a particular court or jurisdiction where he feels he will receive the most favorable judgment or verdict.").

17 The exception involving those marriages declared void by the domicile would seem to correspond roughly to those marriages which would be deemed obnoxious by the domicile.

18 For example, some states may decide to do away with no-fault divorce. See Karen Peterson, "Saying 'No' to the Notion of No-Fault Divorce," *USA Today*, January 25, 1996, at 1D ("No-fault divorce, available in some form in all 50 states, is under attack."). They may then decide that they

want the option of not recognizing a no-fault divorce decree obtained in another state.

19 See Pub. L. 104–199, 110 Stat. 2419.

20 Ironically, when Congress passed the Full Faith and Credit for Child Support Orders Act, it did include a provision regarding choice of law. See 28 United States Code Annotated (U.S.C.A.) Sec. 1738B(g).

21 See 142 *Cong. Rec.* S4870 (Sen. Nickles) (May 8, 1996) ("This bill does not change State law, but allows each state to decide for itself with respect to same-sex marriage.").

22 Cf. id. ("This effort hardly seems to be news as it reaffirms current practice and policy.").

23 For related discussion concerning how judges acting in good faith should deal with the choice-of-law issues which will likely occur should Hawaii recognize same-sex marriages, see Strasser, "Judicial Good Faith and the *Baehr* Essentials."

24 See id.

25 See 142 *Cong. Rec.* S4870 (May 8, 1996) (Sen Nickles).

26 See *Treines v. Sunshine Mining Co.*, 308 U.S. 66, 77 (1940).

27 317 U.S. at 303–4.

28 Id. at 303.

29 See U.S. Const., Art. IV, Sec. 1.

30 28 U.S.C.A. Sec. 1738A.

31 A Lexis search of the briefs for docket no. 86–964 did not reveal either petitioner's or respondent's discussing the constitutionality of the PKPA.

32 See *Thompson v. Thompson*, 484 U.S. 174, 183 (1988) (suggesting that this was an appropriate use of power by Congress under the Full Faith and Credit Clause).

33 Cf. *United States v. Lopez*, 115 S. Ct. 1624, 1626 (1995) ("The Constitution creates a Federal Government of enumerated powers.").

34 See 28 U.S.C.A. sec. 1738A.

35 See 28 U.S.C.A. sec. 1738B.

36 Cf. Laurence Tribe, *American Constitutional Law*, 1427 (2d ed., 1988) ("The Court's error in *Hardwick* [*Bowers v. Hardwick*, 478 U.S. 186 (1986)] was that it used the wrong level of generality to conceptualize the plaintiff's claim of liberty.").

37 See 142 Cong. Rec. S4870 (Sen. Nickles) (May 8, 1996) ("This bill would . . . allow States to make the final determination concerning same-sex marriages without other States' law interfering.").

38 *Estin*, 334 U.S. at 545–46.

39 Cf. *Yarborough v. Yarborough*, 290 U.S. 202, 215 n.2 (1993) (Stone, J., dissenting: "The mandatory force of the full faith and credit clause as defined by this Court may be, in some degree not yet fully defined, . . . contracted by Congress.")

40 201 U.S. 562 (1906), overruled by *Williams I*, 317 U.S. 287 (1942).

41   *Williams I*, 317 U.S. at 304.

42   See 142 *Cong. Rec.* S5932 (statement of Sen. Kennedy before the Senate Judiciary Comm. on S. 1740, the Defense of Marriage Act) (June 6, 1996) (introducing letter written by Laurence Tribe suggesting that the constitutionality of DOMA would imply that Congress would have the power to negate the Full Faith and Credit Clause).

43   U.S. Const., Amend. xiv, Sec. 5.

44   *Hogan*, 458 U.S. at 732 (quoting *Ex parte* Virginia, 100 U.S. 339, 346 (1880)).

45   Id. (quoting *Katzenbach v. Morgan*, 384 U.S. 641, 651 n.10 (1966)).

46   Id. at 732–33 (citing *Califano v. Goldfarb*, 430 U.S. 199, 210 (1977); *Williams v. Rhodes*, 393 U.S. 23, 29 (1968)).

47   466 U.S. 429, 433 (1984).

48   388 U.S. 1 (1967) (striking down Virginia's antimiscegenation statute).

49   See id. at 11.

50   Id. at 12.

51   See generally Mark Strasser, "Domestic Relations Jurisprudence and the Great, Slumbering *Baehr*: On Definitional Preclusion, Equal Protection and Fundamental Interests," 64 *Fordham L. Rev.* 921 (1995).

52   For an argument suggesting that they should be so recognized, see generally Mark Strasser, "Suspect Classes and Suspect Classifications: On Discriminating, Unwittingly or Otherwise," 64 *Temple L. Rev.* 937 (1991).

53   See *Bowers*, 478 U.S. at 196 n.8.

54   *Romer*, 116 S. Ct. at 1625.

55   Id. at 1628.

56   See 1996 WL 10829444 (statement of Sen. Kennedy before the Senate Judiciary Comm. on S. 1740, the Defense of Marriage Act) (July 11, 1996) ("The bill before us is called the Defense of Marriage Act, but a more accurate title would be the Defense of Intolerance Act"); 142 *Cong. Rec.* E1320 (Rep. Collins) (July 18, 1996) ("The so-called Defense of Marriage Act should really be called the Republican Offense on People Who are Different Act because it is nothing more than blatant homophobic gay-bashing.").

57   See 142 *Cong. Rec.* S4948 (May 9, 1996) (Sen. Coats).

58   See *McLaughlin v. Florida*, 379 U.S. 184, 193 (1964).

59   See id. at 196.

60   See 142 *Cong. Rec.* H-7279 (Rep. McInnis) (July 11, 1996).

61   See 142 *Cong. Rec.* H4791 (Rep. Canady) (July 12, 1996).

62   For a critical assessment of Supreme Court invidious discrimination jurisprudence, see generally Mark Strasser, "The Invidiousness of Invidiousness: On the Supreme Court's Affirmative Action Jurisprudence," 21 *Hastings Const. L. Q.* 323 (1993–1994).

63   See 1996 WL 10829470 (statement of Mr. Wardle before the Senate Judiciary Comm. on S. 1740, the Defense of Marriage Act) (July 11, 1996) ("A

state may have or may create conflict of laws rules that would recognize same-sex marriages if legal in other states.").

64 See 1996 WL 10829443 (statement of Sen. Hatch before the Senate Judiciary Comm. on S. 1740, the Defense of Marriage Act) (July 11, 1996) ("Thus, it would not be surprising that persons who want to invoke the legitimacy of 'marriage' for same-sex unions will travel to Hawaii to become 'married'. Then, they will return to their home states where it would be expected that the state recognize, as valid, a Hawaii marriage certificate."); 1996 WL 10829445 (statement of Rep. Largent before the Senate Judiciary Comm. on S. 1740, the Defense of Marriage Act) (July 11, 1996) ("If the state court in Hawaii legalizes same-sex marriage, homosexual couples from other states around the country will fly to Hawaii to 'marry'. These same couples will then go back to their respective states and argue that the Full Faith and Credit Clause of the U.S. Constitution requires their home state to recognize their union as a 'marriage'.").

65 Cf. Sanford Caust-Ellenbogen, "False Conflicts and Interstate Preclusion: Moving Beyond a Wooden Reading of the Full Faith and Credit Statute," 58 *Fordham L. Rev.* 593, 594 (1990) ("the Supreme Court has often used its plain meaning approach to the full faith and credit statute in its pronouncements on interstate preclusion.").

66 See 1996 WL 256695 (written statement of Mr. Wardle before the House of Rep. Judiciary Comm. on H. 3396, the Defense of Marriage Act) (May 15, 1996) (a main principle underlying DOMA is a "respect for federalism").

67 See generally Michael Gottesman, "Draining the Dismal Swamp: The Case for Federal Choice of Law Statutes," 80 *Geo. L. J.* 1 (1991).

68 See id. at 11–16.

69 Cf. 1996 WL 324365 (Rep. Schroeder before the House of Rep. Judiciary Comm. on H. 3396, the Defense of Marriage Act) (June, 12, 1996) (offering amendment which would "say that a person's second or third or fourth marriage will not be recognized for purposes of federal law unless the prior marriages were terminated by a court proceeding that takes into account the fault factors that led to the dissolution of the marriage"). Congress might incorporate the spirit of Congresswoman Schroeder's remarks by allowing states not to recognize later marriages unless fault had been taken into account. Or, perhaps, Congress might allow each state to decide whether to recognize such marriages at all.

70 When legislation is designed to impose undeserved burdens on disfavored minorities, incentives are skewed both with respect to how carefully the policy implications are weighed and with respect to how much weight certain effects are given. This is yet another reason for courts to closely examine the rationality and legitimacy of statutes like DOMA.

71 *United States v. Guest*, 383 U.S. 747, 757 (1966).

72 *Shapiro v. Thompson*, 394 U.S. 618, 629 (1969).

73 *Haig v. Agee*, 453 U.S. 280, 307 (1981) (citing *United States v. Guest*, 383 U.S. 745, 757–58) (1966).

74 *Twining v. New Jersey*, 211 U.S. 78, 97 (1908). See also *Edwards v. California*, 314 U.S. 160, 178 (1941) (Douglas, J., concurring).

75 *Memorial Hospital v. Maricopa County*, 415 U.S. 250, 254 (1974).

76 73 U.S. (6 Wallace) 35, 39 (1867).

77 Id. at 46.

78 394 U.S. 618 (1969).

79 Id. at 629. See also *Edwards v. California*, 314 U.S. 160 (1941) (striking prohibition against transporting indigent non-residents into the state).

80 *Shapiro*, 394 U.S. at 638.

81 See *San Antonio Indep. Sch. Dist. v. Rodriguez*, 411 U.S. 1 (1973).

82 *Shapiro*, 494 U.S. at 641.

83 *New York v. United States*, 505 U.S. 144, 182 (1992).

84 Pub. L. 104-199, 110 Stat. 2419.

85 See, for example, *In re Jobes*, 529 A.2d 434, 445 (N.J. 1987) ("Family members are best qualified to make substituted judgments for incompetent patients."). See also 1996 WL 10829448 (Ms. Henderson before the Senate Judiciary Comm. on S. 1740, the Defense of Marriage Act) (July 11, 1996) ("On the afternoon of Jan. 3, 1994 our son, James Henderson, felt ill and came home from his office early. By evening, when his partner of nine years, Ray, arrived home he found Jamie delirious from pain, unable to reach the phone. Ray immediately rushed Jamie to the hospital. But there was a problem. Although they have been a couple for nine years, Ray is not legally related to Jamie, so he was left outside in the waiting room—unable to get information about Jamie's condition, and unable to give permission for treatment.").

86 See, for example, *Elden v. Sheldon*, 758 P.2d 582 (Cal. 1988) (in bank) (denying nonmarital partner right to sue for loss of consortium).

87 See *Baehr v. Lewin*, 852 P.2d 44, 59 (1993) (right to sue for wrongful death a privilege of marriage).

88 But see generally Strasser, "Domestic Relations Jurisprudence and the Great, Slumbering *Baehr*."

89 See *Romer*, 116 S. Ct. at 1628 (discussing laws which "raise the inevitable inference that the disadvantage imposed is born of animosity toward the class of persons affected").

90 See *Second Restatement*, Sec. 283, Cmt. b ("Protection of the justified expectations of the parties is a basic policy underlying the field of marriage.").

91 See Strasser, "Judicial Good Faith and the *Baehr* Essentials" (discussing some of the reasons that courts tend to uphold marriages).

92 See *Second Restatement*, Sec. 283. Cf. *In re Marriage of Reed*, 226 N.W.2d

795 (Iowa 1975) (marriage invalid because the law of the state with the most significant contacts, California, would not have recognized it).

93   See *Second Restatement*, Sec. 15, 16, 18. See also Eugene Scoles and Peter Hay *Conflicts of Laws* (2d ed., 1992), Sec. 4.18 "(The element of physical presence is essential to confirm the requisite attitude of mind contemplated by the concept of domicile. As a consequence, a person who is to acquire a domicile of choice at a place must actually be present at that place during the time in which the intention to make it his home exists.)."

94   It is not clear that the *Second Restatement* would allow the marriage to be considered void in this case. See id. Cmt. j ("To date, a marriage has been held invalid in such circumstances only when it violated a strong policy of a state where at least one of the spouses was domiciled at the time of the marriage and where both have made their home immediately thereafter.").

95   A separate question for the trier of fact to determine would be whether the couple in fact had had the intention of moving to State X at the time of the marriage. The difficulty of making such a factual determination is one of the reasons that "[p]hysical presence in a particular area is essential for the acquisition in that area of a domicil of choice." Id., Sec. 16, Cmt. a.

96   See *Jones v. Helms*, 452 U.S. 412, 417–18 (1981).

97   *Dunn v. Blumstein*, 405 U.S. 330, 341 (1972) (citing *Shapiro*, 394 U.S. at 643).

98   *Zobel v. Williams*, 457 U.S. 55, 76–77 (1982) (O'Connor, J., concurring in the judgment).

99   *Attorney General of New York v. Soto-Lopez*, 476 U.S. 898, 907 (1986).

100 Cf. *Edwards v. California*, 314 U.S. 160, 176 (1941) ("The prohibition against transporting indigent non-residents into one State is an open invitation to retaliatory measures.").

101 Pub. L. 104-199, 110 Stat. 2419.

102 *United States Dept. of Agriculture v. Moreno*, 413 U.S. 528, 534 (1973).

103 *Mugler v. Kansas*, 123 U.S. 623, 661 (1887).

104 482 U.S. 78, 95–96 (1987).

105 See id. at 96.

106 For further discussion of this point, see Strasser, "Domestic Relations Jurisprudence and the Great, Slumbering *Baehr*," at 962–63.

107 *United States v. Yazell*, 382 U.S. 341, 353 (1966).

108 *Ex parte Burrus*, 136 U.S. 586, 593–94 (1890).

109 *McCarty v. McCarty*, 453 U.S. 210, 237 (1981) (Rehnquist, J., dissenting) (citations omitted). See also *Lopez*, 115 S. Ct. at 1632 (casting doubt on the appropriateness of Congress's regulating family law).

110 *Mansell v. Mansell*, 490 U.S. 581, 587 (1989).

111 Id.

112 The state's own law could not violate the guarantees offered by the Due

Process Clause of the Fourteenth Amendment, which would prevent any state from having a say in the validity of a marriage where the state had no connection to either of the parties or the marriage itself.

113 Cf. 1996 WL 10829449 (Statement of Cass Sunstein before the Senate Judiciary Comm. on S. 1740, the Defense of Marriage Act) (July 11, 1996) (suggesting that DOMA "gives states no authority that they lack").

114 See Pub. L. 104-199, 110 Stat. 2419.

115 *De Sylva v. Ballentine*, 351 U.S. 570, 580 (1956).

116 Id.

117 481 U.S. 619, 625 (1987) (citing *Hisquierdo v. Hisquierdo*, 439 U.S. 572, 581 (1979), quoting *United States v. Yazell*, 382 U.S. 341 352 (1966)).

118 See *McCarty v. McCarty*, 453 U.S. 210, 221 (1981) (describing California system in which retirement pay earned during marriage is included within community property). For a definition of community property, see *Black's Law Dictionary*, 280 (6th ed., 1990) (Community Property: "Property owned in common by husband and wife each having an undivided one-half interest by reason of their marital status. . . . Under a community property system, one-half of the earnings of each spouse is considered owned by the other spouse.").

119 Thus, this case is distinguished from *McCarty* in which the Court ruled that the type of benefit at issue was not properly included within community property. See *McCarty*, 453 U.S. at 232–33.

120 *Hisquierdo*, 439 U.S. at 581 (quoting *Yazell*, 382 U.S. at 352).

121 See *Wissner v. Wissner*, 338 U.S. 655, 660–61 (1950) (upholding serviceman's right to make insurance benefit "payable to the relative of his choice," as legitimate because it "might well directly enhance the morale of the serviceman." The exemption involved an end which was "a legitimate one within the congressional powers over national defense."). See also *Mansell v. Mansell*, 490 U.S. 581, 583 (1989) (state courts may not "treat as property divisible upon divorce military retirement pay waived by the retiree in order to receive veterans' disability benefits"); *Ridgway v. Ridgway*, 454 U.S. 46, 55 (1981) (upholding Servicemen's Group Life Insurance Act under which the "insured service member possesses the right freely to designate the beneficiary and to alter that choice at any time by communicating the decision in writing to the proper office"); *McCarty v. McCarty* 453 U.S. 210 (1981) (upholding right to Congress not to have "application of community property principles to military retired pay").

122 See generally Mark Strasser, "Unconstitutional? Don't Ask; If It Is, Don't Tell: On Deference, Rationality and the Constitution," 66 *U. Colo. L. Rev.* 375 (1995) (arguing that current policy with respect to gays in the military is unconstitutional).

123 See *Hisquierdo v. Hisquierdo*, 439 U.S. 572 (1979).

124 See *United States v. Yazell*, 382 U.S. 341, 348 (1966) (not allowing government to ignore state rule of coverture, while recognizing "there is always a

federal interest to collect moneys which the Government lends."). See *Black's Law Dictionary*, 366 (6th ed., 1990) (defining coverture as the legal disability "whereby the wife could not own property free from the husband's claim or control").

125 See, e.g., 142 *Cong. Rec.* S4871 (Sen. Nickles) (May 8, 1996); 142 *Cong. Rec.* H7277 (July 11, 1996) (Rep. Hoke).

126 See 142 *Cong. Rec.* H7277 (Rep. McInnis) (July 11, 1996); id. at 7275 (Rep. Barr) (July 11, 1996).

127 See 142 *Cong. Rec.* S4947 (Sen. Coats) (May 9, 1996).

128 For a more general discussion comparing the former prohibition of interracial marriage and the current prohibition of same-sex marriage, see Mark Strasser, "Family, Definitions, and the Constitution."

129 See 142 *Cong. Rec.* H7276 (Rep. Largent) (July 11, 1996) (testifying as concerned parent).

130 Cf. 142 *Cong. Rec.* H7273 (Rep. Schroeder) (July 11, 1996) ("if there are two individuals and they are willing to make a commitment to each other under the civil law of a State and a State decides to recognize it, what right does the Federal Government have to say, no, they cannot do that?").

131 *Adarand Constructors, Inc. v. Pena*, 115 S. Ct. 2097, 2120 (Stevens, J., dissenting).

132 *Romer*, 116 S. Ct. at 1628.

133 852 P.2d 44, 59 (Haw. 1993) (plurality decision).

134 Id.

135 See *Chae Chan Ping v. United States*, 130 U.S. 581, 599 (1889) ("the last expression of the sovereign will must control").

136 Cf. *The Cherokee Tobacco*, 78 U.S. 616, 623 (1870) (Bradley, J., dissenting) (In every case the intent of the legislature is to be sought, and in the case of such special and local exemptions the general rule for ascertaining whether the legislature does not intend to repeal or affect them, is to inquire whether they are expressly named; if not expressly named, then whether the language is such, nevertheless, as clearly to indicate the legislative intent to repeal or affect them.)

137 *Wetmore v. Markoe*, 196 U.S. 68, 77 (1904).

138 See 1996 WL 10829470 (statement of Mr. Wardle before the Senate Judiciary Comm. on S. 1740, the Defense of Marriage Act) (July 11, 1996) (explaining that section 2 of DOMA would affect divorce, custody, alimony, property division, etc.).

139 For a discussion of some of the disturbing trends in the Supreme Court's affirmative action jurisprudence, see generally Mark Strasser, "The Invidiousness of Invidiousness: On the Supreme Court's Affirmative Action Jurisprudence," 21 *Hastings Const. L. Q.* 323 (1994).

140 See *Casey*, 505 U.S. at 984 (Scalia, J., concurring in part and dissenting in part, suggesting that abortion, like sodomy, is not entitled to constitutional protection).

141   See *Turner*, 482 U.S. at 95–96.

142   *Zablocki*, 434 U.S. at 386.

143   See *Romer*, 116 S. Ct. at 1629 (Scalia, J., dissenting, "This Court has no business imposing upon all Americans the resolution favored by the elite class from which the Members of this institution are selected, pronouncing that 'animosity' towards homosexuality . . . is evil.").

BIBLIOGRAPHY

FEDERAL COURTS

Supreme Court

Adamson v. California, 332 U.S. 46 (1947)

Adarand Constructors, Inc. v. Pena, 115 S. Ct. 2097 (1995)

Alaska Packers Ass'n v. Industrial Accident Commission of California, 294 U.S. 532 (1935)

Allied Stores of Ohio, Inc. v. Bowers, 358 U.S. 522 (1959)

Allstate Insurance Co. v. Hague, 449 U.S. 302 (1981)

American Sugar Ref. Co. v. Louisiana, 179 U.S. 89 (1900)

Anderson v. Martin, 375 U.S. 399 (1964)

Andrews v. Andrews, 188 U.S. 14 (1903)

Arlington Heights, Village of, v. Metropolitan Hous. Dev. Corp., 429 U.S. 252 (1977)

Attorney General of New York v. Soto-Lopez, 476 U.S. 898 (1986)

Bain Peanut Co. v. Pinson, 282 U.S. 499 (1931)

Barbier v. Connolly, 113 U.S. 27 (1885)

Barnes v. Glen Theatre, Inc., 501 U.S. 560 (1991)

Baxstrom v. Herald, 383 U.S. 107 (1966)

Belle Terre, Village of, v. Boras, 416 U.S. 1 (1974)

Bellotti v. Baird, 443 U.S. 622 (1979)

Bell's Gap R.R. Co. v. Pennsylvania, 134 U.S. 232 (1890)

Board of Directors of Rotary International v. Rotary Club of Duarte, 481 U.S. 537 (1987)

Bob Jones Univ. v. United States, 461 U.S. 574 (1983)

Boddie v. Connecticut, 401 U.S. 371 (1971)

Bolling v. Sharpe, 347 U.S. 497 (1954)

Bowers v. Hardwick, 478 U.S. 186 (1986)

Bradford Electric Light Co. Inc. v. Clapper, 286 U.S. 145 (1932)

Bradwell v. Illinois, 83 U.S. (16 Wall.) 130 (1872)

Brown v. Board of Education, 347 U.S. 483 (1954)

Brown v. Louisiana, 383 U.S. 131 (1966)

Burlington N.R.R. v. Ford, 504 U.S. 648 (1992)

Burnham v. Superior Court, 495 U.S. 604 (1990) (plurality opinion)

Burrus, Ex parte, 136 U.S. 586 (1890)

Caban v. Mohammed, 441 U.S. 380 (1979)

Carey v. Population Servs. Int'l, 431 U.S. 678 (1977)

Capitol Square Review and Advisory Board v. Pinette, 115 S. Ct. 2440 (1995)

Carolene Products Co., United States v., 304 U.S. 144 (1938)

Carrington v. Rash, 380 U.S. 89 (1965)

Chae Chan Ping v. United States, 130 U.S. 581 (1889)

Cheely v. Clayton, 110 U.S. 701 (1884)

Church of the Lukumi Babalu Aye, Inc. v. City of Hialeah, 508 U.S. 520 (1993)

City of (see name of city)

Cleburne, City of, v. Cleburne Living Center, 473 U.S. 432 (1985)

Cleveland Bd. of Educ. v. LaFleur, 414 U.S. 632 (1974)

Coates v. City of Cincinnati, 402 U.S. 611 (1971)

Coe v. Coe, 334 U.S. 378 (1948)

Cook v. Cook, 342 U.S. 126 (1951)

Craig v. Boren, 429 U.S. 190 (1976)

Crawford v. United States, 212 U.S. 183 (1909)

Dandridge v. Williams, 397 U.S. 471 (1970)

Davis v. Davis, 305 U.S. 32 (1938)

De Sylva v. Ballentine, 351 U.S. 570 (1956)

Dunn v. Blumstein, 405 U.S. 330 (1972)

Durfee v. Duke, 375 U.S. 106 (1963)

Edmonds, City of, v. Oxford House, Inc., 115 S. Ct. 1776 (1995)

Edwards v. California, 314 U.S. 160 (1941)

Eisenstadt v. Baird, 405 U.S. 438 (1972)

Employment Div. Dep't of Human Resources of Oregon v. Smith, 494 U.S. 872 (1990)

Erznoznik v. Jacksonville, 422 U.S. 205 (1975)

Estin v. Estin, 334 U.S. 541 (1948)

F.S. Royster Guano Co. v. Virginia, 253 U.S. 412 (1920)

Fauntleroy v. Lum, 210 U.S. 230 (1908)

Foley v. Connelie, 435 U.S. 219 (1978)

Foman v. Davis, 371 U.S. 178 (1962)

Frontiero v. Richardson, 411 U.S. 677 (1973)

Georgia v. Nationalist Movement, 505 U.S. 123 (1992)

Goldman v. Weinberger, 475 U.S. 503 (1986)

Gomez v. Perez, 409 U.S. 535 (1973)

Grayned v. City of Rockford, 408 U.S. 104 (1972)

Griffin v. Griffin, 327 U.S. 220 (1946)

Griffin v. Illinois, 351 U.S. 12 (1955)

Griffin v. McCoach, 313 U.S. 498 (1941)

Griswold v. Connecticut, 381 U.S. 479 (1965)
Guest, United States v., 383 U.S. 747 (1966)
Gulf, Colorado & Santa Fe R.R. Co. v. Ellis, 165 U.S. 150 (1897)
Haddock v. Haddock, overruled by *Williams v. North Carolina*, 317 U.S. 287 (1942)
Haig v. Agee, 453 U.S. 280 (1981)
Halvey v. Halvey, 330 U.S. 610 (1947)
Hampton v. M'Connel, 16 U.S. (3 Wheat) 234 (1818)
Harper v. Virginia Board of Elections, 383 U.S. 663 (1966)
Hilton v. Guyot, 159 U.S. 113 (1895)
Hirabayashi v. United States, 320 U.S. 81 (1943)
Hisquierdo v. Hisquierdo, 439 U.S. 572 (1979)
Hughes v. Fetter, 341 U.S. 609 (1951)
In re (see name of party)
International Shoe Co. v. Washington, 326 U.S. 310 (1945)
International Union, UAW v. Johnson Controls, 499 U.S. 187 (1991)
Johnson v. Muelberger, 340 U.S. 581 (1951)
Jones v. Helms, 452 U.S. 412 (1981)
Jones v. Meehan, 175 U.S. 1 (1899)
Kagama, United States v., 118 U.S. 375 (1886)
Kenney v. Supreme Lodge of the World, 252 U.S. 411 (1920)
Keyishian v. Board of Regents, 385 U.S. 589 (1967)
Korematsu v. United States, 323 U.S. 214 (1944)
Kramer v. Union Free Sch. Dist., 395 U.S. 621 (1969)
Kulko v. Superior Court, 436 U.S. 84 (1978)
Lafayette Insurance Co. v. French, 59 U.S. (18 Howard) 404 (1855)
Lassiter v. Dept of Social Services, 452 U.S. 18 (1981)
Lawton v. Steele, 152 U.S. 133 (1894)
Lehr v. Robertson, 463 U.S. 248 (1983)
Levy v. Louisiana, 391 U.S. 68 (1968)
Lindsley v. Natural Carbonic Gas Co., 220 U.S. 61 (1911)
Lopez, United States v., 115 S. Ct. 1624 (1995)
Loughran v. Loughran, 292 U.S. 216 (1934)
Louisville Gas & Elec. Co. v. Coleman, 277 U.S. 32 (1928)
Loving v. Virginia, 388 U.S. 1 (1967)
Magnolia Petroleum Co. v. Hunt, 320 U.S. 430 (1943)
Mansell v. Mansell, 490 U.S. 581 (1989)
Massachusetts Board of Retirement v. Murgia, 427 U.S. 307 (1976)
Mathews v. Lucas, 427 U.S. 495 (1976)
May v. Anderson, 345 U.S. 528 (1953)
Maynard v. Hill, 125 U.S. 190 (1888)
McCabe v. Atchison, Topeka, & Santa Fe Ry., 235 U.S. 151 (1914)
McCarty v. McCarty, 453 U.S. 210 (1981)
McLaughlin v. Florida, 397 U.S. 184 (1964)

Memorial Hospital v. Maricopa County, 415 U.S. 250 (1974)

Meyer v. Nebraska, 262 U.S. 390 (1923)

Michael H. v. Gerald D., 491 U.S. 110 (1989)

Michael M. v. Sonoma County Superior Court, 450 U.S. 464 (1981)

Mills v. Duryee, 11 U.S. (7 Cranch) 481 (1813)

Mills v. Habluetzel, 456 U.S. 91 (1982)

Milwaukee County v. M.E. White Co., 296 U.S. 268 (1935)

Mississippi University for Women v. Hogan, 458 U.S. 718 (1982)

Missouri ex rel. Gaines v. Canada, 305 U.S. 337 (1938)

Modern Woodmen of America v. Mixer, 267 U.S. 544 (1925)

Moore v. City of East Cleveland, 431 U.S. 494 (1977)

Morey v. Doud, 354 U.S. 457 (1957)

Morris v. Jones, 329 U.S. 545 (1947)

Mugler v. Kansas, 123 U.S. 623 (1887)

Nevada v. Hall, 440 U.S. 410 (1979)

New Orleans, City of, v. Dukes, 427 U.S. 297 (1976)

New York v. Miln, 36 U.S. (11 Pet.) 102 (1837)

New York v. United States, 505 U.S. 144 (1992)

Norwood v. Harrison, 413 U.S. 455 (1973)

O'Brien, United States v., 391 U.S. 367 (1968)

O'Connor v. Donaldson, 422 U.S. 563 (1975)

Ohio Oil Co. v. Conway, 281 U.S. 146 (1930)

Orr v. Orr, 440 U.S. 268 (1979)

Oyama v. California, 332 U.S. 633 (1948)

Pace v. Alabama, 106 U.S. 583 (1882)

Palmer v. Thompson, 403 U.S. 217 (1971)

Palmore v. Sidoti, 466 U.S. 429 (1984)

Parham v. Hughes, 441 U.S. 347 (1979)

Pennoyer v. Neff, 95 U.S. 714 (1877)

Personnel Administrator of Massachusetts v. Feeney, 442 U.S. 256 (1979)

Phillips Petroleum Co. v. Shutts, 472 U.S. 797 (1985)

Pickett v. Brown, 462 U.S. 1 (1983)

Pierce v. Society of Sisters, 268 U.S. 510 (1925)

Planned Parenthood of Southeastern Pennsylvania v. Casey, 505 U.S. 833 (1992)
    (plurality opinion)

Plessy v. Ferguson, 163 U.S. 537 (1896)

Plyler v. Doe, 457 U.S. 202 (1982)

Poe v. North Carolina, 445 U.S. 947 (1980)

Poe v. Ullman, 367 U.S. 497 (1961)

Powell v. Texas, 392 U.S. 514 (1968)

Prince v. Massachusetts, 321 U.S. 158 (1944)

Quilloin v. Wolcott, 434 U.S. 246 (1978)

Railway Express Agency, Inc. v. New York, 336 U.S. 106 (1949)

Reed v. Reed, 404 U.S. 71 (1971)

Reitman v. Mulkey, 387 U.S. 369 (1967)
Reynolds v. Sims, 377 U.S. 533 (1964)
Reynolds v. United States, 98 U.S. 145 (1878)
Richards v. United States, 369 U.S. 1 (1962)
Richardson v. Belcher, 404 U.S. 78 (1971)
Richmond v. J.A. Croson Co., 488 U.S. 469 (1989)
Ridgway v. Ridgway, 454 U.S. 46 (1981)
Riley v. New York Trust Co., 315 U.S. 343 (1942)
Robel, United States v., 389 U.S. 258 (1967)
Roberts v. United States Jaycees, 468 U.S. 609 (1984)
Robinson v. California, 370 U.S. 660 (1962)
Rochin v. California, 342 U.S. 165 (1952)
Roe v. Wade, 410 U.S. 113 (1973)
Romer v. Evans, 116 S. Ct. 1620 (1996)
Rosado v. Wyman, 397 U.S. 397 (1970)
Rose v. Mitchell, 443 U.S. 545 (1979)
Rose v. Rose, 481 U.S. 619 (1987)
Rowland v. Mad River Local Sch. Dist., 470 U.S. 1009 (1985)
Saint Francis College v. Al-Khazraji, 481 U.S. 604 (1987)
San Antonio Indep. Sch. Dist. v. Rodriguez, 411 U.S. 1 (1973)
Santosky v. Kramer, 455 U.S. 745 (1982)
Shapiro v. Thompson, 394 U.S. 618 (1969)
Shelley v. Kraemer, 334 U.S. 1 (1948)
Sherbert v. Verner, 374 U.S. 398 (1963)
Sherrer v. Sherrer, 334 U.S. 343 (1948)
Skinner v. Oklahoma ex rel. Williamson, 316 U.S. 535 (1942)
Slaughter House Cases, (In re) 83 U.S. (16 Wallace) 36 (1873)
Smith v. Organization of Foster Families for Equality and Reform (OFFER), 431
    U.S. 816 (1977)
Sniadach v. Family Finance Corp. of Bay View, 395 U.S. 337 (1969)
Soon Hing v. Crowley, 113 U.S. 703 (1885)
Sosna v. Iowa, 419 U.S. 393 (1975)
Stanley v. Illinois, 405 U.S. 645 (1972)
Stanton v. Stanton, 421 U.S. 7 (1975)
Steele v. Louisville & Nashville R.R., 323 U.S. 192 (1944)
Strauder v. West Virginia, 100 U.S. 303 (1879)
Sugarman v. Dougall, 413 U.S. 634 (1973)
Sun Oil Co. v. Wortman, 486 U.S. 717 (1988)
Sutton v. Leib, 342 U.S. 402 (1952)
Takahashi v. Fish and Game Comm'n, 334 U.S. 410 (1948)
The Cherokee Tobacco, 78 U.S. 616 (1870)
Thomas v. Washington Gas Light Co., 448 U.S. 261 (1980)
Thompson v. Thompson, 484 U.S. 174 (1988)
Treines v. Sunshine Mining Co., 308 U.S. 66 (1940)

Trimble v. Gordon, 430 U.S. 762 (1977)

Turner v. Safley, 482 U.S. 78 (1987)

Twining v. New Jersey, 211 U.S. 78 (1908)

Underwriters National Assurance Co. v. North Carolina Life and Accident and Health Insurance Guaranty Association, 455 U.S. 691 (1982)

Union National Bank v. Lamb, 337 U.S. 38 (1949)

United States Dep't of Agric. v. Moreno, 413 U.S. 528 (1973)

United States v. ——— (see opposing party)

Univ. of Cal. v. Bakke, 438 U.S. 265 (1978)

Vanderbilt v. Vanderbilt, 354 U.S. 416 (1957)

Wards Cove Packing Co. v. Atonio, 490 U.S. 642 (1989)

Washington v. Davis, 426 U.S. 229 (1976)

Weber v. Aetna Casualty, 406 U.S. 164 (1972)

Wetmore v. Markoe, 196 U.S. 68 (1904)

Whitney v. California, 274 U.S. 357 (1927)

Williams v. North Carolina, 317 U.S. 287 (1942) (*Williams I*)

Williams v. North Carolina, 325 U.S. 226 (1945) (*Williams II*)

Williams v. Rhodes, 393 U.S. 23 (1968)

Williamson v. Lee Optical, 348 U.S. 483 (1955)

Wisconsin v. Yoder, 406 U.S. 205 (1972)

Wissner v. Wissner, 338 U.S. 655 (1950)

Yarborough v. Yarborough, 290 U.S. 202 (1933)

Yazell, United States v., 382 U.S. 341 (1966)

Yick Wo v. Hopkins, 118 U.S. 356 (1886)

Zablocki v. Redhail, 434 U.S. 374 (1978)

Zobel v. Williams, 457 U.S. 55 (1982)

Courts of Appeal

Adoption of a Minor, In re, 228 F.2d 446 (D.C. App. 1955)

Barrons v. United States, 191 F.2d 92 (9th Cir. 1951)

Collin v. Smith, 578 F.2d 1197 (7th Cir. 1978), cert. denied, 439 U.S. 916 (1978)

DeSantis v. Pacific Tel. & Tel. Co., 608 F.2d 327 (9th Cir. 1979)

Franz v. United States, 707 F.2d 582 (D.C. Cir.), supplemented by 712 F.2d 1428 (D.C. Cir. 1983)

Harding, United States v., 971 F.2d 4140 (9th Cir. 1992), cert. denied, 506 U.S. 1070 (1993)

High Tech Gays v. Defense Indus. Sec. Clearance Office, 895 F.2d 563 (9th Cir. 1990)

IDK, Inc. v. County of Clark, 836 F.2d 1185 (9th Cir. 1988)

Lovisi v. Slayton, 539 F.2d 349 (4th Cir.), cert. denied sub nom. Lovisi v. Zahradnick, 429 U.S. 977 (1976)

Moe v. Dinkins, 669 F.2d 67 (2d Cir.), cert. denied, 459 U.S. 827 (1982)

Padula v. Webster, 822 F.2d 97 (D.C. Cir. 1987)

Potter v. Murray City, 760 F.2d 1065 (10th Cir.), cert. denied, 474 U.S. 849 (1985)

Pruitt v. Cheney, 943 F.2d 989 (9th Cir.), superseded, 963 F.2d 1160 (9th Cir. 1991), cert. denied, 506 U.S. 1020 (1992)

Shahar v. Bowers, 70 F.3d 1218 (11th Cir. 1995), reh'g en banc granted, opinion vacated, 78 F.3d 499 (11th Cir. 1996), reh'g 114 F.3d 1097 (11th Cir. 1997) (en banc), aff'g 836 F. Supp. 859 (N.D. Ga. 1993)

Steffan v. Perry, 41 F.3d 677 (D. C. Cir. 1994)

Stevens v. United States, 146 F.2d 120 (10th Cir. 1944)

Urban Jacksonville, Inc. v. Chalbeck, 765 F.2d 1085 (11th Cir. 1985)

Watkins v. United States Army, 837 F.2d 1428 (9th Cir.), superseded, 847 F.2d 1329 (9th Cir. 1988), aff'd, 875 F.2d 699 (9th Cir. 1989), cert. denied, 498 U.S. 957 (1990)

Whetstone v. Immigration and Naturalization Service, 561 F.2d 1303 (9th Cir. 1977)

Woodward v. United States, 871 F.2d 1068 (Fed. Cir. 1989), cert. denied, 494 U.S. 1003 (1990)

District Courts

Adams v. Howerton, 486 F. Supp. 1119 (C.D. Cal. 1980), aff'd, 673 F.2d 1036 (9th Cir. 1982), cert. denied, 458 U.S. 1111 (1982)

Alsager v. District Court, 406 F. Supp. 10 (S.D. Iowa 1975)

Baker v. Wade, 553 F. Supp. 1121 (N.D. Tex. 1982), rev'd, 769 F.2d 289 (5th Cir. 1985), cert. denied, 478 U.S. 1022 (1986)

Brodie, In re, 394 F. Supp. 1208 (D. Or. 1975)

Dahl v. Secretary of the United States Navy, 830 F. Supp. 1319 (E.D. Cal. 1993)

Equality Found. of Greater Cincinnati, Inc. v. City of Cincinnati, 860 F. Supp. 417 (S.D. Ohio 1994), rev'd, 54 F.3d 261 (6th Cir.), cert. granted and judgment vacated, 116 S. Ct. 2519 (1996), on remand to 128 F.3d 289 (6th Cir. 1997)

Gibson v. Hughes, 192 F. Supp. 564 (S.D.N.Y. 1961)

Hann v. Housing Auth., 709 F. Supp. 605 (E.D. Pa. 1989)

High Tech Gays v. Defense Indus. Sec. Clearance Office, 668 F. Supp. 1361 (N.D. Cal. 1987), rev'd in part, vacated in part, 895 F.2d 563 (9th Cir. 1990)

Jantz v. Muci, 759 F. Supp. 1543 (D. Kan. 1991), rev'd, 976 F.2d 623 (10th Cir. 1992), cert. denied, 508 U.S. 952 (1993)

Kinney, Ex parte, 14 Fed. Cas. 602 (E.D. Va. 1879)

Labady, In re, 326 F. Supp. 924 (S.D.N.Y. 1971)

Madewell v. United States, 84 F. Supp. 329 (E.D. Tenn. 1949)

McLaughlin v. Pernsley, 693 F. Supp. 318 (E.D. Pa. 1988), aff'd, 876 F.2d 308 (3rd. Cir. 1989)

Metropolitan Life Insurance Co. v. Spearman, 334 F. Supp. 665 (M.D. Ala 1972)

Rovira v. AT&T, 817 F. Supp. 1062 (S.D.N.Y. 1993)

Shahar v. Bowers, 836 F. Supp. 859 (N.D. Ga. 1993), affirmed in part, vacated in part by 70 F.3d 1218 (11th Cir. 1995), reh'g en banc granted, opinion vacated by 78 F.3d 499 (11th Cir. 1996), reh'g 114 F.3d 1097 (11th Cir. 1997) (en banc), aff'g 836 F. Supp. 859 (N.D. Ga. 1993)

Steffan v. Cheney, 780 F. Supp. 1 (D.D.C. 1991), aff'd sub nom. Steffan v. Perry, 41 F.3d 677 (D. C. Cir. 1994)

Union Pacific Railroad Co. v. Bolton, 840 F. Supp. 421 (E.D. La. 1993)

United States ex rel. Devine v. Rodgers, 109 F. 886 (E.D. Pa.)

STATE COURTS

A. v. A., 514 P.2d 358 (Or. App. 1974)

A.C. v. C.B., 829 P.2d 660 (N.M. App. 1992), cert. denied, 827 P.2d 837 (N.M. 1992)

A.J.J., In re, 438 N.Y.S.2d 444 (Sur. Ct. 1981)

Adams v. Gay, 19 Vt. 358 (1847)

Adoption of a Child by A.R., In re, 378 A.2d 87 (N.J. Super. 1977)

Adoption of a Child by J.M.G., In re, 632 A.2d 550 (N.J. Super. Ct. Ch. Div. 1993)

Adoption of Adult Anonymous, In re, 435 N.Y.S.2d 527 (Fam. Ct. 1981)

Adoption of Charles B., In re, 552 N.E.2d 884 (Ohio 1990)

Adoption of Children by D., In re, 293 A.2d 171 (N.J. 1972)

Adoption of Evan, In re, 583 N.Y.S.2d 997 (Sur. Ct. 1992)

Adoption of Robert Paul P., In re, 471 N.E.2d 424 (N.Y. 1984)

Adoption of Swanson, In re, 623 A.2d 1095 (Del. 1993)

Adoption of Syck, In re, 562 N.E.2d 174 (Ill. 1990)

Adoption of Tammy, 619 N.E.2d 315 (Mass. 1993)

Adoption of Two Children by H.N.R., In re, 666 A.2d 535 (N.J. App. 1995)

Adoption of Zachariah K., 8 Cal.Rptr.2d 423 (Ct. App. 1992)

Adoptions of B.L.V.B. and E.L.V.B., 628 A.2d 1271 (Vt. 1993)

Adult Anonymous II, In re, 452 N.Y.S.2d 198 (App. Div. 1982)

Alexander v. Alexander, 445 So.2d 836 (Miss. 1984)

Alison D. v. Virginia M., 572 N.E.2d 27 (N.Y. 1991)

Alison D. v. Virginia M., In re, 552 N.Y.S.2d 321 (App. Div. 1990), aff'd, 572 N.E.2d 27 (N.Y. 1991)

Angel Lace M., In re, 516 N.W.2d 678 (Wis. 1994)

Anonymous Adoption, In re, 31 N.Y.S.2d 595 (Sur. Ct. 1941)

Anonymous v. Anonymous, 325 N.Y.S.2d 499 (Sup. Ct. 1971)

Appeal in Pima County Juvenile Action B-10489, In re, 727 P.2d 830 (Ariz. App. 1986)

Ashling v. Ashling, 599 P.2d 475 (Or. App. 1979)

Atkinson v. Atkinson, 408 N.W.2d 516 (Mich. App. 1987)

Atkisson v. Kern County Hous. Auth., 130 Cal.Rptr. 375 (Ct. App. 1976)

Atlanta, City of, v. McKinney, 454 S.E.2d 517 (Ga. 1995)

Baby Girl Eason, In re, 358 S.E.2d 459 (Ga. 1987)

Baehr v. Lewin, 852 P.2d 44 (Haw.), reconsideration granted in part, 875 P.2d 225 (Haw. 1993)

Bagnardi v. Hartnett, 366 N.Y.S.2d 89 (Sup. Ct. 1975)

Baker v. Nelson, 191 N.W.2d 185 (Minn. 1971), appeal dismissed, 409 U.S. 810 (1972)

Banks, In re Estate of, 629 N.E.2d 1223 (Ill. App. 1994)

Barlow v. Blackburn, 798 P.2d 1360 (Ariz. App. 1990)

Beatty v. Truck Ins. Exch., 8 Cal.Rptr.2d 593 (Ct. App. 1992)

Bennett v. Jeffreys, 356 N.E.2d 277 (N.Y. 1976)

Berger v. State, 364 A.2d 993 (N.J. 1976)

Bethlehem Steel Corp. v. G.C. Zarnas Co., 498 A.2d 605 (Md. App. 1985)

Bezio v. Patenaude, 410 N.E.2d 1207 (Mass. 1980)

Bigelow v. Halloran, 313 N.W.2d 10 (Minn. 1981)

Bobala v. Bobala, 33 N.E.2d 845 (Ohio App. 1940)

Bonadio, Commonwealth v., 415 A.2d 47 (Pa. 1980)

Borough of Glassboro v. Vallorosi, 568 A.2d 888 (N.J. 1990)

Bottoms v. Bottoms, 444 S.E.2d 276 (Va. App. 1994), rev'd, 457 S.E.2d 102 (Va. 1995)

Bottoms v. Bottoms, 457 S.E.2d 102 (Va. 1995)

Boyer v. Dively, 58 Mo. 510 (1875)

Braschi v. Stahl Associates Co., 543 N.E.2d 49 (N.Y. 1989)

Brawer v. Pinkins, 626 N.Y.S.2d 674 (Sup. Ct. 1995)

Brenda H., In re, 305 N.E.2d 815 (Ct. Common Pleas Ohio, 1973)

Bridges v. Nicely, 497 A.2d 142 (Md. 1985)

Bronislawa K. v. Tadeusz K., 393 N.Y.S.2d 534 (Fam. Ct. 1977)

Brown v. Brown, 237 S.E.2d 89 (Va. 1977)

Bryan v. Bryan, 645 P.2d 1267 (Ariz. App. 1982)

Bucca v. State, 128 A.2d 506 (N.J. Super. Ct. Ch. Div. 1957)

Burrell, In re, 388 N.E.2d 738 (Ohio 1979)

Cabalquinto v. Cabalquinto, 669 P.2d 886 (Wash. 1983) (En Banc)

Camilla, In re, 620 N.Y.S.2d 897 (Fam. Ct. 1994)

Carroll v. City of Miami Beach, 198 So.2d 643 (Fla. App. 1967)

Carter v. Brodrick, 644 P.2d 850 (Alaska 1982)

Case, Commonwealth v., 189 A.2d 756 (Super. Ct. Pa. 1963)

Catalano v. Catalano, 170 A.2d 726 (Conn. 1961)

Cebrzynski v. Cebrzynski, 379 N.E.2d 713 (Ill. App. 1978)

Champagne v. Welfare Division of Nevada State Dept. of Human Resources, 691 P.2d 849 (Nev. 1984)

Clausen, In re, 502 N.W.2d 649 (Mich. 1993)

Colby v. Colby, 369 P.2d 1019 (Nev. 1962), cert. denied, 371 U.S. 888 (1962)

Collins v. Collins, 1988 WL 30173 (Tenn. App.)

Commonwealth ex rel. (see name of relator)

Commonwealth v. —— (see name of opposing party)

Compo v. Jackson Iron Co., 6 N.W. 295 (Mich. 1883)

Conkel v. Conkel, 509 N.E.2d 983 (Ohio App. 1987)

Constant A. v. Paul C.A., 496 A.2d 1 (Pa. Super. Ct. 1985)

Cooper, In re, 592 N.Y.S.2d 797 (App. Div. 1993), appeal dismissed, 624 N.E.2d 696 (N.Y. 1993)

Cooper, In re Estate of, 564 N.Y.S.2d 684 (Sur. Ct. 1990), aff'd, 592 N.Y.S. 2d 797 (App. Div.), appeal dismissed, 624 N.E.2d 696 (N.Y. 1993)

Corder, In re Estate of, 201 N.E.2d 682 (Ill. App. 1964)

Curran, Petition of, 49 N.E.2d 432 (Mass. 1943)

Custody of H.S.H.-K., In re, 533 N.W.2d 419 (Wis. 1995), cert denied sub nom. *Knott v. Holtzman,* 116 S. Ct. 475 (1995)

Custody of Menconi, In re, 453 N.E.2d 835 (Ill. App. 1983)

Custody of Temos, In re, 450 A.2d 111 (Pa. Super. 1982)

Dalip Singh Bir's Estate, In re, 188 P.2d 499 (Cal. App. 1948)

Dallas v. State, 79 So. 690 (Fla. 1918)

Dana, In re, 624 N.Y.S.2d 634 (App. Div.), rev'd sub nom. *In re Jacob,* 660 N.E.2d 397 (N.Y. 1995)

Dean v. District of Columbia, 653 A.2d 307 (D.C. App. 1995)

Dean v. District of Columbia, Civ. A. No. 90–13892, 1992 WL 685364 (D.C. Super. Ct. June 2, 1992), aff'd, 653 A.2d 307 (D.C. App. 1995)

Dept. of Health and Rehabilitative Services v. Cox, 627 So.2d 1210 (Fla. App. 1993), approved in part, quashed in part, 656 So.2d 902 (Fla. 1995)

Dept. of Health and Rehabilitative Services v. Privette, 617 So.2d 305 (Fla. 1993)

Dept. of Social Services v. Ronald P., 623 P.2d 198 (Cal. 1981)

DiStefano v. DiStefano, 401 N.Y.S.2d 636 (App. Div. 1978)

Dorado Beach Hotel Corp. v. Jernigan, 202 So.2d 830 (Fla. App. 1967), appeal dismissed, 209 So.2d 669 (Fla. 1968)

Elden v. Sheldon, 758 P.2d 582 (Cal. 1988)

Estate of (see name of party)

Etheridge v. Shaddock, 706 S.W.2d 395 (Ark. 1986)

Evans v. Evans, 488 A.2d 157 (Md. 1985)

Evans v. Romer, 854 P.2d 1270 (Colo. 1993) (*Romer I*)

Evans v. Romer, 882 P.2d 1335 (Colo. 1994) (en banc) (*Romer II*), aff'd, 116 S. Ct. 1620 (1996)

Ex parte (see name of party)

Finnerty v. Boyett, 469 So.2d 287 (La. App. 1985)

Fort v. Fort, 425 N.E.2d 754 (Mass. App. 1981)

Ferguson, In re Estate of, 130 N.W.2d 300 (Wis. 1964)

G.A. v. D.A., 745 S.W.2d 726 (Mo. App. 1987)

Gabe Collins Realty, Inc. v. City of Margate City, 271 A.2d 430 (N.J App. 1970)

Gaylord v. Tacoma Sch. Dist. No. 10, 559 P.2d 1340 (Wash.), cert. denied, 434 U.S. 879 (1977)

Gay Rights Coalition of Georgetown Univ. Law Ctr. v. Georgetown Univ., 536 A.2d 1 (D.C. App. 1987) (en banc)

Golden v. Golden, 68 P.2d 928 (N.M. 1937)

Gribble v. Gribble, 583 P.2d 64 (Utah 1978)

Grover v. Phillips, 681 P.2d 81 (Okla. 1984)

Hall v. Taylor, 674 P.2d 245 (Cal. 1984), appeal dismissed, 466 U.S. 967 (1984)

Hall v. Univ. of Nevada, 141 Cal.Rptr. 439 (Ct. App. 1977), aff'd, 440 U.S. 410 (1979)

Hastings v. Farmer, 4 N.Y. 293 (1850)

Haun, In re, 286 N.E.2d 478 (Ohio App. 1972)

Hemingway v. McHehee, 228 N.E.2d 799 (N.Y. 1967)

Hewitt v. Hewitt, 380 N.E.2d 454 (Ill. App. Ct. 1978), rev'd, 394 N.E.2d 1204 (Ill. 1979)

Hinman v. Dept. of Personnel Admin., 213 Cal.Rptr. 410 (Ct. App. 1985)

Horton v. Horton, 198 P. 1105 (Ariz. 1921)

Hudson View Properties v. Weiss, 431 N.Y.S.2d 632 (Civ. Ct. 1980), rev'd, 442 N.Y.S.2d 367 (Sup. Ct. 1981), rev'd, 448 N.Y.S.2d 649 (App. Div. 1982), rev'd, 450 N.E.2d 234 (N.Y. 1983)

Hughes v. Creighton, 798 P.2d 403 (Ariz. App. 1990)

Intercontinental Hotels Corporation v. Golden, 254 N.Y.S.2d 527 (N.Y. 1964)

Interest of J.W.T., In re, 872 S.W.2d 189 (Tex. 1994)

Interest of R.C., In re, 775 P.2d 27 (Colo. 1989) (en banc)

Interest of S.I., In re, 173 A.2d 457 (N.J. Super. 1961)

Interest of Z.J.H., In re, 471 N.W.2d 202 (Wis. 1991), overruled by *In re Custody of H.S.H.-K.*, 533 N.W.2d 419 (Wis. 1995)

Israel v. Allen, 577 P.2d 762 (Colo. 1978) (en banc)

J.L.P.(H.) v. D.J.P., 643 S.W.2d 865 (Mo. App. 1982)

J.M.P. Applying for Adoption, In re, 528 So.2d 1002 (La. 1988)

J.P., In re, 648 P.2d 1364 (Utah 1982)

J.P. v. P.W., 772 S.W.2d 786 (Mo. App. 1989)

J.S. & C., In re, 324 A.2d 90 (N.J. Super. Ch. Div. 1974), aff'd, 362 A.2d 54 (N.J. App. 1976)

Jackson, State v., 80 Mo. 175 (1883).

Jacob, In re, 660 N.E.2d 397 (N.Y. 1995)

Jamal B., In re, 465 N.Y.S.2d 115 (Fam. Ct. 1983)

Jarrett v. Jarrett, 400 N.E.2d 421 (Ill. 1980), cert. denied, 449 U.S. 927 (1980)

Jessica W., In re, 453 A.2d 1297 (N.H. 1982)

Jhordan C. v. Mary K., 224 Cal.Rptr. 530 (Ct. App. 1986)

Jobes, In re, 529 A.2d 434 (N.J. 1987)

John M. v. Superior Court, 248 Cal.Rptr. 669 (Ct. App. 1988) (Ordered not published), cert. denied, 491 U.S. 904 (1989)

Johnson v. Johnson, 104 N.W.2d 8 (N.D. 1960)

Johnson v. Lincoln Square Properties, 571 So.2d 541 (Fla. App. 1990)

Jones v. Hallahan, 501 S.W.2d 588 (Ky. 1973)

K.M., In re Petition of, 653 N.E.2d 888 (Ill. App. 1995)

Karin T. v. Michael T., 484 N.Y.S.2d 780 (Fam. Ct. 1985)

Keith v. Pack, 187 S.W.2d 618 (Tenn. 1945)

Kinkead's Estate, In re, 57 N.W.2d 628 (Minn. 1953)

Kinney v. Commonwealth, 71 Va. 858 (1878)

Kirchner, In re Petition of, 649 N.E.2d 324 (Ill. 1995)

Kirsch Holding Co. v. Borough of Manasquan, 281 A.2d 513 (N.J. 1971)

Klipstein v. Zalewski, 553 A.2d 1384 (N.J. Super. Ch. Div. 1988)

Kobogum v. Jackson Iron Co., 43 N.W. 602 (Mich. 1889)

Kramer v. Kramer, 297 N.W.2d 359 (Iowa 1980)

Kristina L., In re, 520 A.2d 574 (R.I., 1987)

Kulla v. McNulty, 472 N.W.2d 175 (Minn. App. 1991)

L.S. and V.L. for the Adoption of a Minor, Ex Parte in re Petition of, 1991 WL 219598 (D.C. Super.)

Laikola v. Engineered Concrete, 277 N.W.2d 653 (Minn. 1979)

Lanham v. Lanham, 117 N.W. 787 (Wis. 1908)

Leefeld v. Leefeld, 166 P. 953 (Or. 1917)

Lenherr, In re Estate of, 314 A.2d 255 (Pa. 1974)

Leszinske v. Poole, 798 P.2d 1049 (N.M. App.), cert. denied, 797 P.2d 983 (N.M. 1990)

Lilienthal v. Kaufman, 395 P.2d 543 (Or. 1964) (en banc)

Lilly v. City of Minneapolis, No. MC 93–21375, 1994 WL 315620 (Minn. Dist. Ct. June 3, 1994), aff'd, 527 N.W.2d 107 (Minn. App. 1995)

Linton v. Linton, 420 A.2d 1249 (1980) (Md. App. 1980)

Lisa R., In re, 532 P.2d 123 (Cal. 1975) (in bank), cert. denied, 421 U.S. 1014 (1975)

Loucks v. Standard Oil of New York, 120 N.E. 198 (N.Y. 1918)

Loughmiller, In re Estate of, 629 P.2d 156 (Kan. 1981)

Loving v. Commonwealth, 147 S.E.2d 78 (Va. 1966), rev'd, 388 U.S. 1 (1967)

Lucas, Commonwealth ex rel. v. Kreischer, 299 A.2d 243 (Pa. 1973)

M.M.D. & B.H.M., In re, 662 A.2d 837 (D.C. App. 1995)

M.P. v. S.P., 404 A.2d 1256 (N.J. App. 1979)

Mangrum v. Mangrum, 220 S.W.2d 406 (Ky. 1949)

Marks v. Marks, 77 N.Y.S.2d 269 (Sup. Ct. 1948)

Marriage of Allen, In re, 626 P.2d 16 (Wash. App. 1981)

Marriage of D.L.J. and R.R.J., In re, 469 N.W.2d 877 (Wis. App. 1991)

Marriage of Diehl, In re, 582 N.E.2d 281 (Ill. App. 1991), cert. denied sub nom. *Diehl v. Diehl*, 591 N.E.2d 20 (Ill. 1992)

Marriage of Matzen, In re, 600 So.2d 487 (Fla. App. 1992)

Marriage of P.I.M., In re, 665 S.W.2d 670 (Mo. App. 1984)

Marriage of Reed, In re, 226 N.W.2d 795 (Iowa 1975)

Marvin v. Marvin, 557 P.2d 106 (Cal. 1976) (in bank)

May's Estate, In re, 114 N.E.2d 4 (N.Y. 1953)

Mazzolini v. Mazzolini, 155 N.E.2d 206 (Ohio 1958)

McDonald v. McDonald, 58 P.2d 163 (Cal. 1936) (in bank)

Medway v. Needham, 16 Mass. 157 (1819)

Michael B., In re, 604 N.E.2d 122 (N.Y. 1992)

Michaud v. Warwuck, 551 A.2d 738 (Conn. 1988)

Michelle W. v. Randal W., 703 P.2d 88 (Cal. 1988) (in bank), appeal dismissed, 474 U.S. 1043 (1986)

Miller v. Lucks, 36 So.2d 140 (Miss. 1948) (in bank)

Miller v. Miller, 478 A.2d 351 (N.J. 1984)

Miller's Estate, In re, 214 N.W. 428 (Mich. 1927)

Missionaries of Our Lady of La Salette v. Village of Whitefish Bay, 66 N.W.2d 627 (Wis. 1954)

Moorehead, In re, 600 N.E.2d 778 (Ohio App. 1991)

Morgan v. M'Ghee, 24 Tenn. 5 (5 Humphreys 13) (1844)

Morone v. Morone, 413 N.E.2d 1154 (N.Y. 1980)

Mortenson, In re Estate of, 316 P.2d 1106 (Ariz. 1957)

Murnion, In re Estate of, 686 P.2d 893 (Mont. 1984)

N.K.M. v. L.E.M., 606 S.W.2d 179 (Mo. App. 1980)

Naim v. Naim, 87 S.E.2d 749 (Va.) vacated on procedural grounds, 350 U.S. 891 (1955)

Nancy S. v. Michele G., 279 Cal.Rptr. 212 (Ct. App. 1991)

Newsome v. Newsome, 256 S.E.2d 849 (N.C. App. 1979)

Ommang's Estate, In re, 235 N.W. 529 (Minn. 1931)

Opinion of the Justices, In re, 530 A.2d 21 (N.H. 1987)

Orsburn v. Graves, 210 S.W.2d 496 (Ark. 1948)

Ortley v. Ross, 110 N.W. 982 (Neb. 1907)

Pacquette v. Pacquette, 499 A.2d 23 (Vt. 1985)

Paquet's Estate, In re, 200 P. 911 (Or. 1921)

Paternity of D.L.H., In re, 419 N.W.2d 283 (Wis. App. 1987)

Pearson v. Pearson, 51 Cal. 120 (Cal. 1875)

People ex rel. Kropp v. Shepsky, 113 N.E.2d 801 (N.Y. 1953)

People, on Complaint of Kay v. Kay, 252 N.Y.S. 518 (Mag. Ct. 1931)

People v. Ezeonu, 588 N.Y.S.2d 116 (Crim. Ct. 1992)

People v. Jose L., 417 N.Y.S.2d 655 (Crim. Ct. 1979)

People v. Onofre, 415 N.E.2d 936 (N.Y. 1980), cert. denied, 451 U.S. 987 (1981)

Perez v. Lippold, 198 P.2d 17 (Cal. 1948)

Petition for Approval of Forms Pursuant to Rule 10 — 1.1(b) of the Rules Regulating the Florida Bar—Stepparent Adoption Forms, In re, 613 So.2d 900 (Fla. 1992)

Petition of (see name of party)

Phillips v. Wisconsin Personnel Comm'n, 482 N.W.2d 121 (Wis. App. 1992)

Pleasant v. Pleasant, 628 N.E.2d 633 (Ill. App. 1993)

Poe, State v., 252 S.E.2d 843 (N.C. Ct. App. 1979), review denied, appeal dismissed, 259 S.E.2d 304 (N.C. 1979), appeal dismissed sub nom. *Poe v. North Carolina*, 445 U.S. 947 (1980)

R.M.G., In re, 454 A.2d 776 (D.C. App. 1982)

Racquel Marie X, In re, 559 N.E.2d 418 (N.Y. 1990), cert. denied, 498 U.S. 984 (1990)

Robertson v. Western Baptist Hospital, 267 S.W.2d 395 (Ky. 1954)

Root v. Allen, 377 P.2d 117 (Colo. 1962) (en banc)

Rosenstiel v. Rosenstiel, 209 N.E.2d 709 (N.Y. 1965), cert. denied, 383 U.S. 943 (1966)

Ross v. Denver Dept. of Health and Hosps., 883 P.2d 516 (Colo. App. 1994)

Rowsey v. Rowsey, 329 S.E.2d 57 (W.V. 1985)

S. v. J., 367 N.Y.S.2d 405 (Sup. Ct. 1975)

S. v. S., 608 S.W.2d 64 (Ky. App. 1980), cert. denied, 451 U.S. 911 (1981)

S.E.G. v. R.A.G., 735 S.W.2d 164 (Mo. App. 1987)

S.N.E. v. R.L.B., 699 P.2d 875 (Alaska 1985)

Sail'er Inn, Inc. v. Kirby, 485 P.2d 529 (Cal. 1971) (In bank)

Santos, State v., 413 A.2d 58 (R.I. 1980)

Schochet v. Maryland, 541 A.2d 183 (Md. App. 1988), rev'd, 580 A.2d 176 (Md. 1990)

Schwartz v. Schwartz, 236 Ill. App. 336 (1925)

Scott v. State, 39 Ga. 321 (1869)

Seebol v. Farie, Case No. 90–923-CA-18, in Appendix of Dept. of Health and Rehabilitative Services v. Cox, 627 So.2d 1210, 1221 (Fla. App. 1993)

Sheppard v. Sheppard, 630 P.2d 1121 (Kan. 1981), cert. denied, 455 U.S. 919 (1982)

Simpson v. Simpson, 586 S.W.2d 33 (Ky. 1979)

Singer v. Hara, 522 P.2d 1187 (Wash. App. 1974)

Spells v. Spells, 378 A.2d 879 (Super. Ct. Pa. 1979)

Spencer v. People in Interest of Spencer, 292 P.2d 971 (Colo. 1956) (en banc)

State v. —— (see opposing party)

Stepanek v. Stepanek, 14 Cal.Rptr. 793 (Ct. App. 1961)

Stones v. Keeling, 9 Va. (5 Call) 143 (1804)

Stuart v. State of New Hampshire Div. for Children & Youth Servs., 597 A.2d 1076 (N.H. 1991)

Stull's Estate, In re, 39 A. 16 (Pa. 1898)

Succession of Gabisso, 44 So. 438 (La. 1907)

Takahashi's Estate, In re, 129 P.2d 217 (Mont. 1942)

Thigpen v. Carpenter, 730 S.W.2d 510 (Ark. App. 1987)

Thomas S. v. Robin Y., 618 N.Y.S.2d 356 (App. Div. 1994), appeal dismissed, 655 N.E.2d 708 (N.Y. 1995)

333 East 53rd Street Associates v. Mann, 503 N.Y.S.2d 752 (App. Div. 1986), aff'd, 518 N.Y.S.2d 958 (N.Y. 1987)

Toler v. Oakwood Smokeless Coal Corporation, 4 S.E.2d 364 (Va. 1939)

Tooker v. Lopez, 249 N.E.2d 394 (N.Y. 1969)

Toth v. Toth, 212 N.W.2d 812 (Mich. App. 1973)

Tucker v. Tucker, 881 P.2d 948 (Utah App.), rev'd, 910 P.2d 1209 (Utah 1996)

United States ex rel. Davis v. Shanks, 15 Minn. 302 (Minn. 1870)

Vandever v. Industrial Commission of Arizona, 714 P.2d 866 (Ariz. App. 1986)

Wade v. Geren, 743 P.2d 1070 (Okla. 1987)

Wall v. Williams, 11 Ala. 826 (1847)

Walsh, State v., 713 S.W.2d 508 (Mo. 1986) (en banc)

Wasson, Commonwealth v., 842 S.W.2d 487 (Ky. 1993)

Weinschel v. Strople, 466 A.2d 1301 (Md. App. 1983)

Welfare of P.L.C., In re, 384 N.W.2d ??? (Minn. App. 1986)

Whaley v. Whaley, 399 N.E.2d 1270 (Ohio App. 1978)

White Plains, City of, v. Ferraioli, 313 N.E.2d 756 (N.Y. 1974)

Whittington v. McCaskill, 61 So. 236 (Fla. 1913)

Whorton v. Dillingham, 248 Cal.Rptr. 405 (Ct. App. 1988)

Wilkins v. Zelichowski, 129 A.2d 459 (N.J. App. 1957), rev'd, 140 A.2d 65 (N.J. 1958)

Wilson v. Cook, 100 N.E. 222 (Ill. 1912)
Woodruff v. Woodruff, 260 S.E.2d 775 (N.C. App. 1979)
Zack v. Fiebert, 563 A.2d 58 (N.J. App. 1989)
Zimmerman v. Burton, 434 N.Y.S.2d 127 (Civ. Ct. 1980)

SECONDARY LITERATURE

Ali, Shaista-Parveen, Comment, "Homosexual Parenting: Child Custody and Adoption," 22 *University of California at Davis Law Review* 1009 (1989)
American Law Institute (ALI), *Restatement (First) of the Conflicts of Laws*, (St. Paul: American Law Institute, 1934)
——, *Restatement (Second) of the Conflicts of Laws* (St. Paul: American Law Institute, 1971)
Apel, Susan, "Communitarianism and Feminism: The Case against the Preference for the Two-Parent Family," 10 *Wisconsin Women's Law Journal* 1 (1995)
Arsenault, Joseph, Comment, "'Family' but Not 'Parent': The Same-Sex Coupling Jurisprudence of the New York Court of Appeals," 58 *Albany Law Review* 813 (1995)
Averill, Sue Nussbaum, Comment, "Desperately Seeking Status: Same-Sex Couples Battle for Employment-Linked Benefits," 27 *Akron Law Review* 253 (1993)
Avins, Alfred, "Anti-Miscegenation Laws and the Fourteenth Amendment: The Original Intent," 52 *Virginia Law Review* 1224 (1966)
Balian, Habib A., "'Til Death Do Us Part': Granting Full Faith and Credit to Marital Status," 68 *Southern California Law Review* 397 (1995)
Barinaga, Marcia, "Is Homosexuality Biological?" 253 *Science* 956 (1991)
Barnett, Walter, *Sexual Freedom and the Constitution* (Albuquerque: University of New Mexico Press, 1973)
Beck, Phyllis W., "Nontraditional Lifestyles and the Law," 17 *Journal of Family Law* 685 (1978–79)
Beschle, Donald L., "Defining the Scope of the Constitutional Right to Marry: More Than Tradition, Less Than Unlimited Autonomy," 70 *Notre Dame Law Review* 39 (1994)
Bickel, Alexander M., "The Original Understanding and the Segregation Decision," 69 *Harvard Law Review* 1 (1955)
Blackburn, Catherine E., Comment, "Human Rights in an International Context: Recognizing the Right of Intimate Association," 43 *Ohio State Law Journal* 143 (1982)
Blumberg, Grace Ganz, "Cohabitation without Marriage: A Different Perspective," 28 *University of California at Los Angeles Law Review* 1125 (1981)
Borchers, Patrick J., "The Choice-of-Law Revolution: An Empirical Study," 49 *Washington and Lee Law Review* 357 (1992)
——, "Conflicts Pragmatism," 56 *Albany Law Review* 883 (1993)
Bork, Robert H., *The Tempting of America* (New York: Free Press, 1990)

Boswell, John, *Same-Sex Unions in Premodern Europe* (New York: Vintage Books, 1995)

Bowman, Craig A., and Blake M. Cornish, Note, "A More Perfect Union: A Legal and Social Analysis of Domestic Partnership Ordinances," 92 *Columbia Law Review* 1164 (1992)

Bradley, Craig, "The Right Not to Endorse Gay Rights: A Reply to Sunstein," 70 *Indiana Law Journal* 29 (1994)

Bradley, Gerald V., "The Enduring Revolution: Law and Theology in the Secular State," 39 *Emory Law Journal* 217 (1990)

Brandon, Kristin, Comment, "The Liberty Interests of Foster Parents and the Future of Foster Care," 63 *University of Cincinnati Law Review* 403 (1994)

Brest, Paul, "The Fundamental Rights Controversy: The Essential Contradictions of Normative Constitutional Scholarship," 90 *Yale Law Journal* 1063 (1981)

Brown, Jennifer Gerarda, "Competitive Federalism and the Legislative Incentives to Recognize Same-Sex Marriage," 68 *Southern California Law Review* 745 (1995)

Brownstein, Alan, "Harmonizing the Heavenly and Earthly Spheres: The Fragmentation and Synthesis of Religion, Equality, and Speech in the Constitution," 51 *Ohio State Law Journal* 89 (1990)

Buchanan, G. Sidney, "Same-Sex Marriage: The Linchpin Issue," 10 *University of Dayton Law Review* 541 (1985)

Burks, Kristin, "Redefining Parenthood: Child Custody and Visitation When Nontraditional Families Dissolve," 24 *Golden Gate University Law Review* 223 (1994)

Calabresi, Guido, "The Supreme Court, 1990 Term—Foreword: Antidiscrimination and Constitutional Accountability (What the Bork-Brennan Debate Ignores)," 105 *Harvard Law Review* 80 (1991)

Caldwell, Gisela, Note, "The Seventh Circuit in *Ben-Shalom v. Marsh*: Equating Speech with Conduct," 24 *Loyola of Los Angeles Law Review* 421 (1991)

Carr, Kimberly, Comment, "*Alison D. v. Virginia M.*: Neglecting the Best Interests of the Child in a Nontraditional Family," 58 *Brooklyn Law Review* 1021 (1992)

Case, Mary Anne, "Couples and Coupling in the Public Sphere: A Comment on the Legal History of Litigating for Lesbian and Gay Rights," 79 *Virginia Law Review* 1643 (1993)

Caudill, David S., "Legal Recognition of Unmarried Cohabitation: A Proposal to Update and Reconsider Common-Law Marriage," 49 *Tennessee Law Review* 537 (1982)

Caust-Ellenbogen, Sanford, "False Conflicts and Interstate Preclusion: Moving Beyond a Wooden Reading of the Full Faith and Credit Statute," 58 *Fordham Law Review* 593 (1990)

Clark, Homer, *The Law of Domestic Relations in the United States* (St. Paul: West, 2d ed., 1988)

Closen, Michael L., and Carol R. Heise, "HIV-AIDS and the Non-Traditional Family: The Argument for State and Federal Judicial Recognition of Danish Same-Sex Marriages," 16 *Nova Law Review* 809 (1992)

Closen, Michael L., and Joan E. Maloney, "The Health Care Surrogate Act in Illinois: Another Rejection of Domestic Partners' Rights," 19 *Southern Illinois University Law Journal* 479 (1995)

Colker, Ruth, "Marriage," 3 *Yale Journal of Law and Feminism* 321 (1991)

Comment, "Constitutional Aspects of the Homosexual's Right to a Marriage License," 12 *Journal of Family Law* 607 (1972–73)

Comment, "Domestic Relations—Minnesota Marriage Statute Does Not Permit Marriage Between Two Persons of the Same Sex and Does Not Violate Constitutionally Protected Rights," 22 *Drake Law Review* 206 (1972)

Cordell, Robert, II, "Same-Sex Marriage: The Fundamental Right of Marriage and an Examination of Conflict of Laws and the Full Faith and Credit Clause," 26 *Columbia Human Rights Law Review* 247 (1994)

Courson, Marty K., "*Baehr v. Lewin*: Hawaii Takes a Tentative Step to Legalize Same-Sex Marriage," 24 *Golden Gate University Law Review* 41 (1994)

Cox, Barbara J., "Same-Sex Marriage and Choice-Of-Law: If We Marry in Hawaii, Are We Still Married When We Return Home?" 1994 *Wisconsin Law Review* 1033

Cox, Juliet, Comment, "Judicial Enforcement of Moral Imperatives: Is the Best Interest of the Child Being Sacrificed to Maintain Societal Homogeneity?" 59 *Missouri Law Review* 775 (1994)

Cullem, Catherine M., Note, "Fundamental Interests and the Question of Same-Sex Marriage," 15 *Tulsa Law Journal* 141 (1979)

Damslet, Otis R., Note, "Same-Sex Marriage," 10 *New York Law School Journal of Human Rights* 555 (1993)

Davies, Julia Frost, Note, "Two Moms and a Baby: Protecting the Nontraditional Family Through Second Parent Adoptions," 29 *New England Law Review* 1055 (1995)

Davis, Peggy Cooper, "Contested Images of Family Values: The Role of the State," 107 *Harvard Law Review* 1348 (1994)

Deitrich, Jonathan, Comment, "The Lessons of the Law: Same-Sex Marriage and *Baehr v. Lewin*," 78 *Marquette Law Review* 121 (1994)

Delaney, Elizabeth, Note, "Statutory Protection of the Other Mother: Legally Recognizing the Relationship between the Nonbiological Lesbian Parent and Her Child," 43 *Hastings Law Journal* 177 (1991)

"Developments in the Law—The Constitution and the Family," 93 *Harvard Law Review* 1156 (1980)

"Developments in the Law—Sexual Orientation and the Law," 102 *Harvard Law Review* 1508 (1989)

Devlin, Patrick, *The Enforcement of Morals* (Oxford: Oxford University Press, 1959)

Dooley, David, Comment, "Immoral Because They're Bad, Bad Because They're

Wrong: Sexual Orientation and Presumptions of Parental Unfitness in Custody Disputes," 26 *California Western Law Review* 395 (1989/1990)

Duclos, Nitya, "Some Complicating Thoughts on Same-Sex Marriage," 1 *Law and Sexuality* 31 (1991)

Duncan, Richard F., "Who Wants to Stop the Church: Homosexual Rights Legislation, Public Policy, and Religious Freedom," 69 *Notre Dame Law Review* 393 (1994)

Dunlap, Mary C., "The Lesbian and Gay Marriage Debate: A Microcosm of Our Hopes and Troubles in the Nineties," 1 *Law and Sexuality* 63 (1991)

Dworkin, Ronald, "Lord Devlin and the Enforcement of Morals," 75 *Yale Law Journal* 986 (1966)

Ehrenzweig, Albert, "Miscegenation in the Conflict of Laws: Law and Reason Versus The Restatement Second," 45 *Cornell Law Quarterly* 659 (1960)

Elovitz, Marc, "Adoption by Lesbian and Gay People: The Use and Mis-use of Social Science Research," 2 *Duke Journal of Gender, Law, and Politics* 207 (1995)

Ely, John H., *Democracy and Distrust* (Cambridge, MA: Harvard University Press, 1980)

——, "Choice of Law and the State's Interest in Protecting Its Own," 23 *William and Mary Law Review* 173 (1981)

Epstein, Richard, "Caste and the Civil Rights Laws: From Jim Crow to Same-Sex Marriages," 92 *Michigan Law Review* 2456 (1994)

Eskridge, William N., Jr., "A Social Constructionist Critique of Posner's *Sex and Reason*: Steps Toward a Gaylegal Agenda," 102 *Yale Law Journal* 333 (1992)

——, "A History of Same-Sex Marriage," 79 *Virginia Law Review* 1419 (1993)

——, *The Case for Same-Sex Marriage* (New York: Free Press, 1996)

Esseks, James D., "Recent Development, Redefining the Family," 25 *Harvard Civil Rights-Civil Liberties Law Review* 183 (1990)

Ettelbrick, Paula, "Who Is a Parent?: The Need to Develop a Lesbian Conscious Family Law," 10 *New York Law School Journal of Human Rights* 513 (1993)

Evans, Marie Weston, Note, "Parent and Child: *M.J.P. v. J.G.P.*: An Analysis of the Relevance of Parental Homosexuality in Child Custody Determinations," 35 *Oklahoma Law Review* 633 (1982)

Fajer, Marc A., "Can Two Real Men Eat Quiche Together? Storytelling, Gender-Role Stereotypes, and Legal Protection for Lesbians and Gay Men," 46 *University of Miami Law Review* 511 (1992)

Fallone, Edward A., "Preserving the Public Health: A Proposal to Quarantine Recalcitrant AIDS Carriers," 68 *Boston University Law Review* 441 (1988)

Feldblum, Chai R., "Sexual Orientation, Morality, and the Law: Devlin Revisited," 57 *University of Pittsburgh Law Review* 237 (1996)

Fineman, Martha L., "Law and Changing Patterns of Behavior: Sanctions on Non-Marital Cohabitation," 1981 *Wisconsin Law Review* 275

Finnis, John M., *Natural Law and Natural Rights* (Oxford: Clarendon Press, 1980)

——, "Law, Morality and 'Sexual Orientation,'" 69 *Notre Dame Law Review* 1049 (1994)

Flaks, David, "Gay and Lesbian Families: Judicial Assumptions, Scientific Realities," 3 *William and Mary Bill of Rights Journal* 345 (1994)

Friedman, Alissa, "The Necessity for State Recognition of Same-Sex Marriage," 3 *Berkeley Women's Law Journal* 134 (1987–1988)

Friedman, Andrew H., "Same-Sex Marriage and the Right to Privacy: Abandoning Scriptural, Canonical, and Natural Law Based Definitions of Marriage," 35 *Howard Law Journal* 173 (1992)

Gardner, Mary F., Note, "*Braschi v. Stahl Associates Co.*: Much Ado about Nothing?" 35 *Villanova Law Review* 361 (1990)

George, Robert P., and Gerard V. Bradley, "Marriage and the Liberal Imagination," 84 *Georgetown Law Journal* 301 (1995)

Glendon, Mary Ann, "Marriage and the State: The Withering Away of Marriage," 62 *Virginia Law Review* 663 (1976).

Gottesman, Michael, "Draining the Dismal Swamp: The Case for Federal Choice of Law Statutes," 80 *Georgetown Law Journal* 1 (1991)

Grey, Thomas C., "Do We Have an Unwritten Constitution?," 27 *Stanford Law Review* 703 (1975)

Gunther, Gerald, "The Supreme Court, 1971 Term—Forward: In Search of Evolving Doctrine on a Changing Court: A Model for a Newer Equal Protection," 86 *Harvard Law Review* 1 (1972)

——, *Constitutional Law* (Mineola, NY: Foundation Press, 12th ed. 1991)

Hafen, Bruce C., "The Constitutional Status of Marriage, Kinship, and Sexual Privacy—Balancing the Individual and Social Interests," 81 *Michigan Law Review* 463 (1983)

Halley, Janet E., "The Politics of the Closet: Towards Equal Protection For Gay, Lesbian, And Bisexual Identity," 36 *University of California at Los Angeles Law Review* 915 (1989)

——, "Sexual Orientation and the Politics of Biology: A Critique of the Argument from Immutability," 46 *Stanford Law Review* 503 (1994)

Harper, James W., and George W. Clifton, "Heterosexuality; A Prerequisite to Marriage in Texas?" 14 *South Texas Law Journal* 220 (1972–73)

Hart, H.L.A., *Law, Liberty, and Morality* (Stanford: Stanford University Press, 1963)

——, "Social Solidarity and the Enforcement of Morality," 35 *University of Chicago Law Review* 1 (1967)

Hayes, John Charles, Note, "The Tradition of Prejudice Versus the Principle of Equality: Homosexuals and Heightened Equal Protection Scrutiny After *Bowers v. Hardwick*," 31 *Boston College Law Review* 375 (1990)

Heeb, Jennifer L., Comment, "Homosexual Marriage, the Changing American Family, and the Heterosexual Right to Privacy," 24 *Seton Hall Law Review* 347 (1993)

Henkin, Louis, "Morals and the Constitution: The Sin of Obscenity," 63 *Columbia Law Review* 391 (1963)

Henson, Deborah M., "Will Same-Sex Marriages Be Recognized in Sister States?: Full Faith and Credit and Due Process Limitations on States' Choice of Law Regarding the Status and Incidents of Homosexual Marriages Following Hawaii's *Baehr v. Lewin*," 32 *University of Louisville Journal of Family Law* 551 (1994)

Herek, Gregory M., "Myths about Sexual Orientation: A Lawyer's Guide to Social Science Research," 1 *Law and Sexuality* 133 (1991)

Hohengarten, William M., Note, "Same-Sex Marriage and the Right of Privacy," 103 *Yale Law Journal* 1495 (1994)

Hollandsworth, Marla, "Gay Men Creating Families Through Surro-Gay Arrangements: A Paradigm for Reproductive Freedom," 3 *American University Journal of Gender and Law* 183 (1995)

Homer, Steven K., Note, "Against Marriage," 29 *Harvard Civil Rights-Civil Liberties Law Review* 505 (1994)

Horn, Harold L., "The Choice-of-Law Revolution: A Critique," 83 *Columbia Law Review* 772 (1983)

Hovermill, Joseph, "A Conflict of Laws and Morals: The Choice of Law Implications of Hawaii's Recognition of Same-Sex Marriages," 53 *Maryland Law Review* 450 (1994)

Hunter, Nan, and Nancy Polikoff, "Custody Rights of Lesbian Mothers: Legal Theory and Litigation Strategy," 25 *Buffalo Law Review* 691 (1976)

Ingram, John Dwight, "A Constitutional Critique of Restrictions on the Right to Marry—Why Can't Fred Marry George—Or Mary and Alice at the Same Time?" 10 *Journal of Contemporary Law* 33 (1984)

Jackson, Robert H., "Full Faith and Credit—The Lawyer's Clause of the Constitution," 45 *Columbia Law Review* 1 (1945)

Jaffa, Harry V., "'Our Ancient Faith' A Reply to Professor Anastaplo," in *Original Intent and the Framers of the Constitution* (Washington, D.C.: Regnery, 1994)

Juenger, Friedrich K., "Governmental Interests—Real and Spurious—in Multistate Disputes," 21 *University of California at Davis Law Review* 515 (1988)

Karst, Kenneth L., "The Freedom of Intimate Association," 89 *Yale Law Journal* 624 (1980)

———, "Religion, Sex, and Politics: Cultural Counterrevolution in Constitutional Perspective," 24 *University of California at Davis Law Review* 677 (1991)

Keane, Thomas, Note, "Aloha, Marriage? Constitutional and Choice of Law Arguments for Recognition of Same-Sex Marriages," 47 *Stanford Law Review* 499 (1995)

Keller, Christopher J., Comment, "Divining the Priest: A Case Comment on *Baehr v. Lewin*," 12 *Law and Inequality Journal* 483 (1994)

Koppelman, Andrew, Note, "The Miscegenation Analogy: Sodomy Law as Sex Discrimination," 98 *Yale Law Journal* 145 (1988)

———, "Why Discrimination against Lesbians and Gay Men Is Sex Discrimination," 69 *New York University Law Review* 197 (1994)

Kozuma, Scott, "*Baehr v. Lewin* and Same-Sex Marriage: The Continued

Struggle for Social, Political and Human Legitimacy," 30 *Willamette Law Review* 891 (1994)

Kramer, Larry, "Return of the Renvoi," 66 *New York University Law Review* 979 (1991)

Law, Sylvia A., "Homosexuality and the Social Meaning of Gender," 1988 *Wisconsin Law Review* 187

Laycock, Douglas, "Equal Citizens of Equal and Territorial States: The Constitutional Foundations of Choice of Law," 92 *Columbia Law Review* 249 (1992)

Leflar, Robert A., "Conflicts Law: More on Choice-Influencing Considerations," 54 *California Law Review* 1584 (1966)

LeFrancois, Arthur G., "The Constitution and the 'Right' to Marry: A Jurisprudential Analysis," 5 *Oklahoma City University Law Review* 507 (1980)

Leonard, Arthur S., "Lesbian and Gay Families and the Law: A Progress Report," 21 *Fordham Urban Law Journal* 927 (1994)

Lewis, Claudia A., "From This Day Forward: A Feminine Moral Discourse on Homosexual Marriage," 97 *Yale Law Journal* 1783 (1988)

Lilly, Graham C., *An Introduction to the Law of Evidence* (St. Paul: West, 2d ed., 1987)

Link, David, Note, "The Tie That Binds: Recognizing Privacy and the Family Commitments of Same-Sex Couples," 23 *Loyola of Los Angeles Law Review* 1055 (1990)

Lintz, Judith, Casenote, "The Opportunities, or Lack Thereof, for Homosexual Adults to Adopt Children — In re Adoption of Charles B., 50 Ohio St. 3d 88, 552 N.E.2d 884 (1990)," 16 *University of Dayton Law Review* 471 (1991)

Loomis, Jeffrey, Comment, "An Alternative Placement for Children in Adoption Law: Allowing Homosexuals the Right to Adopt," 18 *Ohio Northern University Law Review* 631 (1992)

Macedo, Stephen, "Morality and the Constitution: Toward a Synthesis for 'Earthbound' Interpreters," 61 *University of Cincinnati Law Review* 29 (1992)

Malloy, Denise Glaser, Note, "Another Mother?: The Courts' Denial of Legal Status to the Non-Biological Parent Upon Dissolution of Lesbian Families," 31 *University of Louisville Journal of Family Law* 981 (1992)

Martin, Jorge, "English Polygamy Law and the Danish Registered Partnership Act: A Case for the Consistent Treatment of Foreign Polygamous Marriages and Danish Same-Sex Marriages in England," 27 *Cornell International Law Journal* 419 (1994)

Meyers, Felicia, Note, "Gay Custody and Adoption: An Unequal Application of the Law," 14 *Whittier Law Review* 839 (1993)

Michaelson, Sherryl E., Note, "Religion and Morality Legislation: A Reexamination of Establishment Clause Analysis," 59 *New York University Law Review* 301 (1984)

Mill, John Stuart, *Utilitarianism, Collected Works of John Stuart Mill*, vol. 10, ed. John Robson (Toronto: University of Toronto Press, 1969)

——, "Whewell on Moral Philosophy," *Collected Works of John Stuart Mill*, vol. 10, ed. John Robson, (Toronto: University of Toronto Press, 1969)

——, *On Liberty, Collected Works of John Stuart Mill*, vol. 18, ed. John Robson (Toronto: University of Toronto Press, 1977)

Miller, Harris M., II, "An Argument for the Application of Equal Protection Heightened Scrutiny to Classifications Based on Homosexuality," 57 *Southern California Law Review* 797 (1984)

Minow, Martha, "The Supreme Court 1986 Term—Foreword: Justice Engendered," 101 *Harvard Law Review* 10 (1987)

Moglen, Eben, "Toward a New Deal Legal History," 80 *Virginia Law Review* 263 (1994)

Mohr, Richard D., "Mr. Justice Douglas at Sodom: Gays and Privacy," 18 *Columbia Human Rights Law Review* 43 (1986).

——, *Gays/Justice* (New York: Columbia University Press, 1988)

——, "The Case for Gay Marriage," 9 *Notre Dame Journal of Law, Ethics and Public Policy* 215 (1995)

Morrison, Mary Jane, "Death of Conflicts," 29 *Villanova Law Review* 313 (1983–1984)

Murphy, Arthur A., "Homosexuality and the Law: Tolerance and Containment II," 97 *Dickinson Law Review* 693 (1993)

Nagan, Winston P., "Conflict of Laws: Group Discrimination and the Freedom to Marry—A Policy Science Prologue to Human Rights Decisions," 21 *Howard Law Journal* 1 (1978)

Note, "The Legality of Homosexual Marriage," 82 *Yale Law Journal* 573 (1973)

Note, "On Privacy: Constitutional Protection for Personal Liberty," 48 *New York University Law Review* 670 (1973)

Note, "The Constitutionality of Laws Forbidding Private Homosexual Conduct," 72 *Michigan Law Review* 1613 (1974)

Note, "Homosexuals' Right to Marry: A Constitutional Test and a Legislative Solution," 128 *University of Pennsylvania Law Review* 193 (1979)

Note, "The Constitutional Status of Sexual Orientation: Homosexuality as a Suspect Classification," 98 *Harvard Law Review* 1285 (1985)

Note, "*Doe* and *Dronenberg*: Sodomy Statutes Are Constitutional," 26 *William and Mary Law Review* 645 (1985)

Note, "Joint Adoption: A Queer Option?" 15 *Vermont Law Review* 197 (1990)

Note, "Looking for a Family Resemblance: The Limits of the Functional Approach to the Legal Definition of Family," 104 *Harvard Law Review* 1640 (1991)

Nussbaum, Martha C., "Platonic Love and Colorado Law: The Relevance of Ancient Greek Norms to Modern Sexual Controversies," 80 *Virginia Law Review* 1515 (1994)

Parsons, Barry, Casenote, "*Bottoms* v. *Bottoms*; Erasing the Presumption Favoring a Natural Parent over Third Parties—What Makes This Mother Unfit?" 2 *George Mason Independent Law Review* 457 (1994)

Patterson, Charlotte, "Adoption of Minor Children by Lesbian and Gay Adults: A Social Science Perspective," 2 *Duke Journal of Gender, Law, and Politics* 191 (1995)

Pershing, Stephen B, "'Entreat Me Not to Leave Thee': *Bottoms* v. *Bottoms* and the Custody Rights of Gay and Lesbian Parents," 3 *William and Mary Bill of Rights Journal* 289 (1994)

Polikoff, Nancy, "This Child Does Have Two Mothers: Redefining Parenthood to Meet the Needs of Children in Lesbian-Mother and Other Nontraditional Families," 78 *Geogetown Law Journal* 459 (1990)

——, "Educating Judges about Lesbian and Gay Parenting: A Simulation," 1 *Law and Sexuality* 173 (1991)

Pooley, Lisa, Note, "Heterosexism and Children's Best Interests: Conflicting Concepts in *Nancy S. v. Michele G.*," 27 *University of San Francisco Law Review* 477 (1993)

Posnak, Bruce, "Choice of Law—Interest Analysis: They Still Don't Get It," *Wayne Law Review* 1121 (1994)

Posner, Richard, *The Federal Courts: Crisis and Reform* (Cambridge: Harvard University Press, 1985)

——, *Sex and Reason* (Cambridge: Harvard University Press, 1992)

Pound, Roscoe, "Individual Interests in the Domestic Relation," 14 *Michigan Law Review* 177 (1916)

Rassam, A. Yasmine, Note, "'Mother', 'Parent', and Bias," 69 *Indiana Law Journal* 1165 (1994)

Reese, Willis, "Marriage in American Conflicts of Laws," 26 *International and Comparative Law Quarterly* 953 (1977)

Regan, Milton C., Jr., "Reason, Tradition, and Family Law: A Comment on Social Constructionism," 79 *Virginia Law Review* 1515 (1993)

Reynolds, Noel B., "The Enforcement of Morals and the Rule of Law," 11 *Georgia Law Review* 1325 (1977)

Reynolds, William, "The Iron Law of Full Faith and Credit," 53 *Maryland Law Review* 412 (1994)

Rich, Tracey, "Sexual Orientation Discrimination in the Wake of *Bowers v. Hardwick*," 22 *Georgia Law Review* 773 (1988)

Richards, David A. J., "Unnatural Acts and the Constitutional Right to Privacy: A Moral Theory," 45 *Fordham Law Review* 1281 (1977)

——, "Sexual Autonomy and the Constitutional Right to Privacy: A Case Study in Human Rights and the Unwritten Constitution," 30 *Hastings Law Journal* 957 (1979)

——, "Constitutional Legitimacy and Constitutional Privacy," 61 *New York University Law Review* 800 (1986)

——, "Sexual Preference as a Suspect (Religious) Classification: An Alternative Perspective on the Unconstitutionality of Anti-Lesbian/Gay Initiatives," 55 *Ohio State Law Journal* 491 (1994)

Richardson, David G., "Family Rights for Unmarried Couples," 2 *Kansas Journal of Law and Public Policy* 117 (Spring 1993)

Riley, Marilyn, Note, "The Avowed Lesbian Mother and Her Right to Child Custody: A Constitutional Challenge That Can No Longer Be Denied," 12 *San Diego Law Review* 799 (1975)

Rivera, Rhonda, "Our Straight-Laced Judges: The Legal Position of Homosexual Persons in the United States," 30 *Hastings Law Journal* 799 (1979)

———, "Queer Law: Sexual Orientation in the Mid-Eighties," 11 *University of Dayton Law Review* 275 (1986)

Robson, Ruthann, and S. E. Valentine, "Lov(h)ers: Lesbians as Intimate Partners and Lesbian Legal Theory," 63 *Temple Law Review* 511 (1990)

Rosenblum, David, Comment, "Custody Rights of Gay and Lesbian Parents," 36 *Villanova Law Review* 1665 (1991)

Russman, David, Note, "Alternate Families: In Whose Best Interests?" 27 *Suffolk University Law Review* 31 (1993)

Sage, Candace L., Note, "Sister-State Recognition of Valid Same-Sex Marriages; *Baehr v. Lewin*—How Will It Play in Peoria?" 28 *Indiana Law Review* 115 (1994)

Samar, Vincent J., *The Right of Privacy: Gays, Lesbians, and the Constitution* (Philadelphia: Temple University Press, 1991)

Sandel, Michael, "Moral Argument and Liberal Toleration: Abortion and Homosexuality," 77 *California Law Review* 521 (1989)

Sartorius, Rolf, "The Enforcement of Morality," 81 *Yale Law Journal* 891 (1972)

Schwarzschild, Hannah, "Same-Sex Marriage and Constitutional Privacy: Moral Threat and Legal Anomaly," 4 *Berkeley Women's Law Journal* 94 (1988–1989)

Scocca, Julienne C., Comment, "Society's Ban on Same-Sex Marriages: A Reevaluation of the So-Called 'Fundamental Right' of Marriage," 2 *Seton Hall Constitutional Law Journal* 719 (1992)

Scoles, Eugene, and Peter Hay, *Conflict of Laws* (St. Paul: West, 2d ed., 1992)

Seidelson, David E., "Resolving Choice-of-Law Problems Through Interest Analysis in Personal Injury Actions: A Suggested Order of Priority among Competing State Interests and among Available Techniques for Weighing Those Interests," 30 *Duquesne Law Review* 869 (1992)

Sella, Carmel, "When a Mother Is a Legal Stranger to Her Child: The Law's Challenge to the Lesbian Nonbiological Mother," 1 *University of California at Los Angeles Women's Law Journal* 135 (1991)

Sencer, Myra, Note, "Adoption in the Non-Traditional Family—A Look at Some Alternatives," 16 *Hofstra Law Review* 191 (1987)

Singer, Jana B., "The Privatization of Family Law," 1992 *Wisconsin Law Review* 1443

Stamps, Ron-Christopher, Comment, "Domestic Partnership Legislation: Recognizing Non-Traditional Families," 19 *Southern University Law Review* 441 (1992)

Steenson, Michael K., "Fundamental Rights in the 'Gray' Area: The Right of Privacy Under the Minnesota Constitution," 20 *William Mitchell Law Review* 383 (1994)

Sterk, Stewart, "The Marginal Relevance of Choice of Law Theory," 142 *University of Pennsylvania Law Review* 949 (1994)

Stoddard, Thomas B., "*Bowers v. Hardwick*: Precedent by Personal Predilection," 54 *University of Chicago Law Review* 648 (1987)

Stone, Donald, "The Moral Dilemma: Child Custody When One Parent is Homosexual or Lesbian—An Empirical Study," 23 *Suffolk University Law Review* 711 (1989)

Strasser, Mark, "Family, Definitions, and the Constitution: On the Anti-miscegenation Analogy," 25 *Suffolk University Law Review* 981 (1991)

——, "Suspect Classes and Suspect Classifications: On Discriminating, Unwittingly or Otherwise," 64 *Temple Law Review* 937 (1991)

——, *Agency, Free Will, and Moral Responsibility* (Wakefield: Hollowbrook, 1992)

——, "The Invidiousness of Invidiousness: On the Supreme Court's Affirmative Action Jurisprudence," 21 *Hastings Constitutional Law Quarterly* 323 (1993–1994)

——, "Domestic Relations Jurisprudence and the Great, Slumbering *Baehr*: On Definitional Preclusion, Equal Protection, and Fundamental Interests," 64 *Fordham Law Review* 921 (1995)

——, "Unconstitutional? Don't Ask; If It Is, Don't Tell: On Deference, Rationality, and the Constitution," 66 *University of Colorado Law Review* 375 (1995)

——, "Legislative Presumptions and Judicial Assumptions: On Parenting, Adoption, and the Best Interests of the Child," 45 *University of Kansas Law Review* 49 (1996)

——, "Fit to Be Tied: On Custody, Discretion, and Sexual Orientation," 46 *American University Law Review* 841 (1997)

——, "Judicial Good Faith and the *Baehr* Essentials: On Giving Credit Where It's Due," 28 *Rutgers Law Journal* 313 (1997)

——, "*Loving* the *Romer* Out for *Baehr*: On Acts in Defense of Marriage and the Constitution," 58 *University of Pittsburgh Law Review* 279 (1997)

Sullivan, Andrew, *Virtually Normal* (New York: Alfred A. Knopf, 1995)

Sullivan, Leo, "Same-Sex Marriage and the Constitution," 6 *University of California at Davis Law Review* 275 (1973)

Sunstein, Cass R., "Sexual Orientation and the Constitution: A Note on the Relationship Between Due Process and Equal Protection," 55 *University of Chicago Law Review* 1161 (1988)

——, "Homosexuality and the Constitution," 70 *Indiana Law Journal* 1 (1994)

Susoeff, Steve, Comment, "Assessing Children's Best Interests When a Parent is Gay or Lesbian: Toward a Rational Custody Standard," 32 *University of California at Los Angeles Law Review* 852 (1985)

Taintor, C. W. II, "What Law Governs the Ceremony Incidents and Status of Marriage," 19 *Boston University Law Review* 353 (1939)

——, "Marriage in the Conflict of Laws," 9 *Vanderbilt Law Review* 607 (1956)

Tamayo, Yvonne, "Sexuality, Morality and the Law: The Custody Battle of a Non-Traditional Mother," *Syracuse Law Review* 45 (1994)

Tewksbury, Michael D., Comment, "*Gaylord* and *Singer*: Washington's Place in the Stream of the Emerging Law Concerning Homosexuals," 14 *Gonzaga Law Review* 167 (1978)

Toulon, Eric J., "Call the Caterer: Hawaii to Host First Same-Sex Marriage," 3 *Southern California Review of Law and Women's Studies* 109 (1993)

Treuthart, Mary Patricia, "Adopting a More Realistic Definition of 'Family'," 26 *Gonzaga Law Review* 91 (1990)

Tribe, Laurence, *American Constitutional Law* (Mineola, N.Y.: Foundation Press, 2d ed., 1988)

Trosino, James, Note, "American Wedding: Same-Sex Marriage and the Miscegenation Analogy," 73 *Boston University Law Review* 93 (1993)

Turner, Scott, Comment, "*Braschi v. Stahl Assocs. Co.*: In Praise of Family," 25 *New England Law Review* 1295 (1991)

Veitch, Edward, "Essence of Marriages: A Comment on the Homosexual Challenge," 5 *Anglo-American Law Review* 41 (1976)

Vieira, Norman, "*Hardwick* and the Right of Privacy," 55 *University of Chicago Law Review* 1181 (1988)

Wadlington, Walter, "The *Loving* Case: Virginia's Antimiscegenation Statute in Historical Perspective," 52 *Virginia Law Review* 1189 (1966)

Waldron, Jeremy, "Particular Values and Critical Morality," 77 *California Law Review* 561 (1989)

Weinberg, Louise, "Against Comity," 80 *Georgetown Law Journal* 53 (1991)

——, "Choosing Law: The Limitation Debates," 1991 *University of Illinois Law Review* 638

Weintraub, Russell, *Commentary on the Conflict of Laws* (Mineola, N.Y.: Foundation Press, 2d ed. 1980)

Whitten, Ralph, "The Constitutional Limitations on State Choice of Law: Full Faith and Credit," 12 *Memphis State University Law Review* 1 (1981)

Wilkinson, J. Harvie, III and G. Edward White, "Constitutional Protection for Personal Lifestyles," 62 *Cornell Law Review* 563 (1977).

Wintemute, Robert, *Sexual Orientation and Human Rights* (Oxford: Clarendon Press, 1995)

Wishard, Darryl Robin, Comment, "Out of the Closet and Into the Courts: Homosexual Fathers and Child Custody," 93 *Dickinson Law Review* 401 (1989)

Wolfson, Evan, "Crossing the Threshold: Equal Marriage Rights for Lesbians and Gay Men and the Intra-Community Critique," 21 *New York University Review of Legal and Social Change* 567 (1994)

Zimmer, Lisa R., Note, "Family, Marriage, and the Same-Sex Couple," 12 *Cardozo Law Review* 681 (1990)

Zuckerman, Elizabeth, Comment, "Second Parent Adoption for Lesbian-Parented Families: Legal Recognition of the Other Mother," 19 *University of California at Davis Law Review* 729 (1986)

INDEX

▼